VISUAL QUICKSTART GUIDE

iTunes 4

FOR MACINTOSH AND WINDOWS

Judith Stern and Robert Lettieri

Peachpit Press

Visual QuickStart Guide
iTunes 4 for Macintosh and Windows
Judith Stern and Robert Lettieri

Peachpit Press
1249 Eighth Street
Berkeley, CA 94710
510/524-2178
800/283-9444
510/524-2221 (fax)

Find us on the World Wide Web at: http://www.peachpit.com
To report errors, please send a note to errata@peachpit.com
Peachpit Press is a division of Pearson Education

Copyright © 2004 by Judith Stern and Robert Lettieri

Editors: Cliff Colby and Karen Reichstein
Production Coordinator: Hilal Sala
Copyeditor: Sally Zahner
Compositor: Danielle Foster
Indexer: Joy Dean Lee
Cover design: The Visual Group
Cover production: George Mattingly/GMD

Notice of Rights
All rights reserved. No part of this book may be reproduced or transmitted in any form by any means, electronic, mechanical, photocopying, recording, or otherwise, without the prior written permission of the publisher. For information on getting permission for reprints and excerpts, contact permissions@peachpit.com.

Notice of Liability
The information in this book is distributed on an "As Is" basis, without warranty. While every precaution has been taken in the preparation of the book, neither the authors nor Peachpit Press shall have any liability to any person or entity with respect to any loss or damage caused or alleged to be caused directly or indirectly by the instructions contained in this book or by the computer software and hardware products described in it.

Trademarks
Visual QuickStart Guide is a registered trademark of Peachpit Press, a division of Pearson Education. Apple, Macintosh, Mac, Mac OS, iTunes, AppleScript, iLife, iDVD, iMovie, SuperDrive, iPod, Finder, iPhoto, QuickTime, GarageBand are trademarks or registered trademarks of Apple Computer, Inc., in the United States and/or other countries. Windows XP is a registered trademark of Microsoft Corporation. All other trademarks are the property of their respective owners. Throughout this book, trademarks are used. Rather than put a trademark symbol in every occurrence of a trademarked name, we state that we are using the names in an editorial fashion only and to the benefit of the trademark owner with no intention of infringement of the trademark.

ISBN 0-321-24665-9

9 8 7 6 5 4 3 2 1

Printed and bound in the United States of America

Dedication

To our moms, Lois and Ann, who love music

About the Authors

Judith Stern is an instructional multimedia specialist. Her background includes corporate training, expert systems development, educational research, and multimedia development. She holds degrees in psychology and education from Cornell University and the University of California at Berkeley. She currently works for Educational Technology Services at the University of California at Berkeley, where she provides support and training to faculty and staff using instructional software.

Robert Lettieri has been experimenting and working with digital and analog video for more than 15 years. He has taught many people how to use graphics and desktop publishing software, both individually and in training workshops. He holds degrees from Rutgers University and California State University, Hayward, and is currently working at the Space Sciences Lab at UC Berkeley.

Together, Stern and Lettieri are the authors of several books and articles on multimedia, including all of Peachpit's QuickTime Visual QuickStart Guides.

They can be reached at itunes@judyandrobert.com, and will post updates and corrections to this book at www.judyandrobert.com/itunes.

Special Thanks:

We are especially grateful to our awesome Peachpit editors: Karen Reichstein, who not only did an amazing and careful job of editing, but also added much spice; and Cliff Colby, who gave us a chance at something new, and mused on Muze. Thanks also to all the rest of the folks responsible for the production of this book: Sally Zahner, Hilal Sala, Danielle Foster, and Joy Dean Lee.

We'd also like to thank Mumble and Peg (www.lebofsky.com/music/mumble/) for giving us CDs and permission to use images, and The League Band for use of images from their Web site.

Other folks that helped along the way include Apple folks (Keith Hatounian, Grace Kvamme, Bonnie Kinnare, Chris Bell, Peter Lowe, Tom Dowdy, and Patrick McDermott), friends (Phil Bell, Greg Paschall, Brandon Muramatsu, Ian Sicurella, Jason McPhate, Matt Lebofsky, James Malloy), family (Marvin Stern and Paul Lettieri), and various colleagues at UC Berkeley's Space Sciences Lab and Educational Technology Services.

Last but definitely not least, we couldn't have done this without the cooperation and patience of our wonderful children, Sam and Jake. Nor could we have done it without the assistance of those that helped care for them during the process: Aunt Mona (who also cared for us in so many ways and even did some editing), Phil and Judy, Lara and Michael, Brenda and Geoffrey, Sandy and Michael, Paul and Anne, Karen and Phil, plus others in the NOCSS and Monteverde communities.

Contents at a Glance

Chapter 1:	Getting Started	1
Chapter 2:	Adding Music to your Library	19
Chapter 3:	Finding and Playing Songs	49
Chapter 4:	Shopping at the iTunes Music Store	85
Chapter 5:	Organizing your library	123
Chapter 6:	Burning CDs and Other Disks	153
Chapter 7:	Using iTunes with Your iPod	173
Chapter 8:	Sharing Music Over a Network	193
Appendix A:	iTunes in your iLife (Mac Only)	205
Appendix B:	AppleScripts for iTunes (Mac Only)	215
	Index	221

TABLE OF CONTENTS

Chapter 1: **Getting Started**   **1**
Hardware and Software Requirements 2
Getting the Current Version of iTunes 4
What's New in iTunes 4? 7
Installing iTunes (Windows)................... 9
Installing iTunes (Mac)....................... 11
Launching iTunes............................ 12
Setting Up iTunes 13
Quick Interface Overview..................... 16
About iTunes Preferences 17

Chapter 2: **Adding Music to your Library**   **19**
About the Library............................ 20
Importing an Audio CD 21
Importing Individual Songs
    from an Audio CD 24
Changing Import Preferences for CDs 26
About iTunes Encoding Choices 28
Changing How Songs Are Encoded
    on Import 31
About Custom Encoder Settings............... 32
Adding Audio Files from Your Computer....... 35
Getting Audio Files from Online Sources 38
Converting Songs to a Different
    Audio Format 40
Adding Links to Audio on the Internet 42
Adding Artwork to Your Songs 44

Chapter 3: **Finding and Playing Songs**   **49**
Browsing Through Your Library 50
Searching for Songs 52
Sorting Songs............................... 54
Hiding and Showing Columns 55
Changing Order and Size of Columns 56
Playing and Pausing Songs.................... 58
Moving Around in a Song 61

vii

Table of Contents

Viewing Song Artwork 62
Options for Playing Multiple Songs............ 64
Listening to Radio Streams 66
Customizing the iTunes Window 68
Getting Information About What's Playing..... 70
Controlling Volume 71
Using the Equalizer 72
Saving Equalizer Adjustments as Presets 74
Assigning Equalizer Presets to
   Streams or Songs 76
Adjusting Sound Effects...................... 78
Specifying Start and Stop Times 79
Using the Visualizer........................... 80
Controlling Visualizations..................... 82

Chapter 4: Shopping at the iTunes Music Store   85
About the iTunes Music Store 86
Home and Genre Page Overview 88
Album Page Overview 90
Artist Page Overview 92
Navigating with the Browser.................. 94
Searching the Store 96
Power Searching the Store.................... 98
Previewing Songs 99
About Audiobooks.......................... 101
Saving Links 104
Getting an Account 106
Signing In and Out of the Store 108
Setting iTunes Purchasing Preferences 109
1-Click Purchasing 110
Shopping Cart Purchasing................... 112
Giving Gift Certificates 114
Redeeming Gift Certificates.................. 116
Giving a Music Allowance 119
Managing Your Account 121

Chapter 5: Organizing your library   123
About Song Information 124
Editing Song Information 125
Rating Songs............................... 127
About Playlists............................. 129
Creating a Playlist and Adding Songs to It 130
Creating a Smart Playlist 133
Deleting Songs 137
Reordering the Songs in a Playlist 139

Table of Contents

Organizing Multiple Playlists 140
Deleting Playlists............................ 141
Exporting and Importing Song Lists.......... 143
How iTunes Organizes Files
   on Your Hard Drive...................... 146
Choosing a New iTunes Music Folder 150
Consolidating Songs on Your Hard Drive 151

Chapter 6: Burning CDs and Other Disks — 153
Checking for a Supported Burner 154
Deciding on a CD Format..................... 156
Preparing to Burn Audio CDs................. 158
Burning Audio CDs 160
Preparing to Burn an MP3 CD 162
Making Sure Songs Are MP3s................. 164
Burning an MP3 CD.......................... 166
Creating a Data CD or DVD
   for Archiving Purposes................... 168
Tips for Successful Burning.................. 171

Chapter 7: Using iTunes with Your iPod — 173
Making Sure You Have the Latest Version
   of iPod Software 174
Setting Up Your iPod with iTunes............. 176
Ejecting an iPod............................. 178
Changing iPod Updating Preferences.......... 179
About Automatic Updating 181
Manually Updating Your iPod 184
Creating Playlists for iTunes on Your iPod..... 186
Rating Songs for iTunes on Your iPod......... 189
About Other Portable MP3 Players............ 190

Chapter 8: Sharing Music Over a Network — 193
Making Your Music Available to Others....... 194
Accessing Shared Libraries 196
Disconnecting from a Shared Library.......... 199
Authorizing a Computer to Play
   Purchased Songs......................... 200
Deauthorizing Computers for Your Account .. 202
Dealing with Firewalls....................... 203

Appendix A: iTunes in your iLife (Mac Only) — 205
iTunes and iPhoto 4.......................... 206
iTunes and iMovie 4.......................... 209
iTunes and iDVD 4........................... 211
iTunes and GarageBand 213

Appendix B: AppleScripts for iTunes (Mac Only) **215**
Finding and Using AppleScripts for iTunes 216
Some Cool Scripts............................ 218

Index **221**

GETTING STARTED

What types of technologies have *you* used to listen to music in your lifetime? Wax cylinder? Turntable and vinyl? Cassettes? Reel-to-reel tapes? An 8-track player? CD player? Boom box? Walkman? MiniDiscs? Internet music sharing? A portable MP3 player? Depending on your age and personal preferences, you've used some—or maybe all—of these.

If iTunes is new to you, you're about to add something new to your list of ways to listen to music. iTunes, Apple's wildly popular and revolutionary digital jukebox software, not only lets you listen to music from a variety of sources but also lets you burn CDs, purchase music online, synchronize your music collection with a portable music player, and share music with friends and coworkers over a network. Listening to music will never be the same again!

You'll enjoy using iTunes because it lets you do all this with ease. It's well designed and has an intuitive interface. Even so, for almost all of iTunes' functions, there are multiple ways (some not all that apparent) to accomplish the same task; some methods are more convenient, faster, or more fun than the one that's most obvious. Plus, if you understand some of iTunes' quirks and some of its "under-the-hood" workings, you'll have a better iTunes experience. In this book, we cover iTunes from all these angles.

This chapter helps you install or update iTunes, and gives you a quick overview of the software.

Hardware and Software Requirements

To run iTunes on a Macintosh, you need:

- Mac OS X version 10.1.5 or later
- 400-MHz PowerPC G3 processor or better
- 128 MB RAM

To run iTunes in Windows, you need:

- Windows XP or 2000
- 500-MHz Pentium-class processor or better
- QuickTime 6.4 or later (included when you install iTunes)
- 128 MB RAM minimum

Recommended enhancements for both platforms

- **256 MB RAM**

    For faster performance and fewer problems with other applications open, you'll want at least 256 MB RAM.

- **Internet connection**

    If you want to use the iTunes Music Store, download or stream music from any online source, or have information automatically added about songs you copy from an audio CD, you'll need an Internet connection; you'll want this to be a DSL, cable modem, or other high-speed Internet connection if you don't want to go nuts waiting for screens to update and music to download.

- **CD or DVD burner**

    If you want to burn CDs, you'll want a CD or DVD writer. All Macintosh internal writers, such as the built-in SuperDrive or combo drive, will work. Most external writers will also work on both platforms, as will most internal writers for Windows computers.

What's Different Between the Mac and Windows Versions?

As you read this chapter, you'll find large blocks of text devoted to a single platform, which may lead you to believe that the Mac and Windows versions of iTunes are quite different. Not so. While iTunes installation differs on the two platforms, you'll find that when it comes to *using* iTunes, the two versions are remarkably similar.

Most differences are largely due to operating system interface standards. For example, on the Mac you'll find the Preferences menu choice under the iTunes menu, and in Windows it's under the Edit menu. Modifier keys and window control buttons are also platform-appropriate. On occasion, one platform or the other will have an extra option, an extra setting, or an extra feature.

In this book, we use screen shots from both platforms interchangeably, since the majority of menus and windows contain the same content on both platforms.

When keys, names of screen elements, or procedures differ between the two platforms, we note both options—for example, "Press the Option key (Mac OS X) or the Alt and Ctrl keys (Windows)."

In the very few cases in which a feature is available on only one platform, or when the sequence of steps to follow is significantly different, we'll label the section accordingly (for example, "Mac OS X only").

Recommended enhancements for Mac OS X

- Mac OS X v10.2.4

    If you want to burn DVDs (covered in Chapter 6) or share music (Chapter 8), you'll want Mac OS X version 10.2.4. You can't burn DVDs or share music over a network with earlier versions of Mac OS X.

- QuickTime 6.2 or greater

    If you want your audio files encoded using AAC (an encoder that gives the highest audio quality for the smallest file size), you'll want at least QuickTime 6.2 (but we recommend getting the most current version, which is QuickTime 6.5 at this writing). To get the latest version of QuickTime, you can download it from Apple's Web site: www.apple.com/quicktime/download.

    You can also use Mac OS X's built-in Software Update feature, which automatically checks Apple's Internet servers for updates to your Mac OS X software, letting you download and install them, as you choose.

Recommended enhancements for Windows

- **Latest Windows service packs**

    Downloading the latest Windows *service pack* (Microsoft's collection of driver updates, bug fixes, minor software upgrades, and security patches) helps ensure that your PC runs as smoothly as possible. If you're using Windows XP, use the Automatic Update feature to choose how and when updates are installed on your PC, or visit the Microsoft Update Web site at http://windowsupdate.microsoft.com.

Still Using Mac OS 9?

Apple stopped developing iTunes for Mac OS 9 several versions ago. If you're still using Mac OS 9, the best you can do is use iTunes version 2.0.4, available at http://docs.info.apple.com/article.html?artnum=120073. This older version has a similar-looking user interface but, as you'd expect, is missing many of version 4's features. We won't be covering this older version in this book. (It's really time you upgraded, anyway!)

Chapter 1

Getting the Current Version of iTunes

You'll want to have the current version of iTunes (iTunes 4.2), which with the revolutionary iTunes Music Store and new Windows compatibility offers the most features of any iTunes version so far. Some of you (most likely Windows users) may need to download this version anew. If you're a Mac OS X user, odds are very good that you have some version of iTunes already preinstalled on your computer. iTunes has come installed with every version of Mac OS X since Mac OS X 10.1. If you already own iTunes, it's probably already up-to-date, since both the Windows and Mac versions of iTunes prompt you to update if you don't have the current version. Just in case, however, we'll explain how to update an older version of iTunes.

Ways to determine which version of iTunes you have:

◆ (Windows) Find the iTunes.exe icon (most likely in the Programs Files folder in a folder called iTunes), and then right-click and choose Properties. Click the Version tab; you'll see the version number listed at the top of the tab (**Figure 1.1**).

◆ (Mac OS X) Locate iTunes in your Applications folder. Select the iTunes icon while in column view, and you'll see the version number (**Figure 1.2**).

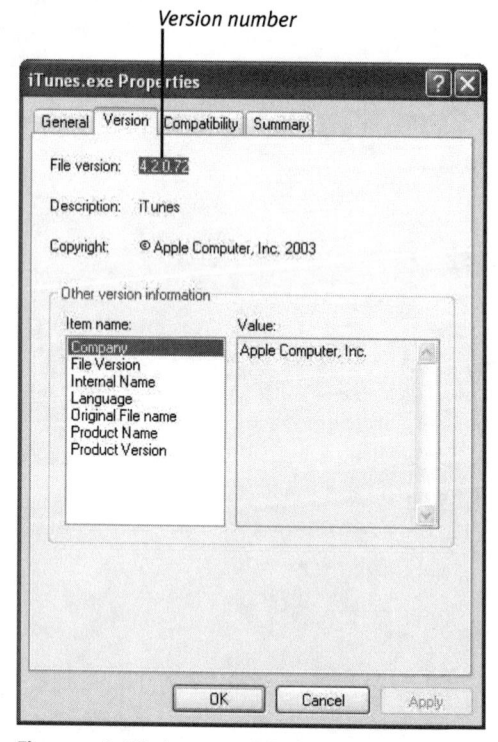

Figure 1.1 In Windows, you'll find the iTunes version number in the Version tab of the Properties window for the iTunes.exe file.

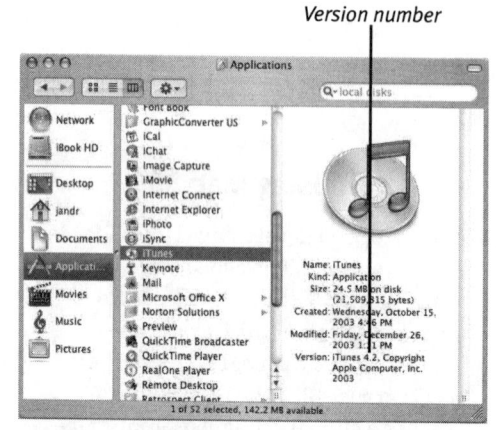

Figure 1.2 In Mac OS X, you can determine which version of iTunes you have by selecting the iTunes icon in the Finder's column view.

4

Figure 1.3 (Windows) Choose About iTunes from the Help menu to open the About iTunes window.

Figure 1.4 (Mac) Choose About iTunes from the iTunes menu to open the About iTunes window.

Figure 1.5 When you open the About iTunes window, the version number is the first line of text that scrolls off the screen.

- Once you launch iTunes, select About iTunes from the Help menu (Windows; **Figure 1.3**) or from the iTunes application menu (Mac; **Figure 1.4**); you'll see a window with scrolling text, starting with the version number (**Figure 1.5**).

✔ Tip

- In the About iTunes window, text scrolls out of view pretty quickly! On either platform, however, you can reverse the direction of the scrolling text: Hold down the Alt key (Windows) or Option key (Mac OS X).

Ways to get iTunes:

- **Download it.** You can find it at www.apple.com/iTunes/download. This is the best way to ensure that you have the most up-to-date version. You'll need to install it; we cover this later in this chapter.

- **Buy a new Mac.** iTunes comes preinstalled on all new Macs. (You may still want to check the version number. As of this writing, iTunes 4.2 wasn't yet shipping on new Macs.)

✔ Tip

- Want to save keystrokes? Hate typing URLs? In the address field of most Web browsers you can simply type itunes.com (just iTunes in virtually all Mac browsers), which automatically takes you to Apple's iTunes Web page at www.apple.com/itunes. On this page you'll see a "Download now" button; click it, and you'll be taken to the iTunes Download page. Or, if you're a Windows user with an older version of iTunes, choose Check for iTunes Updates in the iTunes Help menu, and you'll be taken to the iTunes Download page.

Chapter 1

Ways to update an existing version of iTunes:

◆ Download the current version from the iTunes download page (www.apple.com/iTunes/download) and install it (see next page); the new version will overwrite any older version. (Be reassured, however, that your existing iTunes library won't be touched.).

◆ (Mac) In System Preferences, click the Software Update icon to open the Software Update pane, then click Check Now (**Figure 1.6**). In the window that appears, make sure the check box next to iTunes is checked, and click Install (**Figure 1.7**).

◆ (Windows) From the Help menu, choose Check for iTunes Updates (refer to Figure 4.3). If a new version is available, iTunes tells you so, and asks if you want to download it. Click Yes.

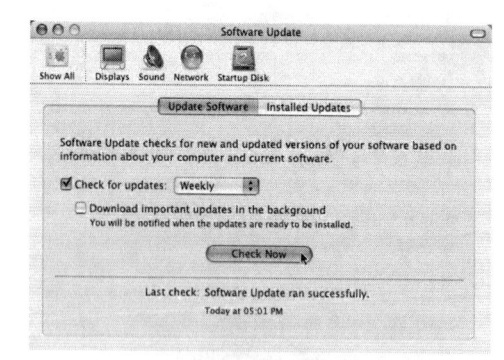

Figure 1.6 In the Mac OS X Software Update pane (which you'll find in System Preferences), click Check Now to find the latest Mac OS X software updates.

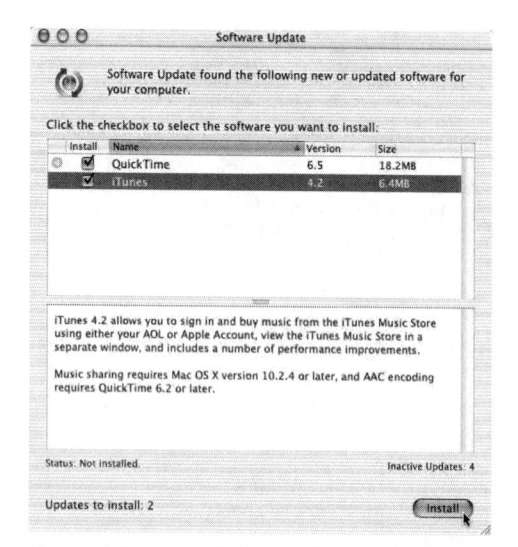

Figure 1.7 Make sure the iTunes check box is checked, then click Install. The iTunes installer downloads and automatically runs.

What's New in iTunes 4?

If you've been using iTunes for a while, you may want to know what's changed over the past few versions and dot-release updates.

What Changed from Version 3 to 4?

iTunes 4, released in April 2003, offered a number of improvements over iTunes 3, most notably the integration of the iTunes Music Store and the ability to play and encode audio using AAC (a high-quality, low-bandwidth encoder). It also introduced music sharing (for personal use), burning to DVD discs, and the ability to add album art. Apple also made a few changes in the organization of some windows (such as the Song Information window) and enhanced performance.

What Changed from Version 4 to 4.1?

iTunes 4.1, the first version available for *both* Mac and Windows, offered a few interesting new features when it was introduced in October 2003: It let you burn a long playlist (or a single long item, such as an audiobook) across multiple CDs, and it could do error correction when importing audio CDs (to ensure fewer problems with older CD drives). When version 4.1 was introduced, Apple also added several new features to the iTunes Music Store: You could save links to specific places in the iTunes Music Store (for bookmarking purposes or to share with friends) buy audiobooks, give gift certificates, and set up an allowance for a child. iPod users (with version 2.1 of the iPod software) could, for the first time, transfer playlists and voice notes to iTunes.

Chapter 1

What changed from Version 4.1 to 4.2?

iTunes 4.2, introduced only a couple of months after version 4.1 (and a couple of weeks before this book was completed), offers only a few new features. You'll find a new field in the information window for songs, called *grouping*; this is most often used to indicate that a song is part of a larger piece, as occurs frequently in the case of classical music, but many iTunes users are finding it convenient for specifying a secondary genre. On Windows, switching from the full iTunes window to a small player now conforms better to Windows interface standards: You no longer click the Maximize button to switch to a smaller window. AOL users can now purchase from the iTunes Music Store without getting an Apple account. And, all users can open the iTunes Music Store in its own window.

Installing iTunes (Windows)

For the most part, installing iTunes is pretty straightforward. It's merely a matter of launching the installer and clicking through several dialogs.

To install iTunes:

1. Locate and install a copy of iTunes on your PC, as described earlier in this chapter.

    If you've downloaded from the iTunes Web site, the InstallShield Wizard should open automatically.

2. If the InstallShield Wizard isn't already open, locate the file iTunesSetUp, and double-click to open it.

3. Follow the Wizard's prompts, clicking Next to move from screen to screen (click Yes to agree to the license agreement).

    Most of the screens you see will be similar to those you've seen in other software installations. When you see the Setup Type screen (**Figure 1.8**), choose from the following options:

    continues on next page

What's QuickTime Got to Do With It?

Wondering why the you're being asked about QuickTime? QuickTime is Apple's media architecture, and it provides various audio services to iTunes. (The most significant example is iTunes's highly touted ability to encode and play AAC audio; iTunes actually relies on QuickTime to do this.)

Thus, on Windows computers, QuickTime is installed with iTunes. (On the Mac, users already have QuickTime preinstalled.)

Since QuickTime is being installed, the iTunes Installer asks you a QuickTime configuration question: Do you want QuickTime Player (an application that gets installed as part of QuickTime) to become the default player for media files? You don't have to worry that agreeing to this will allow QuickTime to take over all media types; for the most part, it's just the ones that are Apple-bred, such as QuickTime movies and PICT files, plus a few others, such as MPEG-4 and DV. To see or change the list of file types that QuickTime can play, go to the QuickTime control panel (Start > Settings > Control Panel > QuickTime), choose File Type Associations, and then click the File Types button.

Chapter 1

- **Install desktop shortcuts**. This installs an iTunes icon on your desktop and in your Quick Launch toolbar.
- **Use iTunes as the default player for audio files.** This sets iTunes as the player to open audio files that you double-click or encounter on the Internet. Think of it as a temporary setting, however, since the default player changes under a variety of circumstances. (See sidebar, "Choosing a Default Audio Player for Windows," later in this chapter.)
- **Use QuickTime as the default player for media files**. This sets the QuickTime Player application to open any video, audio, and animation files that QuickTime is capable of handling and that iTunes doesn't handle. (That is, most audio files will be handled by iTunes.)

When you double-click other media files (video, animation, MIDI, certain sound files), they'll open in QuickTime Player.

When you double-click most audio files in Windows Explorer or click links to audio files in a Web browser, the files will open in iTunes.

Puts iTunes icons on your desktop and your Quick Launch toolbar

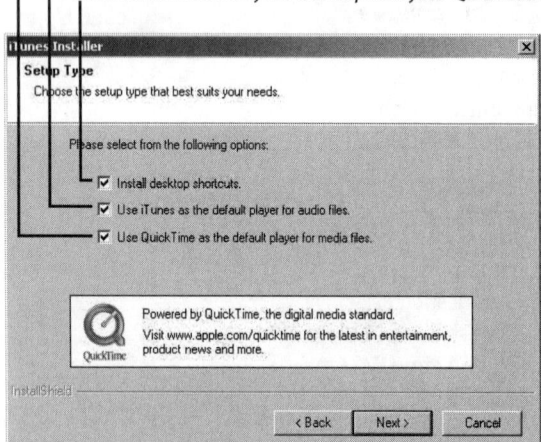

Figure 1.8 Use the Setup Type screen in the Install Wizard to choose where you place iTunes icons and to set up a default player for your audio files.

Getting Started

Figure 1.9 When you download iTunes from Apple's Web site, you download the iTunes *disk image* onto your computer—a single file that contains all the software you need to install iTunes.

Figure 1.10 When you double-click the disk image file, the iTunes 4.2 folder appears.

Figure 1.11 When you double-click the disk icon, this iTunes4.mpkg file appears. Click it to run the installer.

Figure 1.12 During installation, you'll need to enter your username and password. (This assumes you have administrative privileges on the computer on which you are installing.)

Installing iTunes (Mac)

If you've downloaded iTunes from the iTunes download Web page, you'll need to manually run the installer, as we describe on this page. But if you run Software Update, skip this page; iTunes is installed automatically.

To install iTunes:

1. On your Mac, locate and double-click the file called iTunes4.dmg.

   The iTunes4.dmg file (**Figure 1.9**) is a *disk image,* which is downloaded to your computer when you download iTunes from Apple's Web site. When double-clicked, it is automatically turned into a folder called iTunes 4.2 (**Figure 1.10**).

2. Double-click the iTunes 4.2 folder.

   You'll see a file called iTunes4.mpkg appear in the folder (**Figure 1.11**).

3. Double-click the iTunes4.mpkg file.

   The Installer opens.

4. Follow the prompts, clicking Continue on most screens (and clicking Agree to agree to the license agreement). At the last screen, click Upgrade; you'll be prompted to enter your Mac OS X user name and password (**Figure 1.12**); this needs to be the name and password for an OS X user account with administrative privileges.

   iTunes is installed in your Applications folder.

✔ Tip

- If you're running Safari as your Web browser on Mac OS X 10.3 (Panther), the iTunes disk image, once downloaded, automatically turns into a folder called iTunes 4.2. Therefore, you'll want to skip step one.

Launching iTunes

You have a variety of ways to launch iTunes; use whichever method you find most convenient.

Ways to launch iTunes (Windows):

◆ Use the Start menu. In Windows XP; choose Start > All Programs > iTunes> iTunes (**Figure 1.13**). In Windows 2000; choose Start > Programs > iTunes> iTunes.

◆ If you selected "Install desktop shortcuts" during installation, you'll find an iTunes icon on your computer's desktop and in your Quick Launch toolbar; you can double-click the former, or single-click the latter. (If you're using Windows XP, your Quick Launch toolbar may not be visible; you can show it by right-clicking on the task bar and choosing Toolbars > QuickLaunch.)

Figure 1.13 To open iTunes in Windows, navigate from the Start menu.

Ways to launch iTunes (Mac OS X):

◆ An iTunes icon should be in your Dock, unless you've removed it; single-click it to open iTunes (**Figure 1.14**).

◆ Find iTunes in your Applications directory, and double-click to open it.

Figure 1.14 On the Mac, click the iTunes icon in your Dock to launch it. (You'll also find iTunes in your Applications folder.)

✔ Tips

- On a Mac, you'll find that double-clicking many audio files in the Finder launches iTunes; this method isn't failproof, however, as sometimes other applications open.

- On Windows, if you selected "Use iTunes as the default player for audio files" during installation, double-clicking some audio files will open iTunes.

- If you're running Mac OS X version 10.3 (Panther) or Windows XP and you switch users (without logging out), you'll find that you can't have iTunes open for both users. You'll have to quit iTunes as one user, before opening it as another user.

12

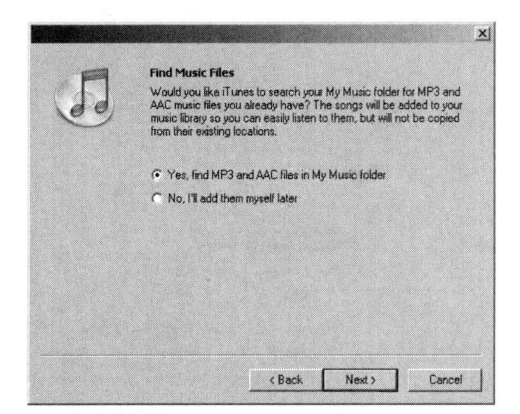

Figure 1.15 If you select Yes, audio files in your My Music folder will be listed in iTunes. Nothing changes on your hard drive.

Figure 1.16 Selecting No is safest. You can change this preference later.

Setting Up iTunes

The first time you launch iTunes, you'll see a Welcome screen, directing you to click Next so you can answer some questions. While the process is mostly self-explanatory, and agreeing to the defaults (by simply clicking Next) is OK in most cases, a few screens require some explanation.

Setup screens on Windows:

◆ **Find Music Files**

You are asked if you want iTunes to search your My Music folder for MP3 and AAC files (**Figure 1.15**). Answering Yes ensures that these music files will be available to you from within iTunes. The screen lets you know that the files will not be copied to a new location; this means that there will be a listing for each of them in iTunes, but the files containing the audio will reside exactly where they were on your hard disk before iTunes installation.

◆ **Keep iTunes Music Folder Organized**

You are asked if you want iTunes to keep your Music Folder organized (**Figure 1.16**). The default is No. We recommend leaving this option set to No for complete safety, though (as you'll find out in Chapter 5) the risks are actually minimal and there are advantages to having iTunes keep your music folder organized. You can always change this setting later, using the Advanced tab in the Preferences window.

✔ Tip

■ You'll understand more about MP3 and AAC files when you read the next chapter.

Setup screens on Mac OS X:

◆ **Internet Audio**

You are asked whether you want iTunes to handle Internet audio content and if it's OK for iTunes to automatically connect to the Internet to get information about CDs you insert (**Figure 1.17**). Saying Yes to both is generally fine for most users. However, don't agree to the first option if you have a different preferred application for handling the audio (typically MP3 files) that you come across when browsing the Web. In addition, you may not want to agree to the second option if you have a dial-up connection, unless having your Mac connect to the Internet every time you insert a CD doesn't bother you.

◆ **Find music files**

You are asked if you want iTunes to search your Home folder for MP3 and AAC files (**Figure 1.18**). Answering Yes ensures that these music files will be available to you from within iTunes. You are told that the files will be copied; this means that each file will be duplicated (with the copy being put in the iTunes Music folder) and that changes made via iTunes will affect only the copies in the iTunes Music folder.

◆ **Keep iTunes Music Folder Organized**

You're asked if you want iTunes to keep your Music Folder organized (**Figure 1.19**). Go ahead and leave the default setting as Yes unless you have previously organized files and folders in your iTunes Music Folder. (In Chapter 5 we explain in detail what keeping your Music Folder organized really means.)

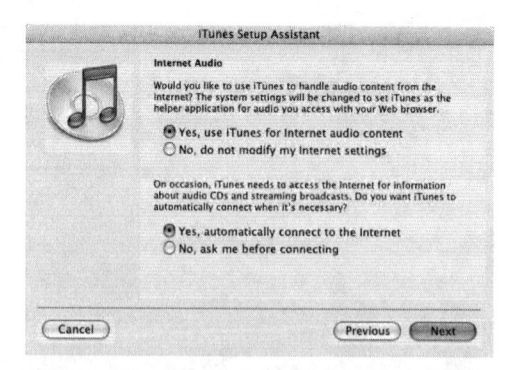

Figure 1.17 Select Yes for using iTunes to play Internet audio content unless you have a different preferred application for handling audio. Select Yes for connecting to the Internet if you want iTunes to be able to get information about the audio CDs you insert.

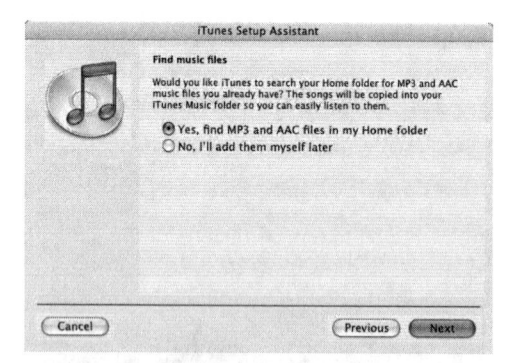

Figure 1.18 Select Yes to have audio files in your Home directory listed in iTunes. Copies of all files will be placed in your iTunes Music folder.

Figure 1.19 Select Yes to keep your iTunes Music Folder organized.

Choosing a Default Audio Player in Windows

You may experience a little struggling between applications as they vie to be the default player of audio files. (The default player is the one that opens when you double-click an audio file's icon. It's also the player that will play most MP3 files you find on Web pages.)

iTunes is your default audio player if you choose this option during the installation process (see Figure 1.8). You can also specify iTunes as the default player by choosing the Set Program Access and Defaults option in your Start menu. (You'll find that you can also make iTunes your default player in the iTunes Preferences window; see "About iTunes Preferences" at the end of this chapter.) Some other audio players, however, may rudely take over as the default audio player without asking when launched.

If iTunes is not your default media player, it will ask you every time you launch it (that is, any time after the first time) whether you want it to become the default player. If you click the Yes button, iTunes will once again become the default player, at least temporarily. (Another audio application may steal the default player title back when launched.)

If you select "Do not show this message again" when you click Yes, iTunes starts acting like the less polite applications, and automatically takes over as the default player each time you open it; it doesn't ask you because it already has your permission.

If you know you *don't* want iTunes to be your default audio player, click No and check "Do not show this message again." iTunes will remain a polite citizen: It won't take over as the default player, nor will it bug you about it again.

Chapter 1

Quick Interface Overview

When you open iTunes, you're presented with the main iTunes window (**Figure 1.20**). You'll find the interface quite easy to use. Let's take a quick look at the various controls and panes. (The majority of these are covered in detail in Chapter 3, "Finding and Playing Music," but many of them come up in other chapters as well.)

What's here changes depending on what's selected in your Source pane. It could be a Browse button, a Burn Disc button, a Refresh button, an Import button, or an Options button.

Playback controls

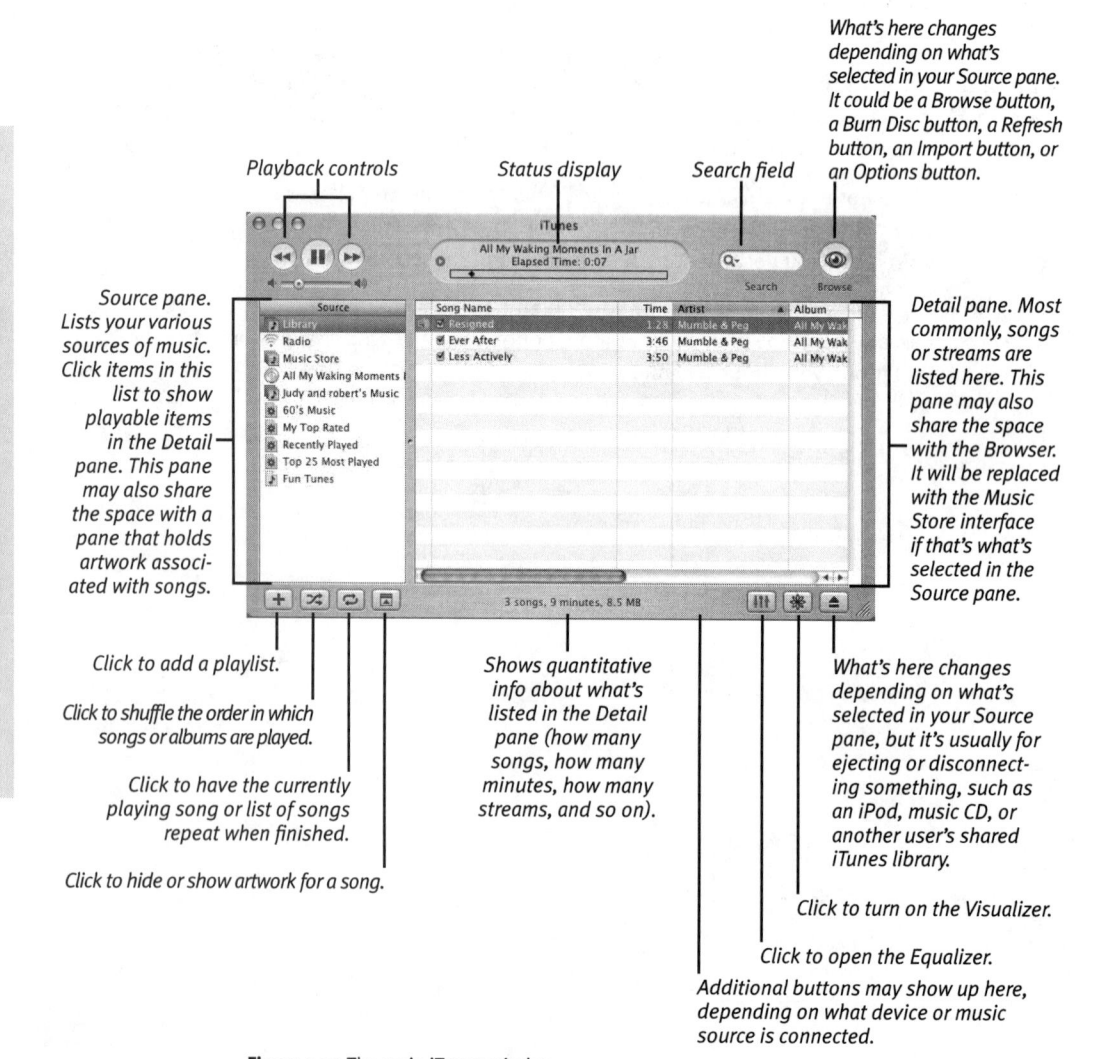

Status display

Search field

Source pane. Lists your various sources of music. Click items in this list to show playable items in the Detail pane. This pane may also share the space with a pane that holds artwork associated with songs.

Detail pane. Most commonly, songs or streams are listed here. This pane may also share the space with the Browser. It will be replaced with the Music Store interface if that's what's selected in the Source pane.

Click to add a playlist.

Click to shuffle the order in which songs or albums are played.

Click to have the currently playing song or list of songs repeat when finished.

Click to hide or show artwork for a song.

Shows quantitative info about what's listed in the Detail pane (how many songs, how many minutes, how many streams, and so on).

What's here changes depending on what's selected in your Source pane, but it's usually for ejecting or disconnecting something, such as an iPod, music CD, or another user's shared iTunes library.

Click to turn on the Visualizer.

Click to open the Equalizer.

Additional buttons may show up here, depending on what device or music source is connected.

Figure 1.20 The main iTunes window.

16

Getting Started

About iTunes Preferences

We've already referenced the iTunes Preferences window several times in this chapter, and you'll be coming across it again during the rest of this book, so we figure it's time for a formal introduction.

The Preferences window is probably the window you'll see second most frequently in iTunes. (The main iTunes window, shown in Figure 1.19, is, of course, the window you'll see most often.)

The Preferences window has more than 40 options you can set; we'll be covering them all in this book. For now, though, we'll just explain how you open this window and briefly describe what you'll find on each tab.

Figure 1.21 (Windows) From the Edit menu, choose Preferences to open the Preferences window.

Figure 1.22 (Mac OS X) From the iTunes application menu, choose Preferences to open the Preferences window.

To open the iTunes Preferences window:

◆ (Windows) From the Edit menu, select Preferences (**Figure 1.21**) or use the keyboard shortcut: Ctrl-, (comma).

◆ (Mac) From the iTunes menu, select Preferences (**Figure 1.22**) or use the keyboard shortcut, Command-, (comma).

The iTunes Preferences window opens, showing the General tab (**Figure 1.23**), unless you previously had it open to another tab.

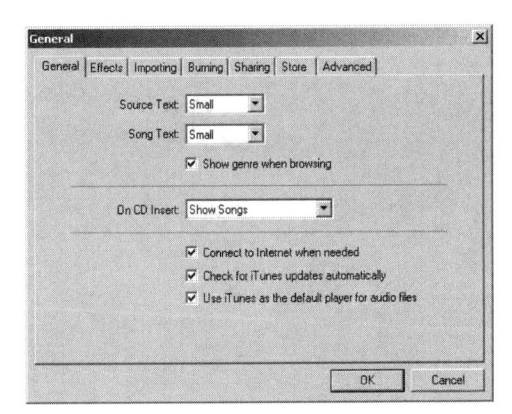

Figure 1.23 The Preferences window lets you set preferences for importing music from CDs, sharing music over a network, displaying special effects, buying music from the iTunes Music Store, and much more.

17

Preferences tabs overview:

- The General tab offers miscellaneous settings, some of which affect the layout of the iTunes window (covered in Chapter 3), one that specifies how iTunes should handle inserted CDs (covered in Chapter 2), and others that specify how and when iTunes should connect to the Internet.

- The Effects tab lets you make choices that impact song playback (covered in Chapter 3).

- The Importing tab provides options for importing music from audio CDs (covered in Chapter 2).

- The Burning tab lets you specify options for burning CDs and DVDs (covered in Chapter 6).

- The Sharing tab is where you'll select your preferences for sharing your music and accessing other people's shared music (covered in Chapter 8).

- The Store tab allows you to tailor your shopping experience in the iTunes Music Store (covered in Chapter 4).

- The Advanced tab is another tab with miscellaneous options, the majority of which have to do with what's happening on your hard drive (covered in Chapter 5). Other options, however, have more to do with playback (covered in Chapter 3).

Adding Music to your Library

If you want to listen to music in iTunes (which is what it's all about, right?), you'll need to start by putting some music into your iTunes library.

Once we provide a quick explanation of the iTunes library, we'll show you what is probably the simplest and cheapest method of adding music: importing (known as *ripping*) songs from a CD. It's the cheapest (for most of you) because you already own CDs. And it's simple because importing an audio CD is basically a one-step process.

Some of you may already have audio files, such as MP3s or WAVs, on your computer, so we'll show you several methods for importing stand-alone audio files into iTunes. We'll also explain your options for getting music from the Internet. (The iTunes Music Store, however, is likely to be your primary source; we'll cover it in detail in Chapter 4.)

Finally, we'll end the chapter with something for your eyes rather than your ears: how to add artwork for albums and songs.

About the Library

Your iTunes library is the central repository of your music. Everything you add to iTunes is listed there. This includes music imported from audio CDs, copied from your hard disk (or any other computer media, such as a Zip disk), or downloaded over the Internet. Your iTunes library can even include links to streaming audio on the Internet.

As you'll see in Chapter 3, even if your library becomes one huge bin of songs—the number can easily mushroom into the thousands—it's still easy to find specific items in it, because you can browse, search, and sort the library in a variety of ways.

The library provides the source for all songs in iTunes playlists. (Chapter 5 covers playlists in depth.) Songs in playlists are merely pointers to songs in the library.

Everything in the library points to an actual file somewhere—usually on your hard drive, but it could also be on the Internet.

To view a list of everything in your library:

◆ Click the library entry in the Source pane. All items in your library are listed in the Detail pane (**Figure 2.1**).

✔ Tips

- To see everything in your library, be sure nothing is typed in the Search field and that you are not using the Browser. This caveat is important (as Chapter 3 will discuss), since both searching and browsing limit what appears in the Detail pane.

- You can rename your library. Just double-click the text of the library entry to make the text editable (**Figure 2.2**). Type a new name for your library, and then click anywhere other than on the text you just edited to make the name change take effect (**Figure 2.3**).

Figure 2.1 When you click Library in the Source pane, all of the songs in your collection are listed in the Detail pane.

Figure 2.2 Double-click to make the name of your library editable.

Figure 2.3 Type a new name, then click away from the text to set the name.

Adding Music to your Library

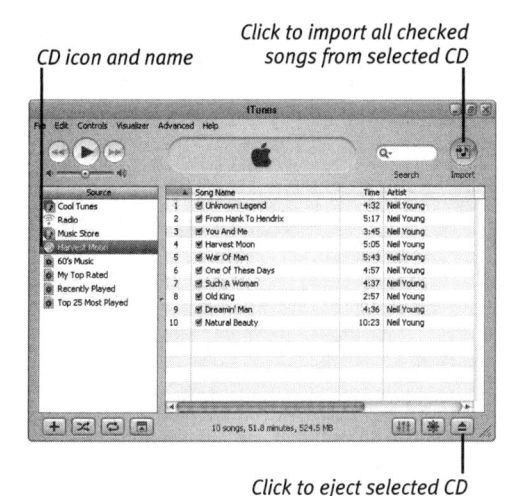

CD icon and name
Click to import all checked songs from selected CD
Click to eject selected CD

Figure 2.4 When you insert a CD, its icon and name appears in the iTunes Source pane; its songs appear in the Detail pane, and the Import button becomes available, as does the Eject button.

Importing an Audio CD

You'll love how easy this is. Grab an audio CD from your shelf and start ripping.

To import all the songs on a CD:

1. Insert the CD into your computer's CD drive.

   The CD icon appears in the iTunes Source pane (sometimes it takes a few seconds, so be patient); the songs on it are likely listed by name, along with additional information such as album and artist (**Figure 2.4**). (See the sidebar "How Does It Know?" for information about how iTunes gets this information, as well as why it might not show any information about the songs other than listing them as Track 1, Track 2, and so on.)

2. Click the Import button (refer to Figure 2.4). iTunes begins to import each song in the list, showing the progress of your import in the status display as it goes (**Figure 2.5**). When iTunes is in the process of importing a song, you'll see an orange circle with a moving wave. Once a song has been imported, you'll see a green circle with a white checkmark.

Indicates how quickly (compared with normal playback speed) song is being imported
Shows progress of the import
Click here to stop importing
Indicates song that has finished importing
Indicates song currently being imported

Figure 2.5 Click the Import button, and iTunes begins to import all the songs.

IMPORTING AN AUDIO CD

21

Chapter 2

Ways to stop an import in progress:

- Click the Import button again.
- Click the tiny "x" icon in the status area (refer to Figure 2.5).

✔ Tips

- To eject a CD from within iTunes, you can select the CD and then either click the Eject Disc button (refer to Figure 2.4), click the Controls menu and choose Eject Disc, or Control-click (Mac) or right-click (Windows) and choose Eject Disc from the contextual menu that appears.

- If you're using an operating system that allows you to do *fast user switching*—a way of logging out of the operating system so that one user's files and programs can remain open while another user logs on— don't switch during a CD import. (Fast user switching is a feature of Mac OS X 10.3 and Windows XP.)

- If you import a lot of CDs in quick succession, you'll save time if you set iTunes to automatically import the songs from a CD once it's inserted and eject the CD when the import is done. To do this, open your Preferences window and, from the General tab's On CD Insert pop-up menu, select Import Songs and Eject (**Figure 2.6**).

- When iTunes is importing, the status area by default shows what's being imported (refer to Figure 2.5). If music is playing at the same time you're importing, you can click the tiny triangular icon on the left side of the status area to show information about what's playing (**Figure 2.7**). If you click it one more time, you'll see a dynamic visual representation of the audio frequencies (which we'll discuss in Chapter 3). Click the icon a third time, and it cycles back to showing the status of the import.

Figure 2.6 If you'll be importing a lot of CDs, you can save time by changing your On CD Insert option to Import Songs and Eject.

Click to cycle among showing status of the import, status of what's currently playing, and a dynamic visual representation of what's playing.

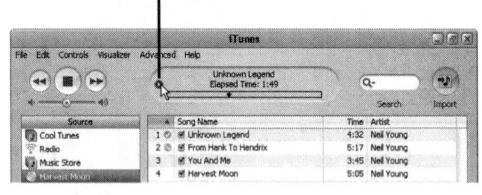

Figure 2.7 You can get information about what's currently playing even while iTunes is busy importing your music.

Adding Music to your Library

How Does It Know?

If you've inserted audio CDs in your computer's CD drive in the past, you've probably found that the CD was generically called "Audio CD" and that the songs were listed as Track 1, Track 2, and so on. iTunes, on the other hand, seems to know the name of the CD, as well as information about the songs on it.

When you insert an audio CD when iTunes is open, iTunes normally connects to a special CD database on the Internet (called the *CDDB*, for Compact Disc Database), retrieves information about that CD and the songs on it, and places that information in the list of songs that appears in the Detail pane. (If you're connected to the Internet, and if you pay attention when you first insert a CD into your computer, you'll see a window appear for a few seconds, entitled "Accessing Gracenote CDDB".)

If you're not connected to the Internet, iTunes obviously can't access CDDB. You can also tell iTunes not to connect to the Internet: In the iTunes Preferences window on the General tab, uncheck the "Connect to Internet when needed" checkbox (refer to Figure 2.6). If you are seeing songs listed only as Track 1, Track 2, and so on, it is likely that this item is already unchecked.

You can manually retrieve information about a CD by clicking the Advanced menu and choosing Get CD Track Names (**Figure 2.8**).

- If iTunes isn't already open when you insert an audio CD, you may find that iTunes opens automatically. On a Windows computer this occurs only if iTunes is set as the default audio player (see Chapter 1). On the Mac, you can change this setting in the CDs and DVDs pane of your System Preferences.

- While it's nice that you get a green check box icon that tells you when a song has finished importing from a CD, iTunes unfortunately won't remember what you've imported from a particular CD the next time you insert it, so you won't see those icons; in other words, when you pop in a CD, iTunes doesn't immediately tell you that you've already imported a particular song. Instead, iTunes will warn you that the song you're trying to reimport is already in your library.

- You can monitor how quickly iTunes is importing by checking in the status area (refer to Figure 2.5); the figure in parentheses indicates how much faster the import speed is than the normal speed of play. (For example, if the figure here averages around "2.0 x", a 2-minute song will be imported in 1 minute.)

Figure 2.8 If you aren't connected to the Internet when you first insert a CD, you can later (when you connect) download album and song information by choosing Get CD Track Names from the Advanced menu.

IMPORTING AN AUDIO CD

23

Chapter 2

Importing Individual Songs from an Audio CD

Sometimes you don't want every song on an audio CD to be imported into your iTunes library.

To import individual songs from a CD (I):

1. Click the check box to the left of each song you *don't* want to import, so that only the songs you want to import are checked (**Figure 2.9**).
2. Click the Import button.

Figure 2.9 Only checked songs get imported when you click the Import button.

To import individual songs from a CD (II):

1. Select the song(s) you want to import by clicking on them.

   Shift-click to select multiple contiguous songs. Command-click (Mac) or Ctrl-click (Windows) to select multiple songs that are not contiguous. (Chapter 5 has more info on making selections.)

2. Click on any of the selected songs and drag to the library in the Source pane (**Figure 2.10**).

   As you drag, you'll see a ghosted version of the song(s); a plus-sign icon appears when you mouse over the Library entry (refer to Figure 2.10), indicating that you've dragged to a source that can receive the songs.

3. Release the mouse button.

   The songs are added to your library.

Figure 2.10 Alternatively, you can select songs and drag them to your library.

Adding Music to your Library

Joining Songs

Some albums contain songs that are meant to be played without pausing, even though they are divided into separate tracks. (The Beatles' Abbey Road is one well-known example.) If you want iTunes to import a number of tracks from a CD as one song, select the songs you want joined and, from the Advanced menu, choose Join CD tracks (**Figure 2.11**). The tracks appear linked (**Figure 2.12**). You'll end up importing a single song, with a name consisting of the names of all the joined songs, separated by hyphens.

(If you don't join songs, you may not notice the pause between tracks if you have "Crossfade playback" checked on the Effects tab of your iTunes Preferences pane; see Chapter 3.)

Figure 2.11 When you want contiguous songs on a CD imported as a single song, select the songs and choose Advanced > Join CD Tracks.

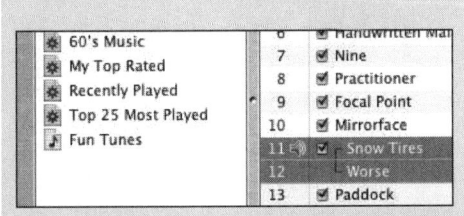

Figure 2.12 iTunes shows that it knows you want the two songs joined. When you import, you end up with a single long song.

✔ Tips

- To quickly add or remove all the checkmarks, Command-click (Mac) or Ctrl-click (Windows) any one of the check boxes.

- Don't confuse the two methods for importing individual songs. Be aware that when you import songs by clicking the Import button, what's *selected* (highlighted in blue) is not necessarily what gets imported—only checked items are imported. If you import songs by dragging them to the Source pane, it doesn't matter what's checked, only what's selected.

- If you opt for the latter method (dragging selected songs), you can drag your selected songs to the white area below your sources (the plus-sign icon will appear when you do) and then release your mouse button to create a new playlist containing those songs. You can also drag to an existing playlist, if you have any. We'll explore these topics in more depth in Chapter 5.

IMPORTING INDIVIDUAL SONGS FROM AN AUDIO CD

25

Chapter 2

Changing Import Preferences for CDs

When you import tracks from a CD, you have a few options to choose from. The defaults are usually fine, but you may find that you want to adjust your encoding settings, or that you'd prefer to have iTunes start playing a CD's songs immediately upon importing, for example.

To change your importing preferences:

1. From the iTunes menu (Mac) or the Edit menu (Windows), choose Preferences (**Figure 2.13**).

2. Click the Importing tab.

   The Importing pane appears (**Figure 2.14**), giving you several encoding and settings options:

Figure 2.13 Open the Preferences window.

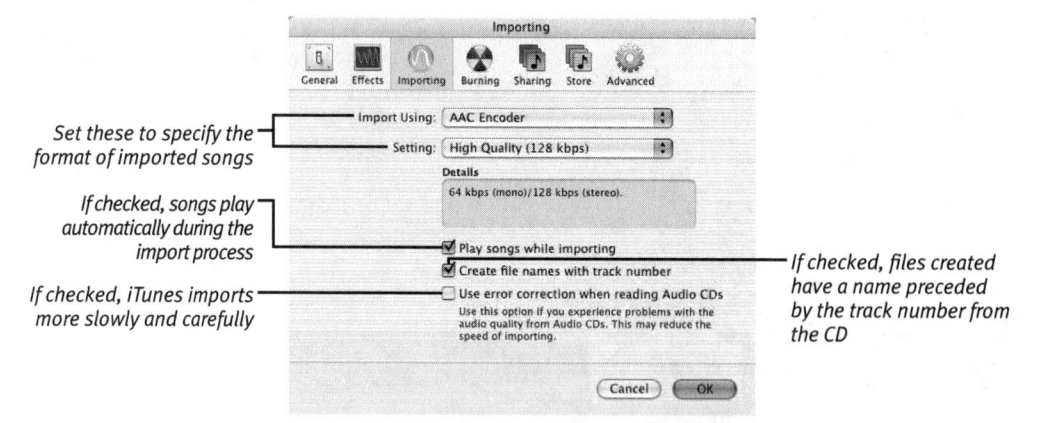

Set these to specify the format of imported songs

If checked, songs play automatically during the import process

If checked, iTunes imports more slowly and carefully

If checked, files created have a name preceded by the track number from the CD

Figure 2.14 The Importing tab of the Preferences window.

Adding Music to your Library

▲ **Import Using** and **Setting.** You can change your encoder and its settings. The section "Changing How Songs Are Encoded on Import" explains these two options.

▲ **Play songs while importing.** Leave this option checked to have your CD begin playing during the import process. If you are encoding songs as AAC, iTunes begins playing the first song only after it is fully imported. For other formats, iTunes can begin playing the song it is importing after only a few seconds. If you uncheck this option, your import happens slightly faster.

▲ **Create file names with track number**. If you leave this option checked, the file that's copied to your hard drive is given a name that begins with the track number. (For example, a file called "Harvest Moon.m4a" would be called "04 Harvest Moon.m4a" if this option were checked.) This is significant only if you will be manipulating your files in the Mac OS X Finder or in Windows Explorer, because if the filenames are preceded with numbers, you won't be able to list them alphabetically.

▲ **Use error correction when reading Audio CDs.** Check this if iTunes has problems importing from your CDs. Checking this option causes iTunes to import data more slowly and carefully than it would otherwise.

27

About iTunes Encoding Choices

In the world of digital media, there are a variety of *file formats,* and a variety of *compressors.* You can think of the file format as specifying the packaging of the media. Not all media in these files is compressed, but when it is, there's always a specific compressor that has done the job. Sometimes a file format and a compressor have the same name; other times they don't.

When iTunes imports audio from a CD, it can change how the music is *encoded,* which can mean a change in file format, in the compressor, or both. iTunes provides four possible encoding choices: AAC, MP3, AIFF, and WAV. We'll go into the mechanics of selecting these a bit later in this chapter; but we'll briefly explain each of these options here.

Different MPEGs

Several file formats bear the MPEG label. (MPEG stands for *Moving Picture Experts Group* and is an organization that has developed all the specifications of the various MPEG standards.)

You'll find three versions of MPEG in use today: MPEG-1, MPEG-2, and MPEG-4.

MPEG-1 is more than 10 years old, but it's still used often because a wide range of media players play MPEG-1 files. In the audio world, in particular, many players play MPEG-1 Layer III, audio—more commonly referred to as MP3. (We hope this clears up a common misconception: MP3 is not MPEG-3; it's most often a form of MPEG-1.)

MPEG-2 is the format used for DVD; MPEG-2 audio files are not all that common, but iTunes can play back some of them. (MPEG-2 Layer III, an extension of MPEG-1 Layer III, is also called MP3, though it's far less common.)

MPEG-4, the new kid on the block, is based on the QuickTime file format. (Like QuickTime, it can contain much more than audio and video and is useful for the Web, CD-ROMs, and a variety of hardware devices, such as handhelds). Not a lot of MPEG-4 audio players are available. iTunes and iPod take full advantage of this format. So, when Apple refers to AAC files, it is *actually* talking about MPEG-4 audio files in which the audio is compressed with the AAC compressor.

MP3

MP3 (which actually stands for MPEG Layer 3) refers to both the name of a file format and the compressor used within files of that format. It has been a very popular choice for encoding audio, due largely to the efficiency of MP3 compression; MP3 files are approximately one-tenth the size of uncompressed audio of equivalent quality. MP3 is not, however, as efficient as the newer AAC.

MP3 is the default encoder for iTunes only if you don't have QuickTime 6.2 or greater installed (which provides access to AAC).

You'll want to encode as MP3 if you will be creating an MP3 CD (covered in Chapter 6) or putting the files on a portable MP3 player that's not an iPod.

AAC

AAC (Advanced Audio Coding) is an audio compressor developed as part of the MPEG-4 standard. MPEG-4 was introduced only in the last few years. As such, files compressed with AAC can't yet play in as many applications or on as many devices as MP3s, but it's more modern and more efficient: You get the same high quality using AAC as with MP3, but in an even smaller file (approximately 80 percent of the size). It's a perfect choice for playback in iTunes or on an iPod.

When AAC is selected as the encoder in iTunes (as it is by default unless you lack QuickTime 6.2 or later), the files created are MPEG-4 files that are compressed using the AAC compressor. (The file extension is .m4a, one of several extensions for MPEG-4 files.)

AIFF

AIFF (Audio Interchange File Format) files contain audio data that is virtually identical to what is stored on an audio CD. Although AIFF files *can* be compressed with a variety of compressors, iTunes applies no compression when you select AIFF as the encoder. (The audio on audio CDs is also uncompressed.)

The main reason for choosing AIFF as your iTunes encoder is if you want a version that's uncompressed (but much larger than MP3 or AAC) so that you can later recompress it in whatever way you need. (See the sidebar "Ripping for the Future".) Highly discriminating listeners may also want an uncompressed version for burning back to audio CD (as we'll cover in Chapter 6).

WAV

WAV is a longtime Windows audio file format. Just about any Windows tool can handle WAV files. WAV files *can* be compressed, but typically they're not. iTunes does not compress when encoding as WAV.

There's no reason to use WAV for importing CDs or for any other iTunes function (playback, burning CDs, or transfer to an MP3 player or iPod). But if you have a need for WAV files (for use with some other Windows program), iTunes will work as a converter. (See "Converting Songs to a Different Audio Format" later in this chapter.)

> **Ripping for the Future**
>
> By default, iTunes is set to compress your audio using what's currently the best and most efficient compressor, AAC. Will this remain the best? Almost certainly not. If you want to be prepared to create audio files using whatever emerges as the best option next, you may want to import as AIFF or WAV. It'll take up more space—much more—but you'll always have an uncompressed version that you can convert to another format. (It's a bad idea to compress something that's already been compressed.)
>
> Remember, however, that AIFF or WAV files are about ten times larger than MP3s or AACs of near-equivalent sound quality. Thus, we recommend importing as AIFF or WAV only if you have a lot of hard drive space or if you're not importing a lot of songs.

Changing How Songs Are Encoded on Import

By default, iTunes 4 is set to convert all imported songs to AAC or MP3. (iTunes defaults to MP3s only if you don't have QuickTime 6.2 or later.) You can change the default encoding format. For example, you may want to import your songs as MP3 files if you plan to burn an MP3 CD (see Chapter 6). You may want an AIFF or WAV file if you want an uncompressed, highest-quality version of your file. And, for any format, you may decide that you want to change encoding settings to improve audio quality or create smaller files.

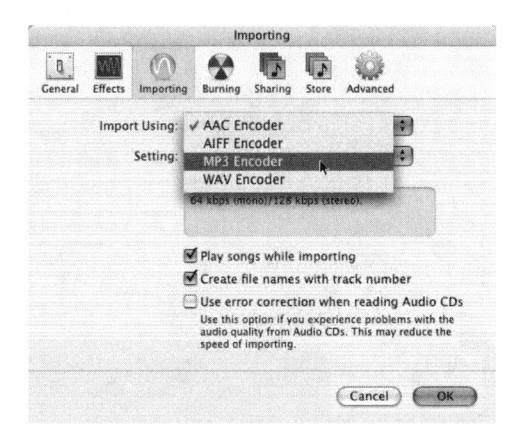

Figure 2.15 Change the encoding format by choosing an option from the Import Using pop-up menu.

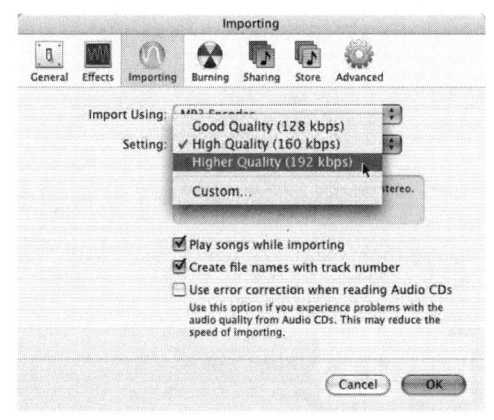

Figure 2.16 Change the settings for the selected encoder by choosing from the Setting pop-up menu.

To change the encoding format and settings:

1. Open the Importing tab of the Preferences window (refer to Figure 2.14).

2. Change the encoding format by choosing from the Import Using pop-up menu (**Figure 2.15**).

3. Change the settings for the selected encoder by choosing from the Setting pop-up menu (**Figure 2.16**).

   For all encoders, you can either select a preset combination of settings or select Custom to pick your own combination.

4. If you've selected Custom, make choices in the window that appears (we cover these options in the following section, "About Custom Encoder Settings"); then click OK.

5. Click the OK button at the bottom of the Preferences window.

   The Preferences window closes. Your encoding settings are saved and will be used the next time you import audio.

✔ Tip

- The changes you make here also apply to files you convert. See "Converting Songs to a Different Audio Format" later in this chapter.

31

Chapter 2

About Custom Encoder Settings

If you select Custom for your encoder setting (refer to Figure 2.16), a new window appears from which you'll pick a variety of settings. The options available differ depending on which encoder you selected. (See **Figures 2.17**, **2.18**, and **2.19**.)

If you opt to pick custom settings, it's because you're not quite satisfied with the results you've achieved from the presets found in the Settings menu. To get results that sound better to your ears, you'll want to understand what each of the options means.

Settings for all formats

- **Sample Rate.** Digitized sound is actually composed of a sequence of individual sound samples. The number of samples per second is the sample rate. The more sound samples per second, the higher the quality of the resulting sound but the larger the file.

  For AAC, you have a choice only of 44.100 and 48.000 kHz (kilohertz); for the other encoders you have choices ranging from 8.000 kHz to 48.000 kHz (**Figure 2.20**). If you choose Auto (the default), it uses the same sample rate as the original, which is generally what you want for audio CD import. (Audio CDs, in case you care, are recorded at 44.1 kHz.)

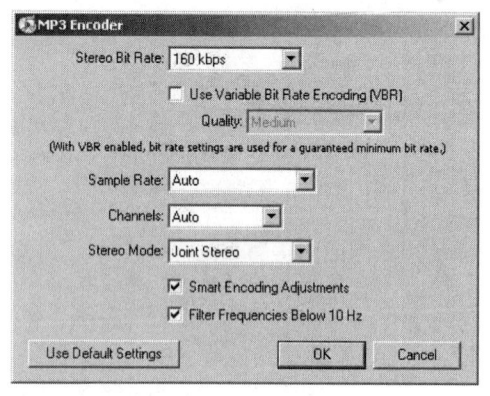

Figure 2.17 The window for setting custom MP3 encoding settings.

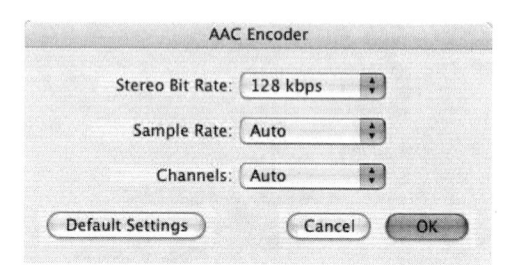

Figure 2.18 The window for setting custom AAC encoding settings.

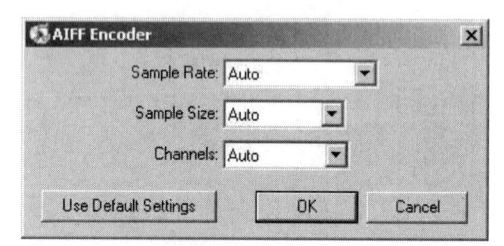

Figure 2.19 The window for setting custom AIFF encoding settings. (These options are identical for WAV custom encoding.).

Adding Music to your Library

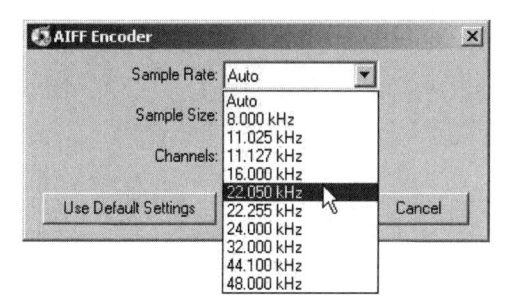

Figure 2.20 You can select a sample rate for all encoders.

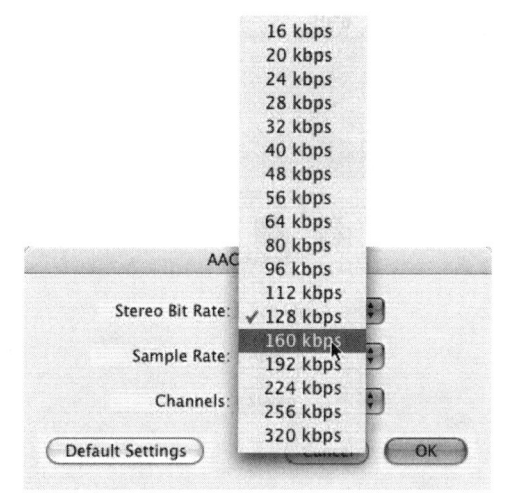

Figure 2.21 For MP3 and AAC, you can also specify a stereo bit rate.

◆ **Channels.** You'll have a choice of Stereo (two channels), Mono (one channel), or Auto (the same number of channels as the original). Most music from CDs has two channels of audio, so you'll want to set this option to Stereo or Auto for importing audio CDs. On the other hand, if you're converting existing audio files on your computer (as we describe later in this chapter), you may be better off with this set to Mono, since odds are that those files were recorded in mono.

Settings for MP3 and AAC only

◆ **Stereo Bit Rate.** Possible bit rates range from 16 to 320 kbps (**Figure 2.21**). This setting specifies the average amount of data per second that is contained in the file (in kilobits per second), assuming that it's encoded in stereo. (If you choose Mono rather than Stereo as your Channels setting, the actual resulting bit rate is half of what you select for Stereo Bit Rate.) Higher bit rates mean higher quality but larger file sizes. A setting of 128 kbps is usually about right for music encoded with AAC, and 160 is good for MP3; these are the defaults.

Settings for MP3 only

◆ **Use Variable Bit Rate Encoding (VBR).** The idea behind variable bit rate encoding is that some parts of an audio recording (for example, where there's a higher range of frequencies) require more bits than others for optimal quality. Checking this box (refer to Figure 2.17) allows the encoder to "rob Peter to pay Paul"—in other words, to devote more bits to the parts that need it and less to the parts that don't, resulting in better overall quality—often without an increase in file size.

ABOUT CUSTOM ENCODER SETTINGS

33

- **Quality.** If you check Use Variable Bit Rate Encoding, you can pick a Quality setting (**Figure 2.22**) that tells iTunes how flexible it can be in devoting extra bits to the "hard parts." The higher the quality setting, the better the resulting sound, but the price you pay is a larger file size.

- **Stereo Mode.** You can choose Joint Stereo or Normal. With Normal chosen, the MP3 file stores a "track" each for the right and the left channels, which can be redundant. Joint Stereo puts similar information in one track and the unique information in the other, producing smaller files; this can give you a better-sounding file when you encode at low bit rates (under 128 kbps).

- **Smart Encoding Adjustments.** If you select this, iTunes may adjust other settings (such as bit rate, number of channels, and sample rate) if it decides that such changes will produce better-sounding audio. It makes adjustments only to settings that you haven't explicitly set.

- **Filter Frequencies Below 10 Hz.** Since frequencies below 10 Hz are essentially inaudible, this removes those frequencies, resulting in a smaller file.

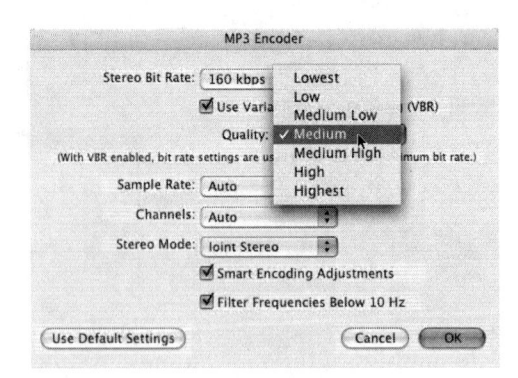

Figure 2.22 For MP3 encoding, you can request variable bit rate encoding at a specified quality level.

Settings for WAV and AIFF only

- **Sample Size.** The size of the audio samples can be either 16 bit or 8 bit. A 16-bit sound sample represents audio more accurately but is twice as large as an 8-bit sound sample; for music you typically want a 16-bit sample size for best quality, but you pay with a file that's twice as large. If you choose Auto (iTunes's default), it uses the same sample rate as the original.

Adding Audio Files from Your Computer

If you've got audio files on your hard drive, a Zip drive, a CD-ROM, or any other type of media that is recognized by your computer, you can add those songs to your iTunes Music library. (You can add a large variety of audio formats; see the table "File Formats iTunes Can Import" later in this chapter.)

Ways to add audio files to your iTunes library:

◆ Select a file(s) or folder(s) in the Finder (Mac) or Windows Explorer (Windows) that you want to add, then drag it to your iTunes Library, located in the Source pane (**Figure 2.23**).

◆ From the File menu, choose Add to Library (Mac), Add File to Library (Windows, **Figure 2.24**), or Add Folder to Library (Windows). Then locate the file(s) or folder(s) you want to add and click Choose.

The files you've selected are added to your library as long as they are music files that iTunes can recognize. If iTunes can't recognize them, it ignores them.

When you add audio files to iTunes, the program may make copies of the files, depending on your iTunes preferences. For Windows users, the default is that files are *not* copied; iTunes points to the file in its original location. For Mac users, iTunes makes a *duplicate* of the file and copies it to your iTunes music folder by default.

Unlike songs imported from an audio CD, audio files on your computer are *not* encoded into a different format when you add them to your iTunes library.

Figure 2.23 Drag audio files directly from Explorer (Windows) or the Finder (Mac) to your library.

Figure 2.24 Alternatively, you can pull down your File menu and choose an Add option.

✔ Tips

- You can change whether or not iTunes copies files by opening your Preferences window, clicking the Advanced tab, and checking or unchecking "Copy files to iTunes music folder when adding to library" (**Figure 2.25**). We'll go into more depth about the structure of the iTunes music folder in Chapter 5.

- If you or iTunes has set your preferences so that files are copied, but you occasionally don't want a file to be copied (if it's very large, for example), you can hold down the Option key (Mac) or Alt key (Windows) when you drag the file, and it won't be copied.

- Windows users can't select multiple files in the Add to Library window, so the select-and-drag method is usually best in situations where you need to add multiple files.

- If the added files are MP3 or MPEG-4 audio files, their entries in the song list may include information in a number of columns in the Detail pane. (Chapter 5 provides details about the information contained in song files.)

- Are you an iPod user? Do you think of your iPod as another hard drive? This isn't a bad way to think about it, but you'll be disappointed if you think you can just drag files from your iPod to iTunes. Read more about using your iPod with iTunes in Chapter 7.

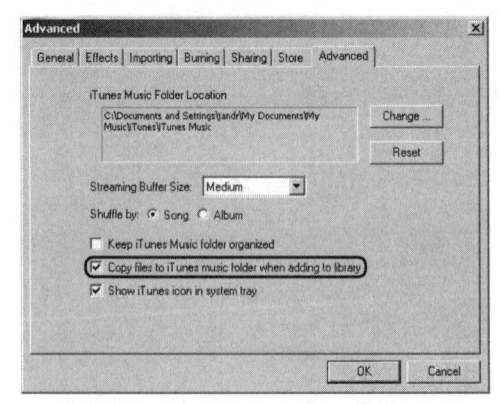

Figure 2.25 You can change whether or not iTunes makes a copy of files you add by checking this box on the Advanced tab of the Preferences window.

Adding QuickTime Movies

You can add a QuickTime movie from your hard drive to your iTunes library, even if it contains a video track or other types of tracks. However, only the audio track(s) will be playable in iTunes.

Information in the QuickTime movie (called an *annotation*) that maps to iTunes columns (Artist, Album, Composer, Comment, and Genre) appears in those columns in the song list. If the movie has a Full Name annotation, this is what's used for the song name.

If your preferences are set to copy files into the iTunes music folder when you add songs (see Figure 2.25), the entire file (including non-audio tracks) is copied. Note that this means you could end up storing a lot of extra data on your hard drive.

Adding Music to your Library

Table 2.1

File Formats iTunes Can Import

File Format	Extension	Description
MIDI	.mid	Musical Instrument Digital interface
*Sound Designer II	.sd2	Works with the professional Sound Designer program
Karaoke	.kar	A variation on MIDI with text; however, no text is allowed into iTunes
MPEG Layer III	.mp3	Popular audio format; includes MPEG-1 Layer III and MPEG-2 Layer III
MPEG Layer II	.mp2	A less popular MPEG-1 format; includes MPEG-1 Layer II and MPEG-2 Layer II.
MPEG-4	.m4a	MPEG-4 AAC audio created with iTunes
MPEG-4	.m4b	MPEG-4 AAC audio for books from iTunes Music Store; copy-protected
MPEG-4	.m4p	MPEG-4 AAC audio for music from iTunes Music Store; copy-protected
MPEG-4	.mp4	MPEG-4 files created by applications other than iTunes
Audible Book	.aa	MP3 Format for Audible.com books
Audio Interchange File	.aif, .aiff, .aifc	Standard audio file format for Mac
Wave	.wav	Standard audio file format for Windows
*System 7 sound	.snd	Old Macintosh file format
QuickTime Movie	.mov	Cross-platform media file format; besides audio can contain video, text, and other types of data.
Nomad Voice File	.nvf	Format for files recorded on some Creative Nomad Audio devices.
Playlist	.pls, .m3u	MP3 playlist

* iTunes can import only on Mac

Moving from Musicmatch Jukebox to iTunes (Windows only)

Prior to October 2003, all Windows iPod models shipped with Musicmatch Jukebox, the popular digital music player. This may mean you have a large Musicmatch collection that you now need to move to iTunes.

Not to worry. Musicmatch stores your ripped music files in the My Music folder on your PC. When you first launched iTunes, iTunes asked if it should search this folder for audio files. If you replied Yes, all of the MP3 files in this folder were automatically added to your iTunes library. If you replied No, it's not too late. You can add them at any time using the methods described for adding files from your computer.

You can also import playlists from Musicmatch Jukebox into iTunes; we'll cover this in Chapter 5.

Adding Audio Files From Your Computer

37

Getting Audio Files from Online Sources

As you're probably well aware, there are numerous Internet sources for downloading audio files. But before you start downloading songs from these sites, it's important to know which sources provide files that are compatible with iTunes.

Files You Download for a Fee

If you want to add purchased songs to your library, the songs need to be in a format that iTunes understands. Virtually all online music stores sell MP3 or Windows Media Audio (WMA) files. In the iTunes world, MP3 is good, and WMA is bad. (See the sidebar "What About Windows Media Audio (WMA)?")

EMusic (www.emusic.com) and MP3.com (www.mp3.com) are examples of stores that sell MP3 files; you can add their songs to your iTunes library without a hitch. But Napster (www.napster.com), BuyMusic (www.buymusic.com), and MusicNow (www.musicnow.com) sell WMA files, and iTunes won't be useful with these. (Other services, such as Listen.com, don't even sell *files* that you can download; instead you purchase access to audio *streams* that play only in streaming media players, such as RealOne and Windows Media Player.)

Files You Download for Free

You'll also come across audio on the Web in a variety of places—on artists' Web sites, educational sites, or personal sites. If the site provides a download button, it's most likely that the format is MP3. For example, Amazon.com's Free Music Download area offers lots of MP3s from independent artists that you can download (**Figure 2.26**).

Figure 2.26 Amazon.com offers a free downloads area where you can download MP3s for your iTunes library. At Amazon's main page, click the Music tab, then the Free Downloads subtab to see what is available.

Adding Music to your Library

Figure 2.27 Windows Internet Explorer users need to right-click the link to an audio file and select Save Target As.

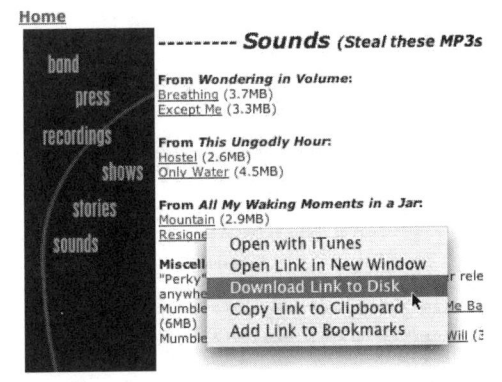

Figure 2.28 Macintosh Internet Explorer and Safari users need to Control-click the link to an audio file and select Download Link to Disk.

On many sites, you'll just find a link that you click to play the audio. Sometimes, such links point to audio *streams* in the WMA format or the Real Media format (another major streaming format); in these cases, there's no file to download. Many sites, however, point to audio *files*—often MP3s—that you *can* download. (See the second tip in this section if you don't know how to do this.) The files you download may be full songs or may only be segments of songs. And, while downloadable files (rather than streams) are not the norm for well-known, established bands, it's worth checking the Web sites of artists you like, especially if they are not yet famous.

✔ Tips

- If you download free audio from an artist's Web site, and you like it enough to keep it in your library, make sure you support their work by *purchasing* some of their music, too.

- Not sure how to download an audio file for which you find only a link? Windows users typically do this in Internet Explorer by right-clicking the link for the file and choosing Save Target As (**Figure 2.27**). Macintosh users typically do this in Internet Explorer or Safari by Control-clicking the link and choosing Download Link to Disk (**Figure 2.28**). The technique will likely be similar in other browsers.

- In Chapter 4, we'll discuss in greater detail how to purchase music from the online iTunes Music Store, which is fully integrated with iTunes; the audio you download is automatically added to your iTunes library. Very convenient!

- Two additional types of files you may come across are those with .m3u or .pls extensions. These are pointers to MP3 files on the Internet. You can download them and add them to your library, but they don't actually contain any music.

- As we'll cover later in the chapter, you can add the Internet address (the URL) of an audio file to your iTunes library as an alternative to downloading and adding the actual file.

GETTING AUDIO FILES FROM ONLINE SOURCES

39

Chapter 2

Converting Songs to a Different Audio Format

iTunes works as a nice little audio-conversion tool. This is useful, since the individual audio files you add from your hard drive don't get automatically converted to AAC or MP3 files, as do imported audio CD files.

To convert songs to a different audio format:

1. Set your encoding options in the Importing tab to indicate the format to which you want to convert. (See "Changing How Songs Are Encoded on Import" earlier in this chapter.)

2. Select the song or songs you want to convert.

3. From the Advanced menu, choose Convert Selection to AAC, Convert Selection to MP3, Convert Selection to AIFF, or Convert Selection to WAV (**Figure 2.29**); only one of these appears depending on which format is selected in the Importing tab.

   iTunes converts the song, informing you of its progress in the status area (**Figure 2.30**). It typically begins playing the converted version of the song a few seconds after starting the conversion process.

   You'll find two versions of the song in your library when done (**Figure 2.31**).

Figure 2.29 From the Advanced menu, you can choose to convert to whatever encoding format is selected in the Importing tab of the Preferences window.

Figure 2.30 The status area shows you the progress of the conversion.

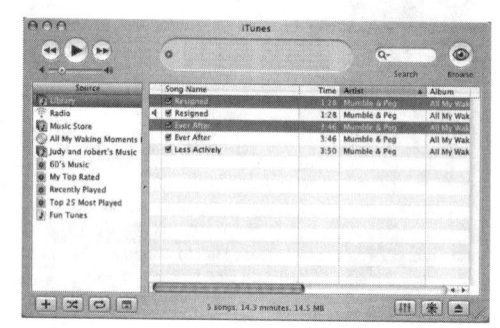

Figure 2.31 Both the original and the converted version are in your library.

40

Converting QuickTime Movies

You'll find that the audio from a QuickTime movie, though playable in iTunes, won't be copied to an iPod, even if the audio in the file is compressed using a compressor that should work, such as MP3. (We've also found that iTunes sometimes crashes when we've asked it to burn a CD from a playlist containing QuickTime movies.)

When you use iTunes to convert a QuickTime movie, the program automatically extracts the audio prior to the conversion, so you are left with a standard audio file. In the Status display, prior to showing you the status of the conversion (refer to Figure 2.27), iTunes will show you the status of the extraction.

What About Windows Media Audio (WMA) Files?

Windows Media Audio, or WMA, is a Microsoft-developed audio file format, designed to work seamlessly with Windows Media Player. You'll find WMA audio files available for download in many online music stores (such as the newly revived Napster), and these files can be played on many portable digital music players, such as the Dell DJ. iTunes and the iPod, however, do *not* support this format.

So what do you do if you've got WMA files that you've downloaded from a Web site or ripped from CDs in the days before you started using iTunes? If you need to, you can *convert* your existing WMA files to the MP3 format with tools that are available at www.wma-mp3.com. The resulting file, however, probably won't sound all that great, since you're recompressing already compressed audio.

✔ Tips

- Depending on your needs, you may want to delete the original file once you have the converted version; one way to do this is to select the file you don't want, and from the Edit menu choose Clear. (In Chapter 5, we cover the ins and outs of deleting files.)

- You can even use iTunes to convert files that aren't already in your library. Hold down the Option key (Mac) or Shift key (Windows) when clicking the Advanced menu, and your Convert choice is different. Instead of "Convert Selection to AAC," for example, the choice is "Convert to AAC." If you select this, a standard window for choosing a file appears. Locate and select the file(s) or folder(s) you want to convert, and click Choose. iTunes performs the conversion, putting the converted version in your library.

- This conversion ability means that iTunes is a free MP3 encoding utility. This is particularly useful if you're dealing with QuickTime files, since MP3 is not one of QuickTime's built-in export options. (See the sidebar "Converting QuickTime Movies" for more information.)

- It's a bad idea to recompress something that's already been compressed. If you convert an MP3 file to AAC, for example, you'll suffer quality loss. It's always best to locate an uncompressed version, often an AIFF or WAV file. In the case of music from an audio CD, you should reimport the file if you don't already have an uncompressed version in your library. (See the sidebar "Ripping for the Future" earlier in this chapter.)

Chapter 2

Adding Links to Audio on the Internet

It's not always necessary to download an audio file in order to add it to your library. If you come across a Web page (such as a favorite musical artist's Web site) that contains a link—textual or graphical—that plays audio when clicked, you can opt to add the Internet address (the URL) of the song to your library, effectively adding the same link to your iTunes library.

You can include links to streams of live or recorded music, as well as to downloadable files on the Internet. The usual caveat applies, however: the link must be pointing to audio that's in a format that iTunes understand, most likely MP3. (Typically, MP3 *streams* have a .pls or .m3u extension and MP3 *files* have a .mp3 extension.)

Figure 2.32 To get the URL for an audio file or stream, right-click (Windows) or Ctrl-click (Mac) and choose the option that copies the address. (This is Internet Explorer on Windows; other browsers have such terms as Copy Link to Clipboard or Copy Link Location.)

To add a link to audio on the Internet:

1. Right-click (Windows) or Control-click (Mac) the link that you normally click to play the music, and choose the option that copies the URL for that link.

   Different browsers label this differently; examples include Copy Shortcut, Copy Link to Clipboard, and Copy Link Location (**Figure 2.32**).

2. In the iTunes Advanced menu, choose Open Stream (**Figure 2.33**)

Figure 2.33 From the Advanced menu, choose Open Stream.

Adding Music to your Library

Figure 2.34 Paste in the URL you copied from the browser.

Figure 2.35 Links added to your library have a broadcast icon as part of their song name.

3. Paste in the URL (**Figure 2.34**), and click OK.

   A new item is added to your library (**Figure 2.35**).

   What's added is not the actual music but a *pointer* to its location on the Internet. If you lose your Internet connection, or the owner of the stream shuts the stream down, you won't be able to play it anymore.

✔ Tips

- Mac users browsing with Safari can Control-click on a link to an MP3 file and choose "Open with iTunes." This also adds the link to your library.

- On some computers, depending on how your system is configured to play MP3 files, simply clicking on a Web page link to an MP3, causes iTunes to add the song to your library and play it.

- In the next chapter we'll cover how you can listen to iTunes Internet radio, which is essentially a collection of URLs to streams that Apple supplies.

Audible.com Books and Subscriptions

At Audible.com (`www.audible.com`), you can download audio files of entire books from all sorts of genres, including fiction, nonfiction, business, biography, and children's literature, to name a few. Audible.com makes it easy to subscribe to audio versions of periodicals, such as the *New York Times*, and get daily (or weekly or monthly) content in digest form. You can even subscribe to radio shows, such as NPR's "Car Talk."

When you download a file from Audible.com, you're given a choice of a number of formats, labeled 1, 2, 3, 4, or 5. As long as you choose formats 2 through 4, the file is MP3-like (even though it bears an *.aa* extension), and you can add it to your iTunes library, just as you add other MP3 files. (You'll find, however, that an Audible.com file is copy-protected and can't be played on more than three different computers.)

ADDING LINKS TO AUDIO ON THE INTERNET

43

Chapter 2

Adding Artwork to Your Songs

Until recently, playing songs in iTunes was a purely auditory experience. Then, in iTunes 4, Apple made it possible to attach artwork to songs, visible in the lower left-hand Artwork pane of the iTunes window. This is particularly cool in light of all the awesome album covers that have been created.

You can add one or more graphics to your songs.

The graphics you add can be in any number of formats, such as JPEG, TIFF, or Photoshop (see the sidebar "Still-Image Formats That Can Be Added as iTunes Artwork," later in this section).

You can add artwork by dragging artwork directly to the artwork pane or by using the iTunes information window; the former is easier but the latter provides an interface for viewing multiple graphics, reordering them, and deleting them.

To add artwork to song(s) by dragging and dropping:

1. If the Artwork pane is not showing, click the rightmost of the four buttons under the Source pane (**Figure 2.36**) to show it.

2. Select the song(s) in the Detail pane.

3. Do one of the following:
   ▲ From the Finder (Mac) or Explorer (Windows), drag the file(s) containing the desired artwork to the artwork pane (**Figure 2.37**)
   ▲ Drag a graphic from an application window to the artwork pane. (This needs to be an application that lets you drag from it. Most Mac applications let you do this; only some Windows applications do.)

   The graphic appears in the artwork pane. (**Figure 2.38**)

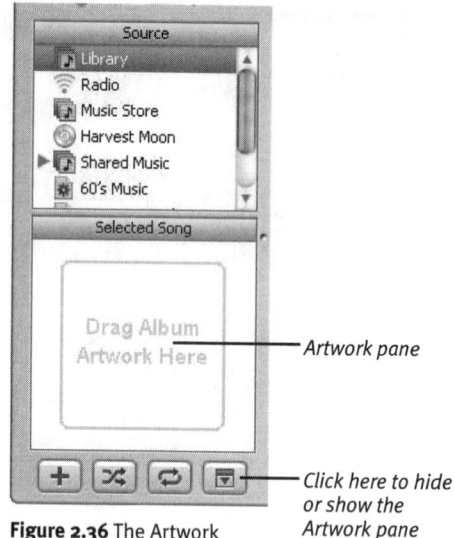

Figure 2.36 The Artwork pane, waiting for artwork. — Artwork pane / Click here to hide or show the Artwork pane

Figure 2.37 Drag files right into the Artwork pane.

Figure 2.38 The Artwork pane, now with artwork.

Adding Music to your Library

Figure 2.39 Select a song and choose Get Info.

To add artwork to a song using the Information window:

1. Select the song in the Detail pane.
2. From the File menu, choose Get Info (**Figure 2.39**) to bring up the iTunes Information window.
3. Click the Artwork tab.
4. Do one of the following:
   - ▲ Click the Add button (**Figure 2.40**), and in the window for choosing a file, navigate to a graphic file and click Open (Windows) or Choose (Mac).
   - ▲ Select and copy the graphic from another application window, click in the Information window, and paste.
   - ▲ Drag from another application to the field in the Artwork tab of the Information window.

   The graphic appears in the window (**Figure 2.41**).

   continues on next page

Figure 2.40 On the Artwork tab, click the Add button (or you can copy and paste a graphic into the field on this tab).

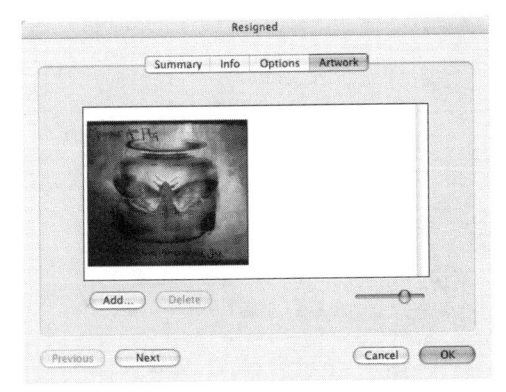

Figure 2.41 The graphic appears here (and will appear in the Artwork pane when you close this window).

Still-Image Formats That Can Be Added as iTunes Artwork

- ◆ BMP
- ◆ FlashPix
- ◆ GIF
- ◆ JPEG
- ◆ MacPaint
- ◆ Photoshop
- ◆ PICT
- ◆ PNG
- ◆ QuickTime Image File
- ◆ SGI
- ◆ Targa
- ◆ TIFF

45

Chapter 2

5. If you want to add additional graphics for this song, repeat step 4. You can reorder these graphics: Click on a graphic and drag to a new position (**Figure 2.42**).

6. Click OK to close the Information window.

   The artwork is added to the song (refer to Figure 2.37). If you have added multiple graphics, the first one in the field (refer to Figure 2.42) shows, but you can view the others by clicking the right-pointing and left-pointing arrow buttons that appear above the artwork pane.

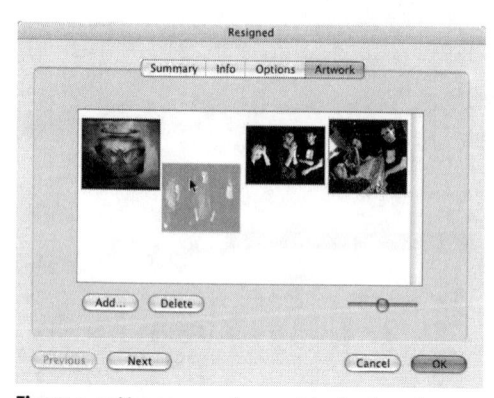

Figure 2.42 You can reorder graphics by dragging them right or left.

✔ Tips

- Mac users can also drag file icons directly from iPhoto; the full-resolution image is added to the iTunes song.

- When you buy music from the iTunes Music Store, album artwork gets added automatically, so you don't have to go through all of these steps.

- To paste into the Information window, Windows users can press Ctrl-V or right-click and choose Paste; Mac users can press Command-V or choose Paste from the Edit menu.

Tools to Help Get Artwork

You can find third-party software (currently only for the Mac) that helps you find and retrieve artwork for iTunes. Here are some that we've tried and liked:

- **Fetch Art** (http://staff.washington.edu/yoel/fetchart/) automatically "fetches" art from Amazon.com (so you don't have to) and lets you add the artwork to iTunes.

- **Clutter** (www.sprote.com/clutter) automatically retrieves artwork from Amazon.com when a song is playing in iTunes. You can tell Clutter to add the artwork to iTunes, or, if you like, you can drag the artwork to your desktop, which creates an icon (cluttering your desktop in the process); when clicked, all the songs in your iTunes library from that album play.

- **Find Album Artwork with Google** is an AppleScript that you'll find at Doug's AppleScripts for iTunes. (www.malcolmadams.com/itunes/index.shtml). Using the album name, it employs Google's image search to look for the artwork.

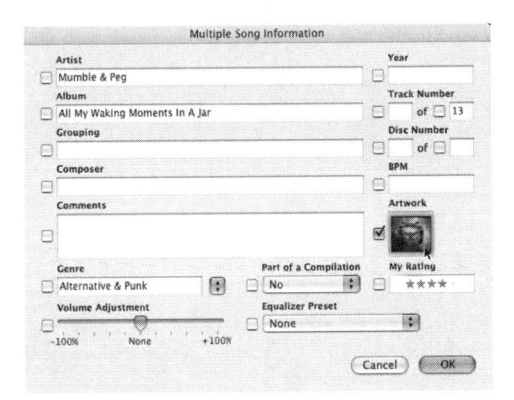

Figure 2.43 Double-click in the artwork field to be able to select a graphic file to be used as artwork for multiple songs. (Or click and paste into this field). The graphic appears in the artwork field, and will appear in the Artwork pane when you close this window.

Places to Find Album Artwork

If you're looking for album artwork to download so you can add it to iTunes, your best bet is to look for Web sites that sell the albums. Amazon.com has the largest collection, but Walmart.com has higher resolution images. (At both of these sites, make sure to click to see the larger image and copy that one.) If you're looking for an independent artist, try allmusic.com. You may also want to try the Web site of the artist in question or try performing image searches at Google (www.google.com) or alltheweb (www.alltheweb.com).

- Be forewarned that when you add art to an iTunes song, the graphic information *also* gets added to the actual song file, thereby increasing its size. (The higher-res graphics you find at Amazon.com, for example, are typically around 25 kilobytes) This makes a difference if you're planning to copy a lot of songs to any limited-space device, such as a small hard drive or a portable player.

- You can also drag a graphic directly from a Web page to the Artwork pane. As of this writing, however, this technique causes the size of the song file to increase by much more than the size of the graphic file. (A 25 kilobyte graphic, for example, increases the file size by 150 kilobytes) This appears to be a bug (that will presumably be fixed in future versions), but in the meantime we suggest that if you need to use a graphic that's on the Web that you download the graphic first and then add it by dragging the file to the Artwork pane.

- To delete a graphic—regardless of the method you have used to add it—select it in the Artwork tab of the Information window (refer to Figure 2.41) and click the Delete button or press the Delete key on your keyboard.

- You can't add artwork to QuickTime movie files.

- If you select multiple songs and then choose File > Get Info, you access the Multiple Song Information window (**Figure 2.43**) on which there is an artwork field. You can double-click this field to open a window in which you can browse your computer for a graphic file; you can also paste a copied graphic or drag a graphic to this field. When you close the Information window the graphic is added to all the songs you had originally selected.

Finding and Playing Songs

3

Once you've added some songs to your library, you'll want to know how to locate specific songs and how to play them.

Of course, you've probably already started poking around in iTunes; it's just too hard not to jump in and start playing your favorite music.

iTunes gives you multiple ways to locate and play songs. You may already know some of them; if you read this chapter, however, you'll likely pick up some new tricks, as well as grasp some nuances of the program that may save you confusion and frustration.

We'll also show you some techniques for enhancing your playback experience, including ways to improve audio quality; and you'll learn how to use the visualizer, iTunes's irresistible—and slightly trippy—visual effects.

Browsing Through Your Library

Just as you navigate through the file system on your computer to get to specific files, you'll need to navigate through the songs in your library to find the ones you want to listen to. One of the easiest ways to do this is to use the iTunes Browser. When the Browser is hiding, you see one long list of songs, as in **Figure 3.1**. When the Browser is showing, however (**Figure 3.2**), it's much easier to locate songs by category.

You can have iTunes list songs by artist or by album. You can also tell it to list songs by genre, though this feature may not yet be enabled for you.

Ways to hide and show the Browser:

◆ Click the Browse button at the top right of your iTunes window (refer to Figure 3.1).

◆ From the Edit menu, choose either Show Browser or Hide Browser. (Or use keyboard shortcuts: Mac users can press Command-B; Windows users can press Ctrl-B.)

The Browser appears in the upper portion of the Detail pane, displaying a column listing artists and a column listing albums (refer to Figure 3.2). Depending on how your preferences are set, a genre column may also appear. If not, you can change your preferences to show it.

Figure 3.1 If you're looking at your library with the Browser hidden, you see one long list of songs.

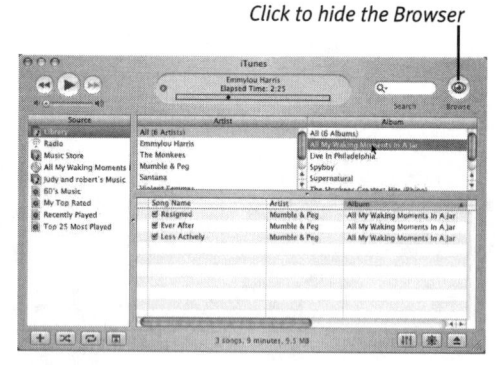

Figure 3.2 Once you show the Browser, you can select a specific artist or album to view.

Finding and Playing Songs

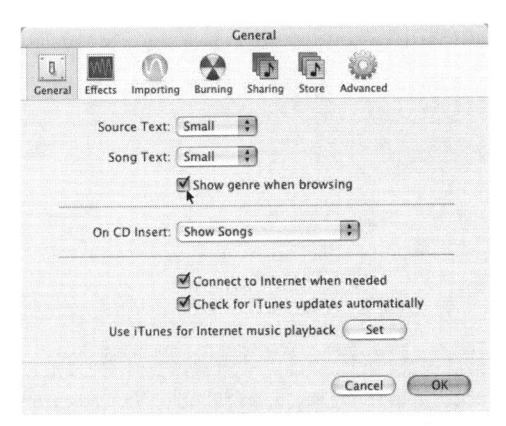

Figure 3.3 Open the Preferences window, and on the General tab, check "Show genre when browsing"...

Figure 3.4 ...to add a Genre column to the Browser.

To show genres when browsing:

1. From the iTunes menu (Mac) or the Edit menu (Windows), choose Preferences to open the Preferences window.

2. On the General tab, click to check "Show genre when browsing" (**Figure 3.3**).

3. Click OK to close the Preferences window. Genre is added as a column for browsing (**Figure 3.4**).

To browse for songs:

◆ With the Browser showing, click a genre, artist, album, or any combination of these. Only songs that match the item(s) you clicked appear in the song list.

✔ Tips

■ The last line that you click in the Browser is selected and is highlighted in blue with white text, to show that the column it's in is active. (In Figure 3.4, Genre is the active column.) Use the up and down arrow keys on your keyboard to select the previous or next album, artist, or genre in the active column.

■ You can select multiple genres, albums, or artists. Shift-click to select contiguous items; Command-click (Mac) or Ctrl-click (Windows) to select items that are not adjacent.

BROWSING THROUGH YOUR LIBRARY

51

Chapter 3

Searching for Songs

Sometimes browsing just doesn't get you where you want to go fast enough. What if all you know, for example, is that either the song title or the album title has the word *Wheels* in it, or that the artist's name starts with *Al*? iTunes has a search feature that will help.

Also, if you have a very large library and you know the exact title of the song you want, the fastest way to get to that song is by using iTunes's search feature.

Figure 3.5 As soon as you start to type in the Search field, iTunes shows only songs that have those characters in the Song Name, Artist, Album, Composer, or Genre column.

To search for a text string:

1. In the Source pane, click the source you want to search to select it.

    Most likely this source will be your library, although you can search playlists and shared libraries in the same way. (You can also search the iTunes Music Store, but the search function doesn't work in exactly the same way; see Chapter 4.)

2. In the Search field, located in the top right corner of the iTunes window, type the text you want iTunes to locate.

    As you type, the song list changes to reflect what you've typed so far. The song list displays all songs that contain—in the Song Name, Artist, Album, Composer, or Genre columns—the text you've typed in the search field. The more you type, the more you narrow the search results (**Figures 3.5** and **3.6**).

Figure 3.6 As you type, the songs that match your search criteria are narrowed down further.

Finding and Playing Songs

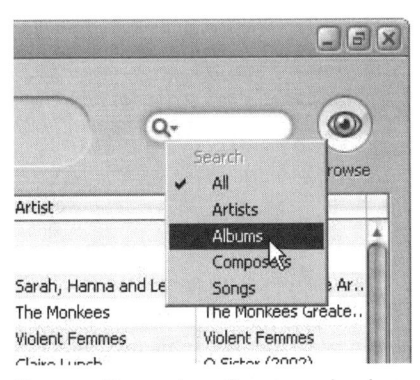

Figure 3.7 You can have iTunes search only a particular column.

Figure 3.8 In this example, we've limited the search to the Album column. That's why the search for "em" doesn't find any songs by Emmylou Harris (even though the Browser shows her as one of the artists in the library).

To limit a search to album, artist, composer, or song name:

1. Click the magnifying glass in the Search field, and select one of the following from the pop-up menu: Artists, Albums, Composers, or Songs (**Figure 3.7**).

2. In the Search field, type the text you want iTunes to locate.

   Again, as you type, the results shown in the song list change to reflect what you've typed. iTunes searches only in the column matching the category you selected (**Figure 3.8**).

✔ Tip

- For a normal (unlimited) search, iTunes checks song name, artist, album, composer, and genre, even if those columns are hidden. It searches the Comment field, too, but only if it is visible. (To learn how to hide and show columns, see "Hiding and Showing Columns" later in this chapter.)

SEARCHING FOR SONGS

53

Chapter 3

Sorting Songs

If browsing or searching yields many songs (or if you're viewing your entire library), it helps to be able to sort the songs that appear in the song list. You may also want to sort your songs in a particular way, since the order they appear in the song list is the order in which they'll play.

To sort by a particular column:

◆ Click the column name (**Figure 3.9**).
The column head becomes highlighted, so you can tell that it's the column by which the entire list is sorted. If the triangle on the right side of the column name points up, everything is sorted in alphabetical or numeric order.

To reverse the order of the sort:

◆ Click the column head again.
The column is now sorted in the reverse order (**Figure 3.10**).

✔ Tips

- When we cover playlists in Chapter 5, you'll see that you can specify the order in which songs play, completely independent of the columns in the song list.

- We find it helpful to sort by the Date Added column; that way, we can easily find the most recent additions to our music collection.

Songs are sorted in alphabetical order, since this triangle points up. Click the triangle to change to reverse alphabetical order.

Figure 3.9 Click any column head to sort by that column.

Figure 3.10 After clicking the column head so the arrow points down, the songs are in reverse alphabetical order.

Finding and Playing Songs

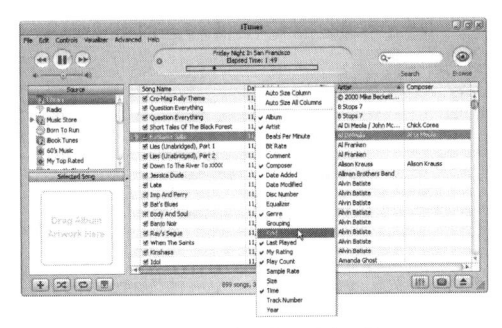

Figure 3.11 Control-click (Mac) or right-click (Windows) any column head to make this pop-up menu appear. Check or uncheck items to show or hide the column of that name.

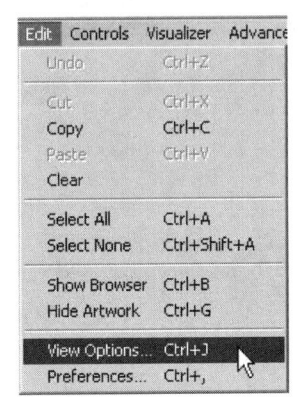

Figure 3.12 From the Edit menu, choose View Options...

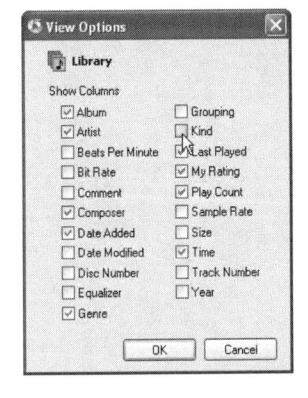

Figure 3.13 ...to open the View Options window. Add checkmarks to indicate which columns you want to have appear.

Hiding and Showing Columns

You can specify the song information you want to display by showing and hiding different columns.

To add or remove columns (I):

1. Control-click (Mac) or right-click (Windows) any column head.

    A pop-up menu appears (**Figure 3.11**).

2. Select any item that has no checkmark to add a column with that name; select an item with a checkmark to remove the column with that name.

    Since you can change only one item at a time, this method works best when you have only one or a few columns to show or hide.

To add or remove columns (II):

1. From the Edit menu, choose View Options (**Figure 3.12**).

    The View Options window appears (**Figure 3.13**).

2. Click items that have no checkmarks to add columns with those names; click items with checks to remove columns with those names.

3. Click OK.

✔ Tips

- Option-click (Mac) or Ctrl-click (Windows) on any one check box in the View Options window to select or deselect all the check boxes at once.

- All those columns provide information about various properties of the song (or stream). Many of these properties are editable; Chapter 5 covers how to do such editing. However, we'll cover the Equalizer setting later in this chapter.

Changing Order and Size of Columns

Once you've decided which columns you want to display, you can change their order and size. For example, you may want to widen the Song Name column so you can view your song titles in their entirety, or you might want to move the Size column to a more visible position, which is helpful when you're choosing songs to burn to a CD.

To change the order of the columns:

1. Click any column (other than Song Name) and drag it to the right or left.

    As you drag to the right of left of other columns, space opens up to show that you can drop the column there (**Figure 3.14**).

2. Release your mouse button when the column is located where you'd like it.

To change the width of a column:

1. Position your cursor over the dividing line between column heads, so that the cursor changes to a vertical bar with double arrows (**Figure 3.15**).

2. Click and drag right or left to widen or narrow the column to the left of the cursor.

    When a column is as small as iTunes will allow, the cursor changes to show a vertical bar with only a right-pointing arrow.

Figure 3.14 You can change the position of columns by dragging a column head. (The Song Name column, however, can't be moved from the far left.)

Figure 3.15 Change the width of columns by clicking the line between column heads and dragging right or left.

Finding and Playing Songs

Figure 3.16 Control-click (Mac) or right-click (Windows) on a column head and choose Auto Size Column to make that column just wide enough to fit the longest item in it.

Figure 3.17 Control-click (Mac) or right-click (Windows) on a column head and choose Auto Size All Columns to make each column just wide enough to fit the longest item in it.

To autosize columns:

◆ Control-click (Mac) or right-click (Windows) the column head and choose Auto Size Column (**Figure 3.16**) to make the column just wide enough to fit the longest item in the column.

◆ Control-click (Mac) or right-click (Windows) on any column head and choose Auto Size All Columns (refer to Figure 3.16) to make all columns just wide enough to fit the longest item in each of them (**Figure 3.17**).

✔ Tips

- Some columns, such as Rating, can't be resized.

- The Song Name column always needs to be at the far left. You can't move it right, and you can't move another column to its left.

- If you want to move a column to a more visible position, it's sometimes quickest to remove the column and then add it back, using the first method covered in "Hiding and Showing Columns" earlier in this chapter.

Chapter 3

Playing and Pausing Songs

Once the songs you want to play are visible in your song list, you have numerous ways to play them. (You've surely discovered some of them by now.)

It gets a little tricky, however, depending on whether or not there's a *current* song. A current song is one that is playing or was just playing; it has a speaker icon next to it.

Ways to play songs:

- Press the Play button (**Figure 3.18**) to play the current song.
- Double-click any song's line to play it.
- Click a song's line in the song list to select it, and press the Return key (Mac) or Enter key (Windows) on your keyboard (refer to Figure 3.18).
- If there's no current song, press the Play button to play whatever song is selected or to play the first song in the list, if nothing is selected (refer to Figure 3.18).
- Double-click a line in the Browser pane to put the songs in that category in the song list and start playing the first of these.

The song that plays becomes the current song; the speaker icon appears next to it with lines emanating from the speaker.

Figure 3.18 iTunes offers you several different ways to play a song.

Finding and Playing Songs

Figure 3.19 Click the Pause button to pause playback of the current song. (When you click the Play button again, playback resumes where you've stopped it.)

Figure 3.20 Notice that the speaker icon no longer has lines emanating from it, indicating that this song is paused. It still shows that the song is current, however.

To pause a song:

◆ Click the Pause button, the button with the parallel lines (**Figure 3.19**).

The speaker icon next to the playing song changes so that there are no sound waves emanating from the speaker (**Figure 3.20**). This song is still the current song, however.

What's Selected Isn't Necessarily What Plays

It can be confusing that one song can be selected (highlighted) while a different song is active (has the speaker icon next to it); see Figure 3.18.

Since the highlighting is so much more prominent than the speaker icon, one might think that clicking the Play button (or choosing Controls > Play or pressing the spacebar) would play the selected song. Not so: The song that gets played is the one that has the speaker icon next to it.

You can, however make the selected song and the current song one-and-the-same: From the File menu, choose Show Current Song (**Figure 3.21**) to select the current song.

Figure 3.21 From the File menu, choose Show Current Song to select the current song.

PLAYING AND PAUSING SONGS

59

Chapter 3

Ways to make the next or previous song current:

- Press the right or left arrow key.
- From the Controls menu, choose Next Song or Previous Song.
- Click the Skip Forward or Skip Backward button (**Figure 3.22**).

    The speaker icon appears to the left of the new current song. If iTunes is playing a song at the time you do any of the above, the new current song begins play from the beginning; otherwise use one of the previously described methods to play the new current song.

Figure 3.22 Click the Skip Forward button to make the next song in the list the current song. (Or click the Skip Backward button, the one with the double arrows pointing left, to make the previous song in the list the current song.)

✔ Tips

- You can also play or pause a song by pressing the spacebar or choosing Play or Pause from the Controls menu.

- Do *not* double-click a paused song to resume playback. It will start from the beginning, not from the point where you paused it.

- If you're trying to play a song that's in someone else's library—something you can do if that person is sharing their iTunes library—you may be asked for a password before you can play a song. (See Chapter 8 for more information on sharing.)

- If you want to make current the next song in the list that's from a different album than the current song, hold down the Shift, Ctrl, and Alt keys (Windows) or the Option key (Mac) while you click the right arrow key. (Doing the same with the left arrow key goes up the song list to find a song that's on a different album.)

Hate Mousing?

You'll find that you can navigate to and play any song in your iTunes collection using just the keys on your keyboard. Using the Tab key, you can jump to different panes and fields: the Search field, the Genre column, the Artist column, the Album column, the song list, and the Source pane. When you're in the Search field, it's bordered in blue, and you can just start typing. When any of the other elements are active, the selected row is highlighted in blue; you can move up and down in the list using your arrow keys. Once you've selected the song you want to play, just press the Return (Mac) or Enter (Windows) key.

Also, it's useful to know that you can press Option-Command-F (Mac) or Ctrl-Alt-F (Windows) to jump directly to the Search field.

Finding and Playing Songs

Drag the diamond to move around in the song.

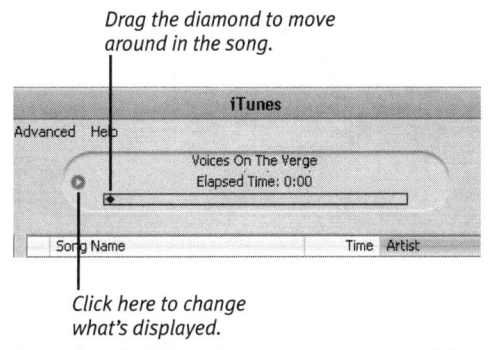

Click here to change what's displayed.

Figure 3.23 The Status display provides several different types of information about the current song.

Figure 3.24 Click and hold the Skip Forward or Skip Backward button to fast forward or fast rewind.

Moving Around in a Song

How do you move around in a song—say, to skip the first 15 seconds or to jump to that cool part near the end that you want your best friend to hear? Try these techniques.

To randomly access portions of a song:

1. If the Status display doesn't show a rectangular bar with a diamond in it as in **Figure 3.23,** click the tiny triangle on the left side of the display until it looks like Figure 3.23.

2. Drag the diamond to the right or left in the bar to get to the portion of the song you want to hear.

To fast forward or fast rewind:

◆ Click and hold the Skip Forward or Skip Backward button (**Figure 3.24**).

✔ Tip

■ When you want to fast forward or fast rewind in a song, it won't work to simply click (that is, press your mouse button down and immediately release) the Skip Forward or Skip Backward button. If you do this, you'll simply make the next or previous song in the list current.

Viewing Song Artwork

If there's artwork associated with a song, it appears in the Artwork pane. (We covered how to add artwork to a song in Chapter 2.) You can do more than just stare at that little pane, however.

Ways to hide or show the artwork pane:

- Click the rightmost of the buttons at the bottom left of the iTunes window. (**Figure 3.25**)
- From the Edit menu, choose Hide Artwork or Show Artwork.

To show the image at full resolution:

- Click the image in the Artwork pane.
  The full-resolution version opens in a separate window (**Figure 3.26**).

To switch between artwork for the selected song and for the playing song:

- Click the bar above the artwork area.
  The text on the bar tells you whether you are looking at the artwork for the selected song (refer to Figure 3.26) or for the currently playing song (**Figure 3.27**).

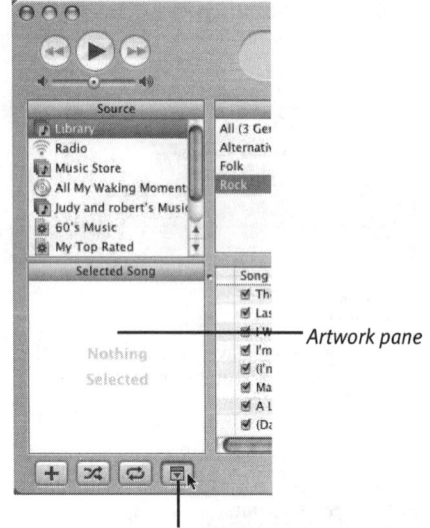

Artwork pane

Click to hide the Artwork pane (or to show it if it's not visible).

Figure 3.25 The iTunes Artwork pane is visible by default. If you find it distracting, simply click it to hide it.

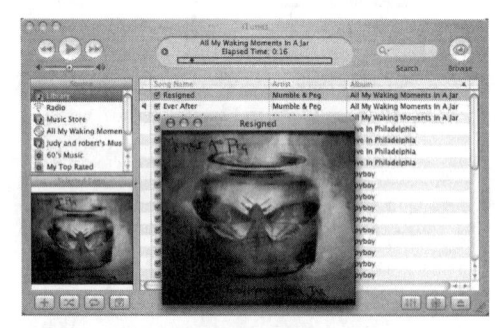

Figure 3.26 When you click a graphic in the Artwork pane, it opens in its own window at full resolution.

Figure 3.27 Clicking the bar at the top of the Artwork pane switches the artwork between that for the playing song and that for the selected song. (Notice that the bar in Figure 3.25 says "Selected Song.")

Finding and Playing Songs

Figure 3.28 Right and left arrow buttons appear at the top of the Artwork pane if there is more than one graphic associated with the song. Click them to show the different graphics.

To switch between multiple images associated with a single song:

◆ Click the previous or next arrows (**Figure 3.28**).

These arrows appear only if there's more than one image associated with the song.

✔ Tips

- The window containing the full-resolution version of the graphic is titled by the name of the song; it is listed in the iTunes Window menu (Mac) or the Windows taskbar (Windows).

- If you have multiple graphics associated with a song, and you open them each in their own full-resolution window, you won't be able to distinguish between them in the Window menu (Mac) or the taskbar (Windows) since they'll all have the same name.

- Close the full-resolution window showing the graphic by clicking the close button at the top of the window.

VIEWING SONG ARTWORK

63

Chapter 3

Options for Playing Multiple Songs

If iTunes is providing the background music for an activity—working, partying, cooking, whatever—you probably want it to keep playing song after song, just as if you were playing a CD. This it does automatically, playing the next song in the list until it reaches the last song in the list.

You can control how iTunes plays music in several ways: repeating, shuffling, and picking particular songs that you don't want to play.

To set iTunes so it repeats the songs in the song list:

◆ Click the Repeat button (located in the lower left of the iTunes window) until it is highlighted blue (**Figure 3.29**).

To set iTunes to play the songs in the song list and then stop:

◆ Click the Repeat button until it's not highlighted (that is, is gray only).

To set iTunes to play the current song repeatedly:

◆ Click the Repeat button until it's highlighted blue and displays the number 1 (**Figure 3.30**).

That little number 1 can be hard to see, but once you've seen it, you'll recognize it when you see it again.

To set iTunes to play the songs in the song list in random order:

◆ Click the Shuffle button so that it's highlighted blue (**Figure 3.31**).

If your library is the selected source, nothing appears to change in the song list, but the songs will be played back in a random order. If a playlist is the selected source, you can see the randomized order if you click the column head for the leftmost column.

Figure 3.29 Click until the Repeat button looks like this (and is highlighted in blue) if you want the current list of songs to repeat. (Click it so it is gray to turn the repeat function off.)

Figure 3.30 Click so the Repeat button looks like this—notice the little number 1—to repeat only the current song.

Figure 3.31 Click the Shuffle button so that it's highlighted in blue if you want the songs to play in random order.

Finding and Playing Songs

Figure 3.32 Songs that are not checked won't play.

Shuffling Albums

If you've turned Shuffle on, iTunes' default behavior is to randomly play all the songs appearing in the Detail pane. However, you can tell it to shuffle by album, in which case it plays all the songs from an album in the order they appear before randomly going to another album, and playing all those songs in the order they appear.

You can switch the Shuffle mode on the Advanced tab of the Preferences window (**Figure 3.33**).

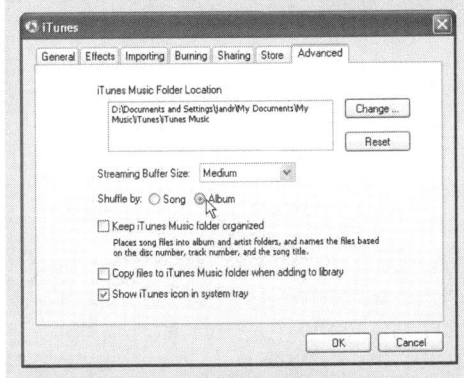

Figure 3.33 On the Advanced tab of the Preferences window you can specify that albums are shuffled; if you do this, all the songs from one randomly selected album play, followed by all the songs from the next randomly-selected album, and so on. Songs on each album play in order.

To specify individual songs that you don't want to play:

◆ Click to remove the checkmark for each song you don't want to play (**Figure 3.32**).

✔ Tips

- If you don't like the way iTunes has shuffled your songs, you can ask for a new random order: Option-click (Mac) or Shift-click (Windows) the Shuffle button.

- If Shuffle mode is on, clicking the Skip Forward or Skip Backward buttons (or using any other method for making the next or previous song current) switches the current song to the next or previous one in the shuffled order, which is not necessarily the song immediately below or above the current song.

- You can put checkmarks next to all the songs in the list or remove them all at once by Command-clicking (Mac) or Ctrl-clicking (Windows) any one check box.

- To play all the songs on an album, by a particular artist, or in a particular genre, just double-click the name of the album, artist, or genre in the Browser.

- If a song is playing when you select a new category from the Browser, iTunes is smart enough to finish playing that song and then stop; it doesn't move on to the song that would have been next. It doesn't, however, start playing your newly selected album, artist, or genre automatically; you need to manually start play.

- Remember that you can use the Browser to select multiple albums, artists, or genres. The combined songs from the selected categories appear in your song list, ready to play.

- You can Command-click (Mac) or Ctrl-click (Windows) an artist, album, or genre, to add to the list of songs even while a song is playing.

OPTIONS FOR PLAYING MULTIPLE SONGS

65

Listening to Radio Streams

The first thing both of us ever used iTunes for was listening to Internet radio streams while working, largely because all we needed in order to gain access to a reasonable selection of music was iTunes and an Internet connection. This is still the case.

iTunes provides access to a fairly large collection of streams. Some of these streams are broadcast by radio stations that also broadcast over the airwaves; others operate like radio stations (playing one song after another) but are Internet-only.

To listen to a radio stream:

1. Click Radio in the Source pane (**Figure 3.34**).

2. Click the disclosure triangle to the left of one of the categories (**Figure 3.35**).

    The triangle turns downward. After a few seconds a list of available radio streams appears. (It takes a bit of time because iTunes is actually contacting a tuning service that returns the list of available streams.)

    Below the Detail pane, the number of streams available to you is listed.

3. Play any of the radio streams listed by double-clicking one (or by using any of the other methods for playing a song described in "Playing and Pausing Songs" earlier in this chapter).

    Sometimes it takes a while to contact the server that's providing the streams.

Figure 3.34 Click Radio in the Source pane to get a list of the categories of streams available to you.

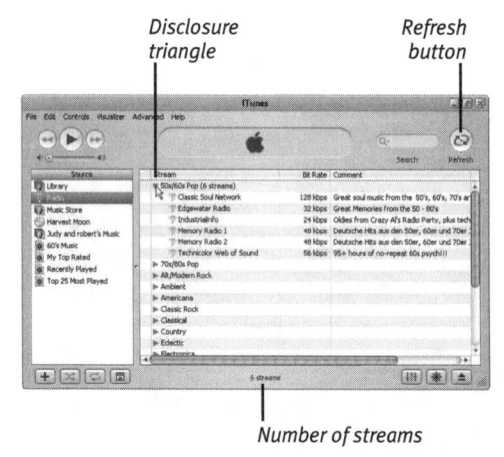

Figure 3.35 Click the disclosure triangle next to a category to have iTunes contact the tuning service and return a list of streams available in that category.

What's the URL, Kenneth?

You can get the URL for any radio stream: Select the stream, choose File > Get Info, and on the Summary tab click the Edit URL button; in the Edit URL window that appears, you'll see the stream's URL, which you can then copy and paste into other applications such as QuickTime Player (in which you'd use the File > Open URL command) or email to a friend.

Finding and Playing Songs

Figure 3.36 When you listen to an Internet radio stream, there's no Pause button—only a Stop button.

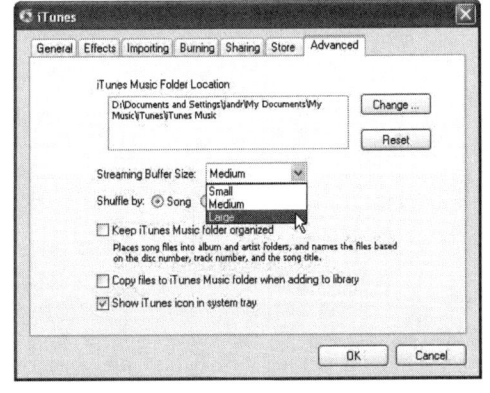

Figure 3.37 If you have a slow Internet connection (such as dial-up), pick a larger buffer size.

Figure 3.38 You can drag radio streams to your library—they'll look like the selected listing above. Notice the broadcast icon and the fact that time is listed as "Continuous."

Ways to stop radio play:

◆ Click the Stop button (the square), located where the Pause button would normally be (**Figure 3.36**).

◆ Press the spacebar.

◆ From the Controls menu, choose Stop.

To view the latest list of categories:

◆ Click the Refresh button at the top right of the iTunes window (refer to Figure 3.35), and iTunes will recontact the tuning service.

✔ Tips

■ Modem users should pick stations that are listed at 56 kbps or less.

■ On the Advanced tab of the Preferences window, you can select a streaming buffer size of Small, Medium, or Large (**Figure 3.37**). The buffer size is a reflection of how much audio data should be downloaded before iTunes will play. If you request a small buffer, the stream will start more quickly, as long as you have a fast connection. If you have a slow connection (such as a modem), you'll want a large buffer, so enough music will be available for playback without stuttering.

■ Once you locate a favorite radio stream, drag it to your library or to a playlist so you can access it quickly (**Figure 3.38**). This also lets you search for it, since iTunes can't search the Radio source. You'll be able to tell which are radio streams by the broadcast icon and by the fact that the time is listed as "Continuous."

■ To open all or close all of the Radio categories, Command-click (Mac) or Ctrl-click (Windows) any one disclosure triangle.

LISTENING TO RADIO STREAMS

67

Customizing the iTunes Window

As you become more familiar with iTunes, you may decide that your main iTunes window isn't precisely as you'd like it. You can make small tweaks to change the size of its elements, or completely shrink the window down to a small window with only basic playback controls.

To change the width of the Source pane:

1. Position your cursor anywhere on the bar to the right of the Source pane.

   The cursor turns into a hand.

2. Press your mouse button and drag to the right or left (**Figure 3.39**).

   The cursor changes to a clenched hand when the mouse button is pressed down. As you drag right, the Source pane widens. As you drag left, it narrows.

To change the height of the Browser pane:

1. Position your cursor anywhere on the bar below the Browser pane.

   The cursor turns into a hand.

2. Press your mouse button and drag up or down to make the Browser pane shorter or taller (**Figure 3.40**).

   The cursor changes to a clenched hand when the mouse button is down.

Click this bar and drag right or left

Figure 3.39 You can widen or narrow the Source pane. This is especially helpful if you've having trouble viewing the full names of your playlists or audio CDs.

Click the bar and drag up or down

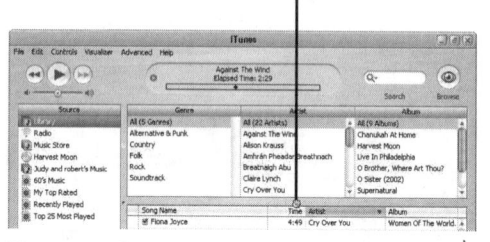

Figure 3.40 If you want to view more (or fewer) songs at one time, you can adjust the Browser area to make it taller or shorter.

Mini Player Alternatives (Mac OS only)

The mini player that iTunes provides isn't the only alternative to displaying the full iTunes window. You can find several add-on programs that provide ways to control iTunes. One example is the $5 shareware application, Synergy (http://synergy.wincent.com); it offers several iTunes enhancements, including one that adds a controller to the menu bar. Other tools provide floating windows, similar to the iTunes mini player, but with additional features. We suggest that you visit www.versiontracker.com and search for "itunes control." (Make sure you're searching for Mac OS X software.) You'll find more than 20 types of controllers for iTunes.

Finding and Playing Songs

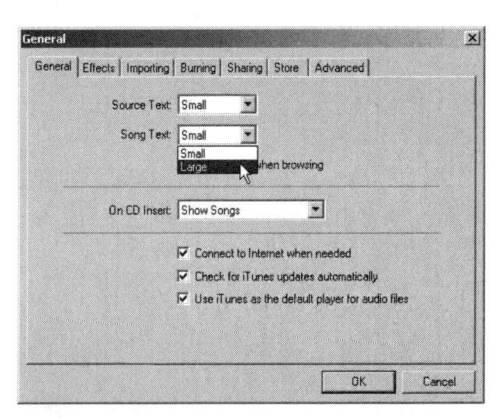

Figure 3.41 Use the General tab of the Preferences window to change the size of the text in the Source and Detail panes.

Figure 3.42 Mac users can click the Zoom button to switch to a mini player.

Figure 3.43 Windows users can choose Advanced > Switch to Mini Player.

Figure 3.44 The mini player—we show both Windows and Mac versions here—includes the basic playback controls and Status display. Click the Zoom button (Mac) or Maximize button (Windows) to return to the full iTunes window.

To change the size of the text:

1. From the iTunes menu (Mac) or the Edit menu (Windows), choose Preferences to open the Preferences window.

2. Choose either Large or Small in the Source Text pop-up menu and the Song Text pop-up menu (**Figure 3.41**).

   Source Text refers to the items in your Source pane. Song Text refers to both the listing of songs and the items in the Browser.

3. Click OK to close the Preferences window.

   The size of the text appears slightly larger or slightly smaller, depending on which option you selected.

To switch between the full iTunes window and a mini player:

◆ Click the Zoom button (Mac; **Figure 3.42**) or from the Advanced menu choose Switch to Mini Player (Windows; **Figure 3.43**).

   The iTunes window shrinks to a mini player window (**Figure 3.44**).

   Clicking the Zoom or Maximize button on the small window expands the window back to the full iTunes window.

✔ Tips

- If you drag the bar below the Browser (refer to Figure 3.40) up all the way, you'll hide the Browser. To reopen it, click the Browse button or choose Edit > Show Browser.

- You can resize the entire iTunes window by dragging on the bottom-right corner, as you can windows in most Mac or Windows applications.

- You can make the mini player even smaller by dragging the bottom right corner to the left; this removes the Status display.

CUSTOMIZING THE iTUNES WINDOW

69

Chapter 3

Getting Information About What's Playing

You've noticed by now that you can get an awful lot of information about a song or stream just by looking at what's listed in the various columns. Here are a few additional methods.

To see total, remaining, or elapsed time:

◆ Click on the text immediately above the progress bar in the Status display.

With each click, the text cycles between showing total, remaining, and elapsed time (**Figures 3.45** and **Figure 3.46**).

Ways to see artist, album, or song name:

◆ Watch the Status display.

Song name, artist, and album entries show one at a time, scrolling off to show the next after a few seconds (refer to Figure 3.46).

◆ Click the line showing artist, album, or song name in the Status display to switch between these three choices.

To get extensive information about a song:

1. Select the song you're interested in.

2. From the File menu, choose Get Info, or press Ctrl-I (Windows) or Command-I (Mac).

3. Click the Summary tab (if it's not currently selected). You'll find some information here (**Figure 3.47**) that you won't find in the columns of the song list or in the Status display.

✔ Tip

■ With songs that weren't encoded by iTunes or that aren't MP3s, the Summary tab won't necessarily list all the information you see in Figure 3.47.

Figure 3.45 Click on the line in the Status display that lists Elapsed Time to show...

Figure 3.46 ...Remaining Time. Click on this line again to show Total Time. Click again to return to Elapsed Time, and so on. (Notice also that the album name is scrolling off and being replaced by the artist name; this happens automatically and independently of clicking the line showing time information.)

Lists the version of the ID3 tagging system used to store information about the song.

Provides information about the song's file format (By the way, MPEG-1, Layer-3 is the same as MP3.)

Tells you which version of iTunes encoded this song.

Tells you the location (on your hard drive or on the Internet) of the file containing this song's audio.

Figure 3.47 This window (which you access by selecting a song and choosing Get Info from the File menu) provides additional information about a selected song.

Finding and Playing Songs

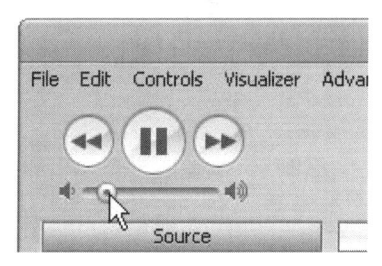

Figure 3.48 Change iTunes's volume using the volume slider.

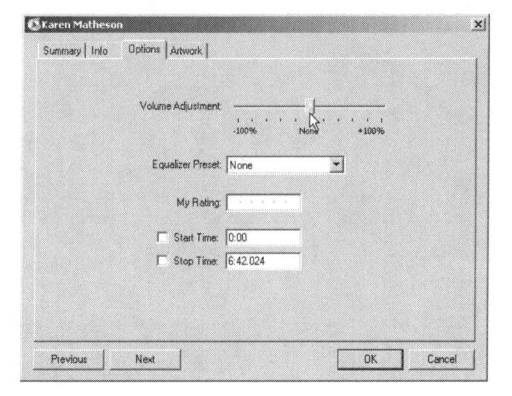

Figure 3.49 Change the default volume for a song in the song's information window, on the Options tab. (Select the song and choose File > Get Info to open this window.)

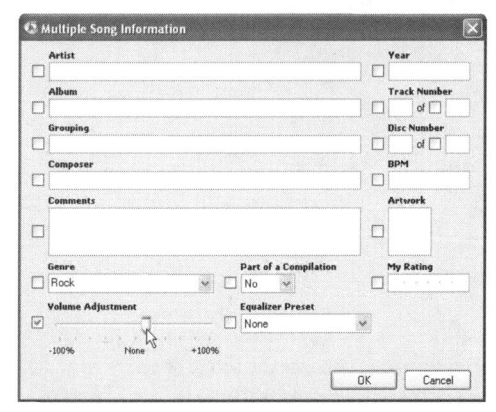

Figure 3.50 You can also change the default volume for a number of songs by selecting them, choosing File > Get Info, and then adjusting the Volume Adjustment slider in this window.

Controlling Volume

You can change the volume for the iTunes application as a whole, or you can change the default volume of specific songs.

Ways to change the volume for all songs:

- Click and drag the volume slider in the iTunes window (**Figure 3.48**).
- Hold down the Command key (Mac) or Ctrl key (Windows) and press the up or down arrow keys on your keyboard.

Setting the default volume for a single song:

1. Click the song in the song list to select it.
2. From the File menu, choose Get Info. The information window for the song appears.
3. Click the Options tab.
4. Select the default volume by adjusting the Volume Adjustment slider (**Figure 3.49**).
5. Click OK to close the window.

Setting the default volume for multiple songs:

1. Shift-click to select multiple contiguous songs or Command-click (Mac) or Ctrl-click (Windows) to select multiple non-contiguous songs in the song list.
2. From the File menu, choose Get Info.
3. If you're asked whether you want to edit information for multiple items, click Yes.
4. Move the Volume Adjustment slider in the lower left corner of the window to adjust the volume (**Figure 3.50**).
5. Click OK to close the window.

✔ Tip

- Your system sound level affects the playback volume, too.

71

Chapter 3

Using the Equalizer

iTunes comes with a standard equalizer that allows you to optimize the tonal quality of your music. Do you prefer a heavier bass sound with your AC/DC? Looking for a clearer treble sound for your Gershwin tracks? The iTunes equalizer lets you tinker to your heart's content.

You can think of the equalizer as functioning somewhat like the bass and treble controls on your stereo, but with more precision and control over different frequencies.

Ways to open the Equalizer window:

◆ Click the Equalizer button, located in the lower right corner of the iTunes window (**Figure 3.51**).

◆ (Mac only) From the Window menu, choose Equalizer.

The Equalizer window appears (**Figure 3.52**).

To choose an equalizer preset:

◆ Select from the pop-up menu at the top of the Equalizer window (**Figure 3.53**).

You should choose an option that seems to describe the song you're listening to (for example, Jazz) or the change you'd like to make (for example, Treble Booster) or the environment in which you're listening (say, Small Speakers).

Figure 3.51 Click the Equalizer button to...

Figure 3.52 ...open the Equalizer window.

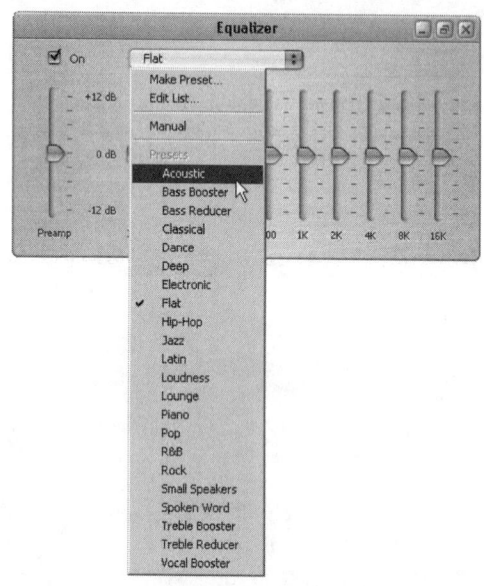

Figure 3.53 To enhance the sound of a song or audio file, you can choose a preset.

To manually adjust frequencies:

- Move any of the sliders up or down (refer to Figure 3.52).

  If you want more or less bass in your music, adjust the three leftmost frequency sliders. If you want more or less high-end frequencies (treble), adjust the rightmost three. If you want more midrange tones (which tends to be the range for voice), adjust the middle four sliders. If you want all frequencies increased or decreased (because the music is too quiet or too loud), adjust the preamp slider.

✔ Tips

- As you adjust the equalizer settings, it helps to keep the markers in a curve; otherwise, the audio will probably sound odd.

- If you've adjusted equalizer settings, but then decide the settings don't apply to what you're currently listening to, you should turn the equalizer off. To do this, uncheck the "On" box in the upper left of the Equalizer window (refer to Figure 3.52).

- To get any one frequency to 0 dB, click its label at the bottom of the slider.

- To return all sliders to 0 dB, click 0 dB or choose Flat from the pop-up menu.

- To shrink the Equalizer window so it shows only the On check box and the pop-up menu for choosing presets, click the Zoom (Mac) or Maximize (Windows) button. Click the same button again to expand the window back to its full size.

What Do Those Sliders Really Mean?

Each of the 10 sliders represents a portion of the sound spectrum (a frequency); 32 Hz is the lowest (bass) and 16 kHz (16,000 Hz) is the highest (treble). The vertical axis is labeled in dB (decibels); this is a measurement of the intensity of the sound for that frequency. When you move a slider up, you're strengthening that frequency; when you move it down, you're decreasing its intensity.

Saving Equalizer Adjustments as Presets

If you've gone to the trouble of creating manual equalizer adjustments, you may want to save those adjustments as *presets*. You can call them up in the future, or you can assign them to specific songs or streams, as we describe in the next section.

To save your manually adjusted equalizer settings as a preset:

1. From the pop-up menu in the Equalizer window, choose Make Preset (**Figure 3.54**).

2. Type in a name and click OK (**Figure 3.55**).

   Your equalizer settings are saved as a preset and now appear in the pop-up menu in the Equalizer window.

To delete a preset:

1. From the pop-up menu in the Equalizer window, choose Edit List (refer to Figure 3.54).

2. In the Edit Presets window (**Figure 3.56**), select the preset you want to delete and click Delete.

3. If you are asked if you're sure you want to delete the preset, click Yes.

4. When you are asked if you want to delete the preset from songs that use it, click Yes.

5. Click Done.

   The preset is removed from the pop-up menu and any songs that use it.

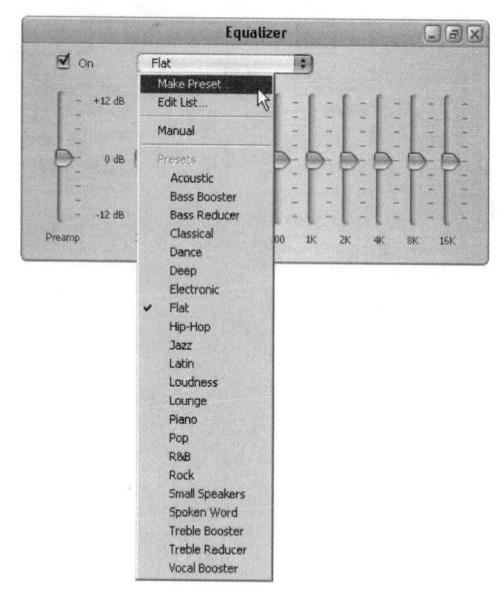

Figure 3.54 If you want to save your current settings as a preset, start by choosing Make Preset.

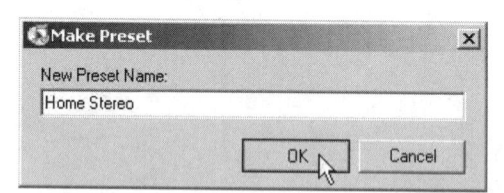

Figure 3.55 Provide a name for your current settings and click OK.

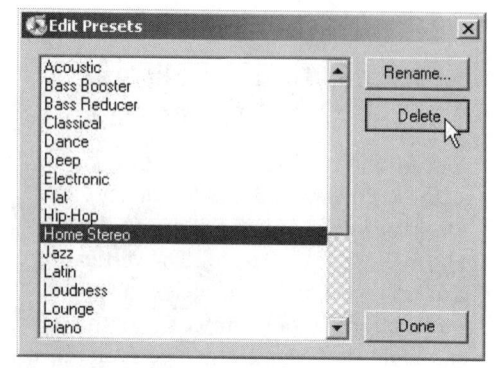

Figure 3.56 If you choose Edit List (refer to Figure 3.53), you can select and delete any preset.

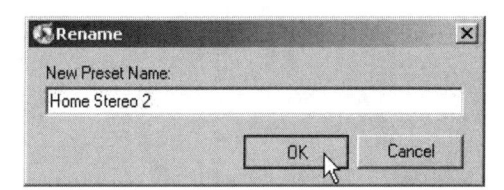

Figure 3.57 You can also choose Rename (refer to Figure 3.55) and then provide a new name in this window.

To rename a preset:

1. From the pop-up menu in the Equalizer window, choose Edit List (refer to Figure 3.54).

2. In the Edit Presets window, select the preset you want to rename (refer to Figure 3.56).

3. Click Rename.

4. In the Rename window, type a new name and click OK (**Figure 3.57**).

5. When you are asked if you want all songs that use the setting with the old name to use the setting with the new name, click Yes.

6. Click Done.

   The preset is renamed.

✔ Tips

- In the window that asks if you're sure you want to delete the preset, you can check "Do not warn me again" to avoid seeing this window in the future.

- If you click No in the window that asks if you want to delete the preset from songs that use it, you'll find that the preset remains assigned to the song, but since it's no longer in the presets pop-up menu, you can no longer apply it to other songs.

Chapter 3

Assigning Equalizer Presets to Streams or Songs

Although it's fine to make equalizer adjustments while you're playing music (just as you make adjustments on your stereo as you're listening), you may want to set equalizer adjustments for particular songs or radio streams.

To assign a preset to an individual song or stream (I):

1. If the Equalizer column is not visible in your song list, make it visible. (Refer to "Hiding and Showing Columns" earlier in this chapter.)

2. Click the pop-up button in the Equalizer column for the song to which you want to assign a preset, and select a preset (**Figure 3.58**).

   The preset you've chosen is applied to the song or stream.

To assign a preset to an individual song or stream (II):

1. Select the song or stream to which you want to assign a particular preset.

2. From the File menu, choose Get Info.

3. Click the Options tab.

4. Choose from the Equalizer presets pop-up menu (**Figure 3.59**).

   The preset you've chosen is applied to the selected song or stream.

Figure 3.58 You can pick any equalizer preset just by clicking on the pop-up icon for the song in the Equalizer column.

Figure 3.59 You can also assign an equalizer preset in the information window for the song. (Select the song, choose File > Get Info, and click the Options tab to get this screen.)

Finding and Playing Songs

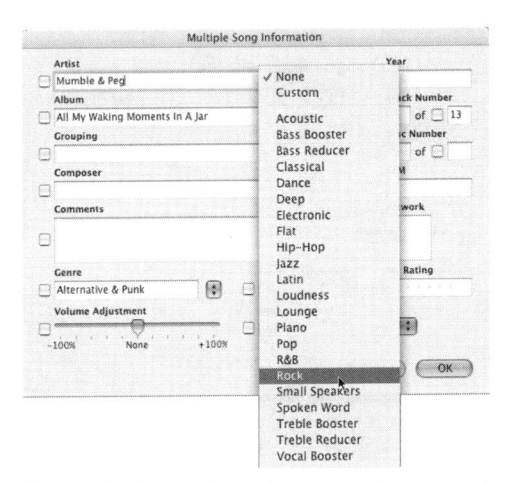

Figure 3.60 You can also assign a preset to a group of songs. (Select the songs and choose File > Get Info to see this screen.)

To assign a preset to multiple songs or streams:

1. Select multiple songs in the song list, or one or more albums, artists, or genres in the Browser.
2. From the File menu choose Get Info.
3. If asked if you're sure you want to edit multiple songs, click Yes.
4. Choose from the Equalizer Preset pop-up menu in the lower right of the window (**Figure 3.60**).
5. Click OK.

Presets That Have Worked Well for Us

Our taste in music is bound to be different than yours, but these are the presets we've used most often.

- **Small Speakers.** We use this when we're using iTunes on computers with inexpensive speakers. (These don't generally produce enough bass; this preset boosts the low-end frequencies.)
- **Spoken Word.** We've used this for news radio streams. This helps because these streams are often quite compressed and benefit from a boost in the middle frequencies.
- **Acoustic.** We like this for a lot of the folk music we like to listen to.

ASSIGNING EQUALIZER PRESETS

77

Chapter 3

Adjusting Sound Effects

Besides the equalizer, iTunes provides a few other controls for enhancing your auditory experience. You'll find these on the Effects tab of the Preferences window.

To change sound effects in iTunes:

1. From the iTunes menu (Mac) or the Edit menu (Windows), choose Preferences.
   The Preferences window appears.

2. Click the Effects tab to open the Effects pane (**Figure 3.61**), then choose from the following options:

   ▲ **Crossfade playback.** This option affects what happens as one song ends and another starts. If it's checked (as it is by default), it causes the first song to fade out while the second song fades in, without any silence between them. The slider determines how long the overlap lasts.

   ▲ **Sound Enhancer.** When you check this, iTunes dynamically adjusts the loudness of various frequencies, as it sees fit. (This is similar to the loudness control on your stereo.) Some people have complained that it has made their MP3-encoded files actually sound worse; you should experiment with this on your own system.

   ▲ **Sound Check.** If you check this, iTunes looks at the volume of each song, compares it to the rest of the songs in your library, and makes adjustments so that all songs are equally loud. (This way, you won't have a situation where one song is relatively quiet and the next is so loud it blasts you out of your seat.)

3. Click OK to close the Preferences window and apply the settings you've chosen.

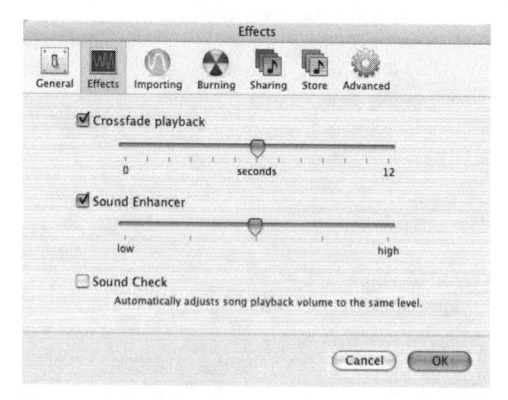

Figure 3.61 The Effects tab of the Preferences window lets you enhance your listening experience.

78

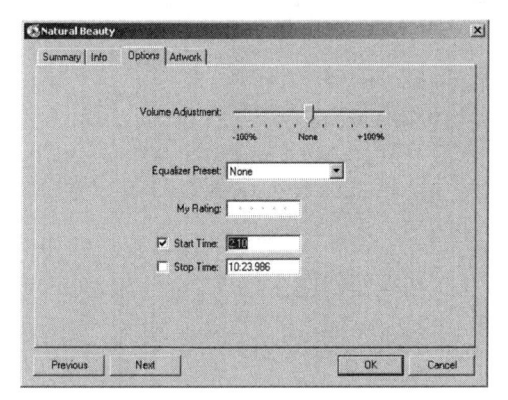

Figure 3.62 Type in a start or stop time if you only want to listen to a specific portion of a song every time it's played.

Specifying Start and Stop Times

Occasionally, you'll find a song you'd rather not listen to from beginning to end. While you can skip over the beginning of a song or stop playing it before it ends, iTunes also lets you assign a start and stop time so that every time you play the song it plays only the portion you like.

To specify start and stop times:

1. Select the song.
2. From the File menu, choose Get Info.
   The information window for the song appears.
3. Click the Options tab.
4. Enter a new time in the Start Time and/or Stop Time fields (**Figure 3.62**).
   You can enter times as seconds or as minutes:seconds:thousandths of a second. For example, if you want 2 minutes and 3.5 seconds, you can enter 123.5 or 2:03:500.
5. Click OK to close the information window.
   Note that the value in the Time column (if it's showing) does not change, since the song itself has not been altered. You have merely told iTunes that, when it plays this song, you only want to hear a portion of it.

Chapter 3

Using the Visualizer

iTunes has one very cool feature for adding a visual component to your listening experience. This, of course, is the *visualizer*, which dynamically creates animated, abstract imagery that accompanies your music as it plays. (*Groovy, trippy*, and *far-out* are words that come to mind.) This is something you absolutely *have* to experience yourself; words are inadequate to describe it.

Figure 3.63 Click the Visualizer button to turn on the visualizer. Click it again to turn it off.

Ways to turn the visualizer on or off:

- Click the Visualizer button, located in the lower-right corner of the iTunes window (**Figure 3.63**).
- From the Visualizer menu, choose Turn Visualizer On or Turn Visualizer Off (**Figure 3.64**).

To choose the size of the visualization:

- From the Visualizer menu, choose Small, Medium, or Large (refer to Figure 3.64).

To turn full-screen mode on or off:

- From the Visualizer menu, choose Full Screen to check or uncheck this option (refer to Figure 3.64).

 If you turn on Full Screen (that is, put a check next to it), the visualizer takes over your whole screen; if you've selected Small or Medium, the actual visualization graphics show in a portion of the screen with a black background (**Figure 3.65**). When the visualizer is off, the visualization occurs only within the confines of the iTunes window (refer ahead to Figure 3.68).

Figure 3.64 You can also turn the visualizer on or off from the Visualizer menu.

✔ Tip

- To turn off the visualizer when it's in full-screen mode, simply click anywhere or press the Esc key.

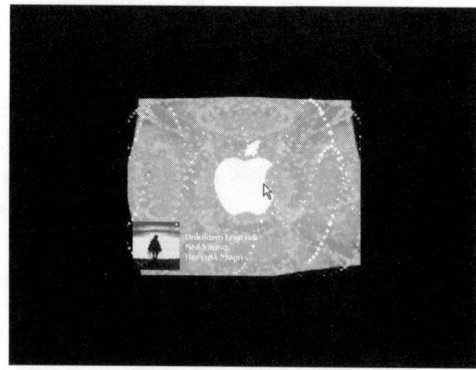

Figure 3.65 This is a result of selecting Small for the size of the visualization, and choosing Full Screen.

Finding and Playing Songs

Figure 3.66 Click the Options button in the top right corner of the iTunes window...

To specify basic visualizer options:

◆ With the visualizer running, click the Options button, located in the upper right corner of the iTunes window. (**Figure 3.66**)

The Visualizer Options window opens and provides a handful of check boxes. (See **Figure 3.67** for a description of these check boxes.)

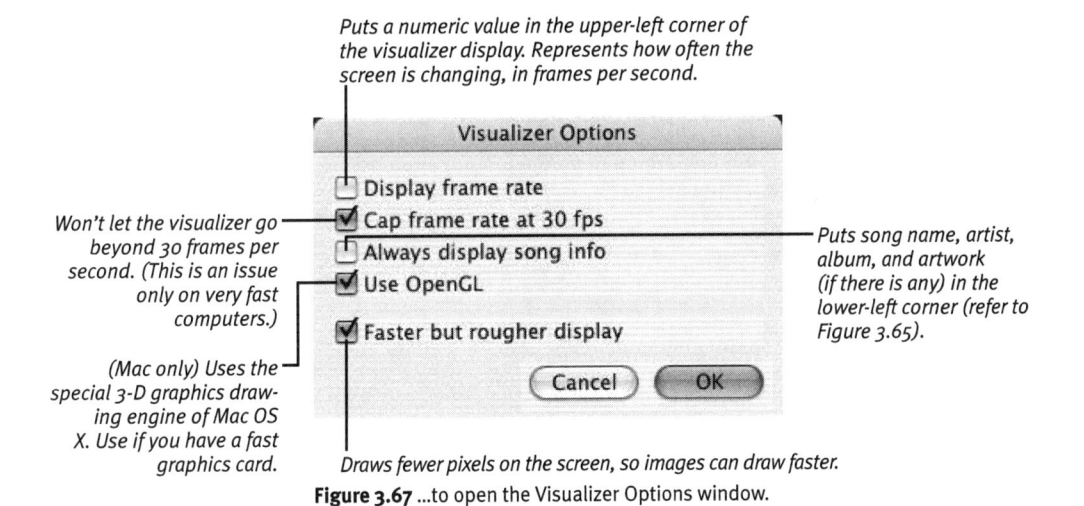

Puts a numeric value in the upper-left corner of the visualizer display. Represents how often the screen is changing, in frames per second.

Won't let the visualizer go beyond 30 frames per second. (This is an issue only on very fast computers.)

(Mac only) Uses the special 3-D graphics drawing engine of Mac OS X. Use if you have a fast graphics card.

Puts song name, artist, album, and artwork (if there is any) in the lower-left corner (refer to Figure 3.65).

Draws fewer pixels on the screen, so images can draw faster.

Figure 3.67 ...to open the Visualizer Options window.

USING THE VISUALIZER

81

Chapter 3

Controlling Visualizations

If you watch the visualizer, you may become curious about what it's doing. There is actually something systematic going on: the visualizer starts with the basic waveform that represents the currently playing audio (which is constantly changing), and applies various graphical manipulations to that form.

Getting a little more specific, there are three properties that are changing as a song plays: waveform representation, effects, and color scheme. The visualizer offers over 75 possible waveform representations, over 150 possible effects, and over 60 possible color schemes. iTunes randomly changes each of these as the music plays. At any time, you can see the current value of each of these three properties, change any one of them, save the current configuration, and reload a configuration—all using keys on your keyboard.

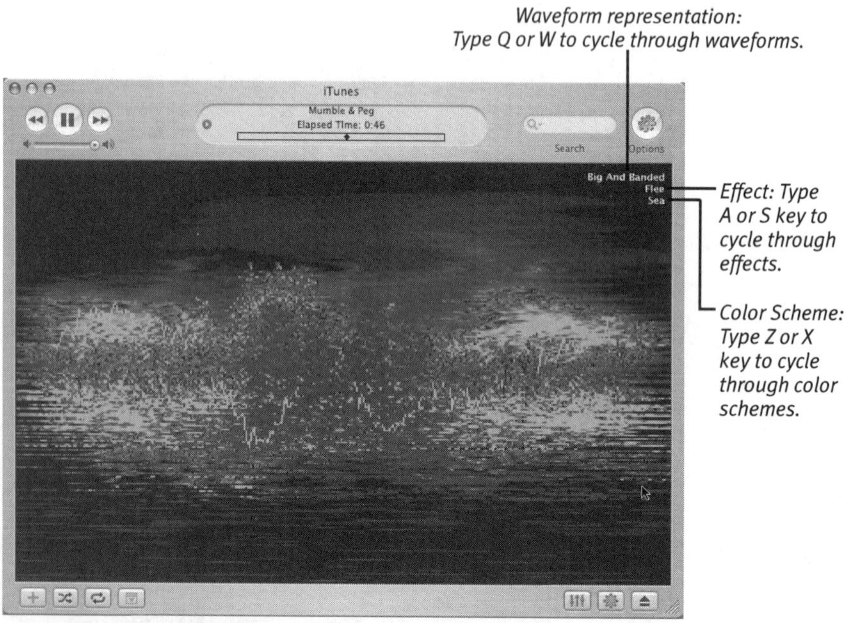

Waveform representation: Type Q or W to cycle through waveforms.

Effect: Type A or S key to cycle through effects.

Color Scheme: Type Z or X key to cycle through color schemes.

Figure 3.68 When you press the C key, the visualizer shows the current waveform, effect, and color scheme.

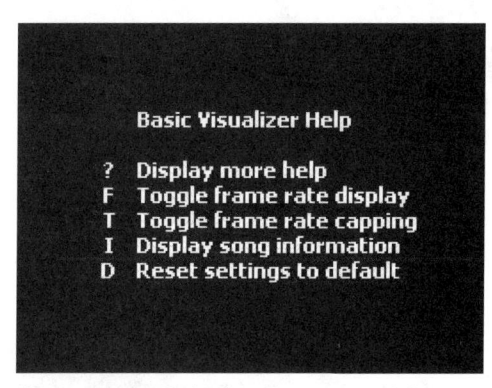

Figure 3.69 Access this list of key commands by pressing the question mark key or the H key.

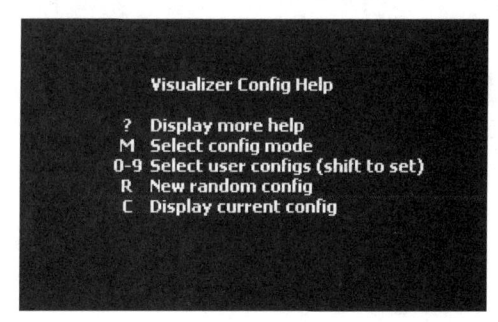

Figure 3.70 Access this list of key commands by pressing the question mark key or the H key a second time.

To see the current configuration:

◆ With the visualizer running, press the C key. Three lines of text appear in the upper-right corner of the visualization (**Figure 3.68**)

 The first line of text represents the name of the current waveform representation; the second line of text represents the name of the current effect; and the third line of text refers to the current color scheme.

To change the current configuration:

◆ Press the Q key or the W key to cycle backward and forward through the list of possible waveform representations.

◆ Press the A or S key to cycle backward and forward through effects.

◆ Press the Z or X key to cycle backward and forward through color schemes.

To save the current configuration:

◆ Press the Shift key, along with any number between 0 and 9.

 You can save up to 10 configurations.

To reload a configuration:

◆ Type the number between 0 and 9 that matches a saved configuration.

✔ Tip

■ Press the question mark key on your keyboard once or twice to get screens that list various keyboard shortcuts; some of which we've covered on this page, and others that we haven't (see **Figures 3.69** and **3.70**). If you want more in-depth coverage, there's a great resource: Susanne Z. Riehemann's iTunes Cheat Sheet, http://doors.stanford.edu/~sr/itunes/. It explains many of these keys and lists all the waveforms, effects, and color schemes available for the visualizer.

Using Other Visualizers

You can find a number of third-party visualizations for iTunes. Some display still images in interesting ways, others play QuickTime movies, and many others show synthetic imagery, similar to the iTunes visualizer.

One that we like displays fountainlike visualizations. It's called Fountain Music, from Binary Minded Software (www.binaryminded.com). Another is G-Force from 55ware (www.55ware.com); it's similar to the iTunes visualizer, but it also incorporates text and unusual graphic objects.

You can find these and many other visualizers listed at VersionTracker, www.versiontracker.com; search the Web site for "iTunes visual."

Once you've downloaded a new visualizer, follow the instructions for installing it in iTunes. Once installed, you can access it from the Visualizer menu (**Figure 3.71**).

Figure 3.71 You're not limited to using the built-in visualizations that ship with iTunes. Try downloading a few third-party visualizations, then access them from the Visualizer menu.

Shopping at the iTunes Music Store

4

It's hard to believe it was less than a year ago that Apple revolutionized the online music business. In spring 2003, they introduced the iTunes Music Store, which provided a legal way to purchase music online at reasonable prices. This is a beautiful thing. You no longer have to fight for parking at the local mall to buy the new Ryan Adams CD—you can simply download it the day it's released, without having to leave your desk.

The basic deal is this: You pay 99 cents for individual songs, or you can purchase entire albums for under $10. You don't pay any monthly subscription fees. You don't have to fear (or feel guilty) that you're downloading music illegally.

There's copy protection on the items you buy, but it's fairly liberal, allowing you to burn songs to CDs, play them on more than one computer, and copy them to iPods. (The iPod is the only device that can play the music from the Store.)

In this chapter, we'll take you on a tour of the store, showing you how to find stuff, how to listen, how to buy songs, and what the limitations are on the music you purchase.

About the iTunes Music Store

The iTunes Music Store is well organized and fun to explore. So long as you're connected to the Internet, you can navigate through the store by clicking through its graphical interface, or you can use a browser, similar to the one you use when browsing through your iTunes library. Using the graphical interface is much like surfing the Web, with clickable graphics and links that let you go down many alternate paths; the Music Store Browser is text-based and reflects a basic hierarchical organization, sorted by genre, then artist, then album.

Either method ultimately takes you to a screen where you can sample and buy songs, but the journey is much more interesting using the graphical interface. In the next few pages of this chapter, we'll go over the three types of screens you're likely to see—the home and genre pages, the album page, and the artist page—when navigating using this graphical interface. We'll cover using the Browser later in this chapter.

But first, let's go to the store.

To go to the iTunes Music Store:

1. Make sure your computer is connected to the Internet.

2. In iTunes, click Music Store in the Source pane.

    iTunes connects to the iTunes Music Store and displays the home page (**Figure 4.1**).

✔ Tips

- Like any good, dynamic Web site, the iTunes Music Store is constantly updated with new content, so what you'll see when you visit probably won't be exactly what you see in these pages.

Shopping at the iTunes Music Store

- You can open the iTunes Music Store in its own window by double-clicking Music Store in the Source pane.

- Keyboard shortcuts for the Forward and Back buttons are Ctrl-] and Ctrl-[(Windows) or Command-] and Command-[(Mac). The keyboard shortcut for the Home button is Shift-Ctrl-H (Windows) or Shift-Command-H (Mac).

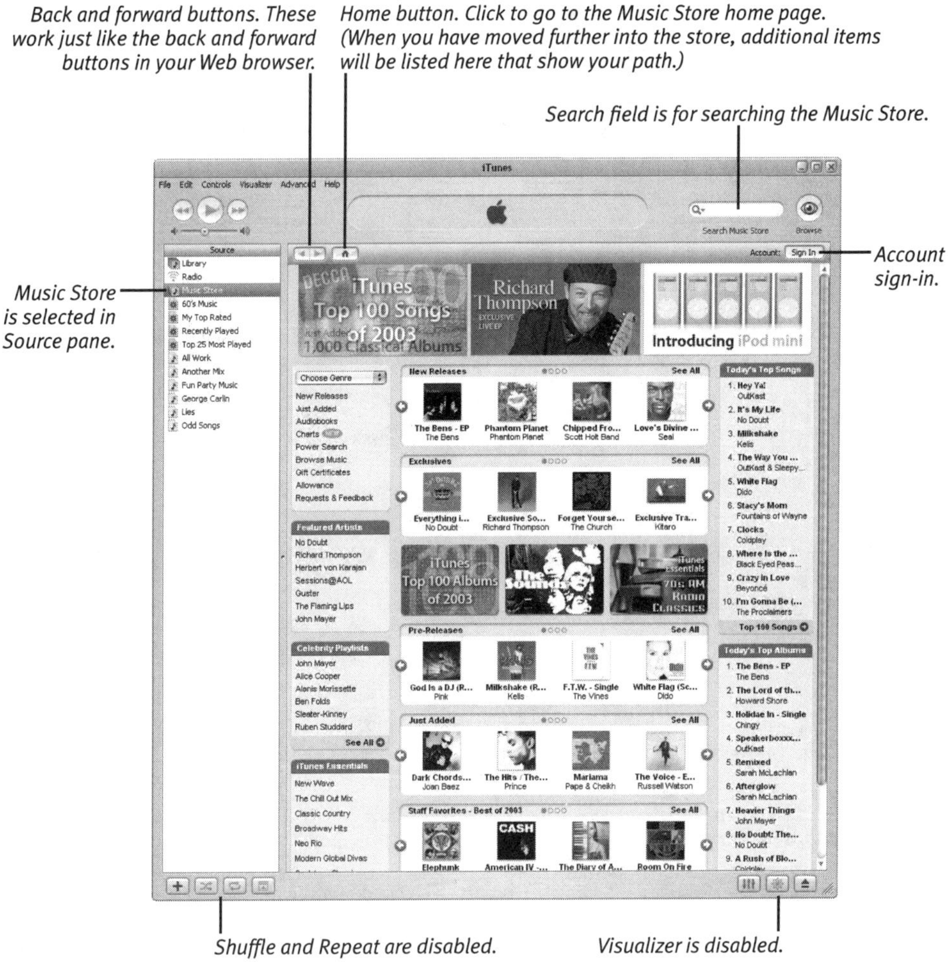

Back and forward buttons. These work just like the back and forward buttons in your Web browser.

Home button. Click to go to the Music Store home page. (When you have moved further into the store, additional items will be listed here that show your path.)

Search field is for searching the Music Store.

Music Store is selected in Source pane.

Account sign-in.

Shuffle and Repeat are disabled.

Visualizer is disabled.

Figure 4.1 The iTunes window, as it appears when you've selected Music Store as your source.

Chapter 4

Home and Genre Page Overview

When you first enter the store, you'll be automatically directed to the iTunes Music Store home page, which offers you a number of ways to visit different sections of the store (**Figure 4.2**).

Click to pick a genre.

Click either of these to see a page listing all New Releases or Just Added albums. (If you're on a genre page, you'll see a list that's particular to that genre.)

Click to scroll to the next set of albums in this category. What you can see in this scrolling field may be a featured subset of the full set of albums in this category.

Click to go to the album that contains this song.

Click to switch to a view that shows all of the albums in this category, which may be more than what's in the scrolling field. (For Exclusives, you'll find many more than are in the scrolling field.)

Click any of these to go an artist page for that artist.

Click to go to this album.

Click to go directly to the 1st, 2nd, 3rd, or 4th subset of albums in the full set.

Figure 4.2 The iTunes Music Store home page (which is similar to a genre page).

Shopping at the iTunes Music Store

If you prefer specific types of music, like pop, jazz, or classical, you'll be happy to know that you can zero in on a specific genre **(Figure 4.3)**. The page for each genre **(Figure 4.4)** offers the same kind of navigational elements as the home page (refer to Figure 4.2).

✔ Tip

- A genre page does not exist for every genre carried in the store, so the options in the pop-up menu for picking a genre are somewhat limited. If you want to view the full list of music genres available at the store, you'll need to use the Browser or the Power Search feature; both are covered later in this chapter.

Figure 4.3 If you prefer to focus on a specific type of music—such as classical or jazz—select a genre.

Shows the genre

Figure 4.4 A genre page looks similar to the iTunes home page, but most of what's shown is particular to the genre.

iTunes Music Store Exclusives

The iTunes Music Store offers "exclusive" content all the time; as of this writing, it lists over 100 exclusive items that you won't find anywhere else—they're not for sale in record stores or at other online sites. You can find exclusive songs, EPs (collections of songs that aren't quite an album), or groups of songs from a wide variety of artists, ranging from the Grateful Dead to Yo-Yo Ma.

When you're at the Music Store home page, click the See All link in the Exclusives scrolling field (refer to Figure 4.2) to view the complete list of exclusive items.

HOME AND GENRE PAGE OVERVIEW

89

Chapter 4

Album Page Overview

No matter how you get to a specific album page in the store, you'll find a basic set of options (**Figure 4.5**) for navigating, previewing and downloading songs.

Click to go to genre page, if it exists. If no page exists for this genre, clicking this button will just take you to the home page.

Click to go the page for this artist.

Songs by this artist that have been downloaded most. Click any of these to select the song in the song list.

These navigational elements tell you where you are in the store.

Click the artist's name to go the page for that artist.

Click to buy all the songs on the album.

Click any column to sort by that column.

Double-click any row to play a preview of the song.

Click any of these buttons to buy the song.

Some albums provide album notes.

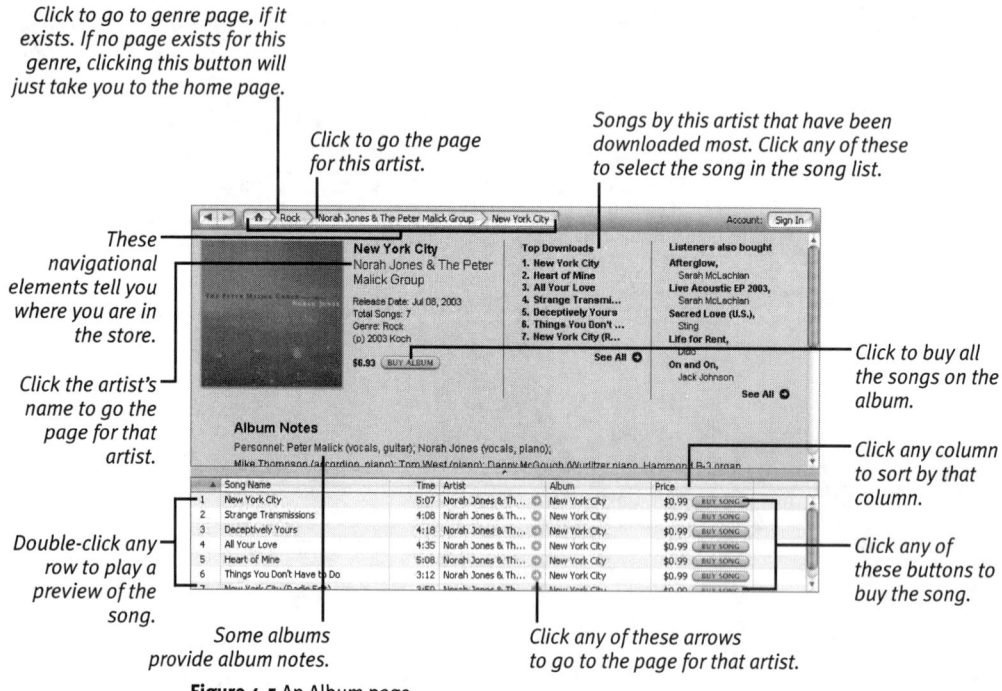

Click any of these arrows to go to the page for that artist.

Figure 4.5 An Album page.

90

Jumping Genres

You go into the store. You pick your favorite genre. You start looking around, clicking links, seeing what's there. Suddenly you realize that the genre has changed. What happened? You may have clicked a Featured Artist link; it's not genre-specific. Or you may have clicked a Listeners Also Bought link; it's reasonable that people buy items in more than one genre.

Another possibility is that some albums are "cross-shelved"—meaning they're categorized in more than one genre. All albums have a primary genre (which you can determine by looking at the navigational indicators next to the back and forward buttons; see Figure 4.5). Poking around in the graphical interface, however, you'll come across plenty of albums whose primary genre is different than the genre you're in. As an example of extreme genre jumping, we went to the Blues genre, located the "Bonnie Raitt Collection" album in the Women in Blues category, clicked it, and found ourselves in the Rock genre; when we clicked to go to Bonnie Raitt's album page we found ourselves in the Pop genre section of the store.

✔ Tips

- You can change the columns that appear in the album page by using the View Options window: Choose Edit > View Options. Or, Control-click (Mac) or right-click (Windows) and choose from the contextual menu that appears.

- See "Previewing Songs" later in this chapter for more information about playing previews of songs on an album page.

- Not all album pages allow you to buy the entire album. There are some albums for which you can only buy the songs individually.

- Depending on your purchasing preferences, you may see Add Song and Add Album buttons rather than Buy Song and Buy Album buttons. Add buttons allow you to add songs or albums to your Shopping Cart. See "Setting iTunes Purchasing Preferences" later in this chapter.

- If a song listed in the Top Downloads area is found on a different album, clicking it causes iTunes to switch to the page for that album.

Chapter 4

Artist Page Overview

Artist pages are not quite as predictable as album pages. All artist pages have a core set of elements; see **Figure 4.6** for an example of an artist page with only a few basic elements. Some artist pages offer much more, as shown in **Figure 4.7**.

Click to go to the genre page if it exists. If no page exists for that genre, clicking this button will take you to the home page.

Choose how you want to sort the list of albums.

Songs by the artist that have been downloaded the most. Click any of these to go to the page for the album on which the song is found. The song will be selected in the song list.

Click the album name to go to the album.

Click the album cover to go to the album.

Click to buy the whole album.

Albums by the artist that have been downloaded the most. Click any of these to go to the page for the album.

Listeners who bought music by this artist also bought music by these other artists. Click any of these to go to the page for that artist.

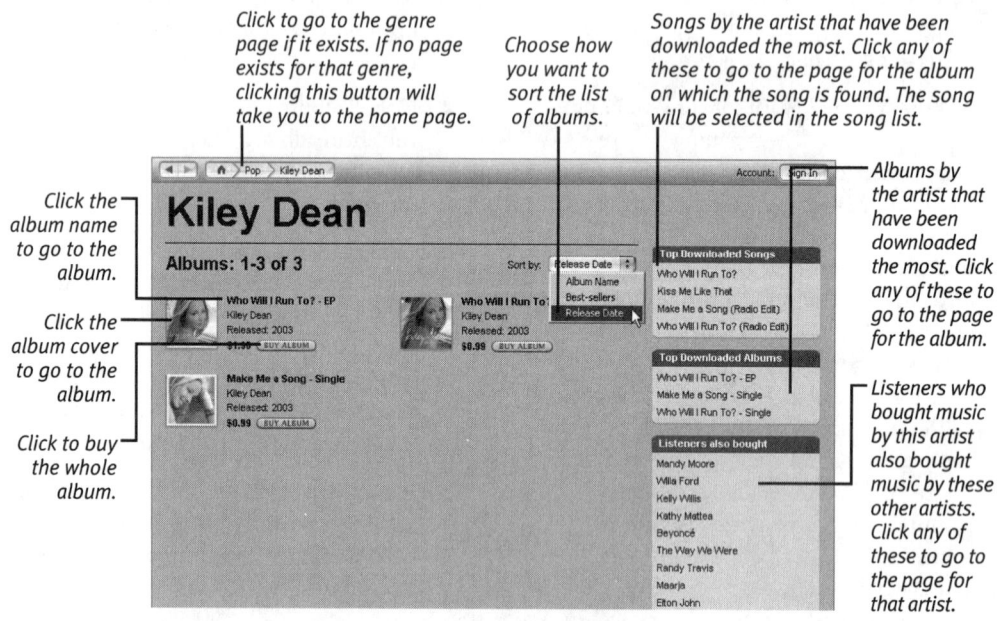

Figure 4.6 An artist page with only a core set of elements.

Behind the iTunes Music Store

You don't have to spend much time in the store before coming across an in-depth artist biography or list of musicians who influenced an artist. Who's coming up with all that? The answer is, Muze. Based in New York, Muze has put together a database with basic biographical information for more than 55,000 artists, plus detailed information for an additional 14,000 artists, as well as data for more than 325,000 albums and millions of songs.

Keeping the database up-to-date is the work of 130 Muze employees and several hundred freelance writers and editors. According to Muze, a group of music experts, musicians, producers, and entertainment-industry pundits puts together each artist's biography and assembles the list of influencers, contemporaries, and followers. Muze defines an *influencer* as a key predecessor to the artist: Bob Dylan is an influencer of the Byrds. A *contemporary* worked within a similar musical and aesthetic context as the artist: Buffalo Springfield is a contemporary of the Byrds. A *follower's* material shows a strong relationship to the artist: R.E.M. is a follower of the Byrds.

Shopping at the iTunes Music Store

Promotional text about the artist, their offerings in the store, or both.

Click to go to a page that puts this artist in context by showing albums that influenced the artist (Influencers), albums that have been influenced by this artist (Followers), and albums by those considered contemporaries of this artist (Contemporaries).

Click to read a musical biography. This biography contains links to albums and artists.

Click to go to what's essentially an album page, where you can sample and buy songs by this artist that are exclusive to the iTunes Music Store.

Click to go to the artist's Celebrity Playlist page, another page that's very much like an album page, with a list of the artist's favorite songs. You can sample or buy these songs or (usually) buy the entire collection as if it were an album.

Click to go to another page (still in the Store) that lets you play a QuickTime music video.

Click to bring your Web browser window to the front and go to the artist's Web site.

Must-have albums by this artist.

Figure 4.7 An artist page with lots of extra features.

ARTIST PAGE OVERVIEW

93

Navigating with the Browser

The iTunes Music Store Browser provides a text-based, hierarchical way to navigate the store. It's probably best for left-brainers (who needs pictures, anyway?) or those who know fairly specifically what they're looking for. It's also faster for those on a slow Internet connection, since you don't have to wait for graphics to download.

To browse for music:

1. If the Browser is not showing, do one of the following:
   - ▲ Click the Browse button in the upper-right corner of the iTunes window (**Figure 4.8**).
   - ▲ Click the Browse Music link in the Music Store interface (refer to Figure 4.8).
   - ▲ From the Edit menu, choose Show Browser. (Or type a keyboard equivalent: Command-B on a Mac or Ctrl-B in Windows.)

   The Browse pane appears.

2. Select the genre you want, then the artist, and then the album (**Figure 4.9**).

   The list of songs on the selected album appears.

Figure 4.8 Click the Browse button or the Browse Music link to switch to the Browser.

Shopping at the iTunes Music Store

✔ Tips

- Once you've browsed to a specific album using the Browser, you can purchase individual songs by clicking the Buy Song (or Add Song) button; but there's no button to buy the entire album. If you want to buy the entire album, click an arrow next to the album name in the song list; the album page shows with its Buy Album button (or Add Album button, depending on your preference settings).

- You can double-click an artist's name in the Browser to bring up the corresponding artist page and switch out of Browse mode.

- You can also double-click a genre name to bring up the corresponding genre page. (If you double-click a genre that has no genre page—such as Children's Music—the Music Store's home page appears.)

Figure 4.9 First select a genre, then an artist, then an album to see a list of songs.

Searching the Store

Do you know the exact name of an artist, album, or song? Can you remember just a fragment of a name? Or are you looking for all songs that have anything to do with a specific topic, such as "war"? If so, use the Search feature.

To perform a general search in the store:

1. In the Search field (located in the top right of the iTunes window), type the text you want iTunes to locate.

    Notice that iTunes doesn't start searching as you type (as occurs when searching your own collection).

2. Press Return (Mac) or Enter (Windows).

    The results of the search are songs that contain the search term(s) in the Artist, Album, or Song Name columns (**Figure 4.10**). The songs are sorted by relevance (a column that's not normally in song lists). When multiple albums are represented, an icon appears for each album at the top of the page. You can click these album icons, or the arrows in the Album column, to go to the corresponding album pages.

To limit a search to album, artist, composer, or song name:

1. If you want to narrow your search, click the magnifying glass and choose Artists, Albums, Composers, or Songs **(Figure 4.11)**.

2. In the Search field, type the text you want iTunes to locate.

    iTunes searches only the column matching the category you selected (**Figure 4.12**).

Click to go to album.   *Search field*

Figure 4.10 The result of a search. (We searched for *Brel*; 38 songs were found.)

You can also click here to go to album.

Figure 4.11 You can have iTunes search only for an album, artist, composer, or song name.

Figure 4.12 Here, we searched for *Brel*, the same term as that shown in Figure 4.10, but we limited the search to Artists. Notice that fewer songs (only 15) were found.

Fun Ways to Discover New Music

Don't necessarily know exactly what you want to buy? Try these other ways to discover new artists or albums:

- **Celebrity Playlists**—accessible from the home or genre pages, as well as some artist pages—are pages in the store with lists of songs chosen by selected artists. Sometimes these pages have quotes by the celebrity regarding how they picked the selected songs, notes about the music they like, or what they think of iTunes.

- **iTunes Essentials**—also accessible from the home or genre pages—are lists of songs that define a category of music. If you're trying to impress your future in-laws with your knowledge of opera, for example, you might want to spend some time with The Beauty of Opera Essentials.

- **Billboard Charts**—a choice in the Genre column of the Browser, as well as on the home page and genre pages—are lists of top songs from various calendar years. Go check out songs from the year your Dad graduated high school!

Just How Big Is This Store?

Apple has received cooperation from the five major music labels (BMG, EMI, Sony Music Entertainment, Universal, and Warner), as well as from over 200 independent artists and labels.

By February 2004, Apple claimed to have over 500,000 songs and was adding hundreds of new ones every week. (Take a look at the Just Added section of the store.)

The store also features more than 5000 spoken-word items, including audiobooks and radio shows from Audible.com.

✔ Tips

- If you type more than one word in the Search field, iTunes searches for songs that have all the words in it, not necessarily in the same order. Thus, a search for *rooster red* will return items containing *red rooster*.

- iTunes ignores certain words and characters in the search field. These include *and, or, not, &, +, -,* and quote marks. In other words, it's smart enough to recognize these as something to ignore, but not smart enough to use them to aid in a search, as a more sophisticated search engine would.

- Relevance is determined by which column, and how many columns, the search term is found in. A song is more relevant, for example, if the search term is located in the Song Name column than if it's located in the Album column (assuming you have not told iTunes to limit the search to a particular column).

- Your search is limited to a maximum of 250 songs. That's usually too many, anyway. Try the Power Search (see next page) to better limit your search.

- If you perform a search and iTunes doesn't find your search term, but finds something similar, it will ask if the similar term is what you meant. You can click on the similar term if that *is* what you meant; otherwise, you can click the word *Request* to fill out a form to request that Apple add to the store a particular song, album, artist, composer, genre, or anything else you can think of. For example, we searched for *Waifs*, whereupon iTunes asked if we meant *Waits;* we didn't, so we clicked Request to request that the iTunes Music Store carry music by The Waifs. We'll check back in a month or two to see if it worked.

Chapter 4

Power Searching the Store

Since the store carries so many items, it provides a Power Search function to help you locate items more precisely. You can specify multiple search terms, each in a different field.

To perform a Power Search:

1. Enter Power Search mode by doing either of the following:
   ▲ Click the magnifying glass in the Search field and choose Power Search (refer to Figure 4.11).
   ▲ Click the Power Search link on the home page, or any genre page (**Figure 4.13**).
   The Power Search pane appears (**Figure 4.14**).
2. Type in any of the fields.
3. Select a genre if you want to limit your search to a particular genre.
4. Click Search.
   The results are displayed in the song list, sorted by relevance (**Figure 4.15**).

✔ Tip

- You may want to limit your use of the genre pop-up menu, as it's sometimes too restricting. It finds only albums that have the selected genre as their primary genre. For example, we used Power Search to search for Alison Krauss under the genre Folk, and didn't find any Alison Krauss albums. Yet, when we used the Browser and selected Folk as the genre and Alison Krauss as the artist, we found multiple albums listed.

Figure 4.13 Click Power Search on the home page or any genre page...

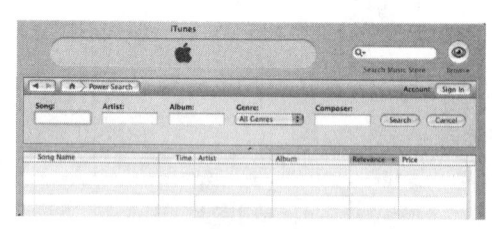

Figure 4.14 ...to show the Power Search pane.

Figure 4.15 Enter search terms and pick a genre (or leave it as All Genres), and then click Search. Here, a search for *war* and *Bruce* brought up songs by both Bruce Springsteen and Bruce Cockburn.

Previewing Songs

Previewing music at the iTunes Music Store is essentially the same as playing music from your own library. On this page, we'll remind you of the methods available to you.

If you're connected to the Music Store over a dial-up modem, you may find that your previewed songs sputter and stop as you listen to them. We'll also show you how you can change your Music Store preferences so that iTunes downloads the song sample before playing it, making for an improved—and less spotty—listening experience.

Ways to preview a song:

◆ Double-click any song's entry in the song list.

◆ If there's no current song (one with a speaker icon), press the Play button to play a preview of whatever song is selected (or the first song in the list if nothing is selected). See **Figure 4.16**.

◆ If there is a current song (one with a speaker icon next to it), click the Play button or press the space bar on your keyboard to play that song.

◆ Click a song's line in the song list to select it, and then press the Return key (Mac) or Enter key (Windows) on your keyboard.

Play button

Selected song: Press Return (Mac) or Enter (Windows) to play. (If there's no current song, you can also play the selected song by clicking the Play button, pressing the space bar, or choosing Controls > Play.)

Current song: Press the space bar (or click the Play button or choose Controls > Play) to play this song.

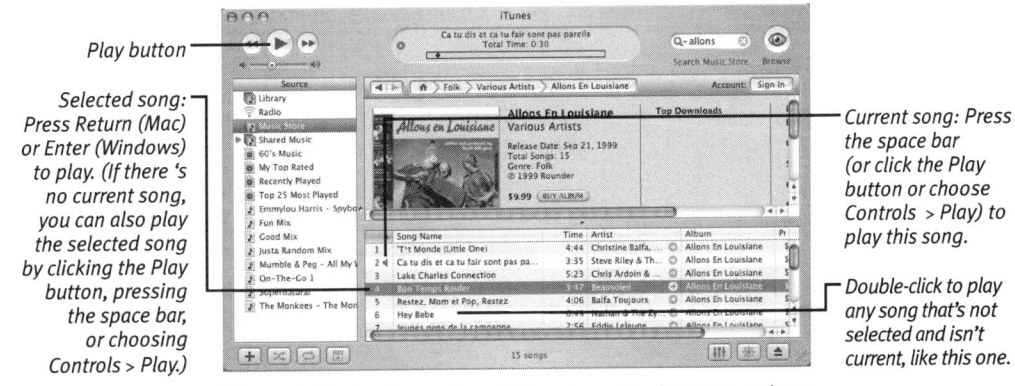

Double-click to play any song that's not selected and isn't current, like this one.

Figure 4.16 You have a number of different ways to play song previews.

Chapter 4

To set iTunes to download complete previews before playing:

1. From the Edit menu (Windows) or iTunes menu (Mac), select Preferences.
2. Click the Store tab.
3. Check the radio button for "Load complete preview before playing" (**Figure 4.17**), then click OK.

✔ Tip

- To preview the previous or next song in a list while a preview is playing, press the left or right arrow key.

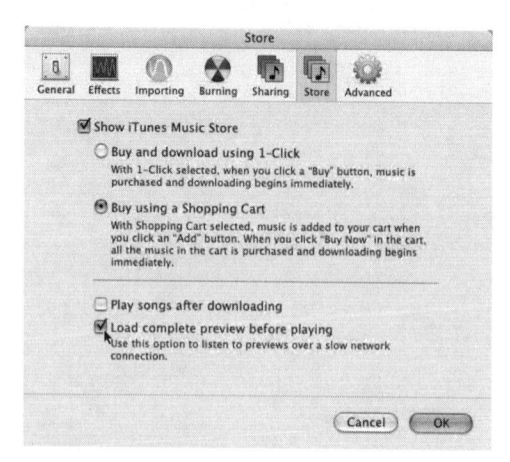

Figure 4.17 You can tell iTunes to download the full preview before playing—a good idea if you're experiencing stuttering.

About Explicit and Clean Lyrics

As you navigate through the iTunes Music Store, you may come across songs or albums labeled "Explicit" or "Clean." The former is a warning that the content may be objectionable; the latter means it is a version of a song or album with explicit lyrics edited out. If you double-click the word *Explicit* or *Clean* on an artist or album page, you'll see a Parental Advisory Screen that explains in detail the system for parental advisory labeling. (Clicking a Parental Advisory or Clean Lyrics icon also loads the Parental Advisory Screen page.)

Click one of these to switch to Browse mode and see all the authors in that category.

Figure 4.18 The Audiobook genre page offers something for everyone—biographies, fiction, comedy, and radio shows, to name a few.

About Audiobooks

You're not limited to listening to music in iTunes. If you realize that you're never going to have time to sit down and read *Bleak House*, or if you enjoy listening to radio programs and interviews, you might try giving audiobooks a listen. In the iTunes Music Store, audiobooks are books read aloud (sometimes abridged), periodicals read aloud (almost always abridged), recorded radio programs, and content created specifically for the audiobook format, such as interviews.

You'll find the store's collection of audiobooks by choosing Audiobooks in the genre pop-up menu that's on the top left of the home page or any genre page (refer to Figure 4.2).

An audiobook page (**Figure 4.18**), at first glance, looks and operates just like a standard genre page, allowing you to click links to go to book or author pages (the equivalent of album and artist pages). What's different is the Categories navigation area on the left; you can think of this as a listing of subgenres within the Audiobooks genre. Another minor difference from other genre pages is the listing of Today's Top Sellers on the right-hand side of the page, rather than Today's Top Songs and Today's Top Albums.

Chapter 4

If you click a category name from the Categories navigation area, iTunes switches to Browse mode and you'll see three columns: Genre (with Audiobooks chosen), Category (with the category you just clicked selected), and Author (**Figure 4.19**). Once you've selected an author, all the books by that author are listed.

The author page will probably look familiar—it's similar to the standard artist page (refer to Figure 4.6), displaying at a minimum a list of the author's audiobooks and a list of the most-downloaded audiobooks by the author.

Figure 4.19 This is Browse mode as it appears in the Audiobook genre. Notice that the columns are Genre, Category, and Author (rather than Genre, Artist, and Album).

The book page (**Figure 4.20**) is *not* like a standard album page. It has a Preview button that you can click to hear a sample of the book's content. (These previews vary in length, but they're generally a few minutes long.) The only button for making a purchase is a Buy Book or Add Book button; and there's no equivalent to a song list, as the book can't be bought in pieces. Usually, you'll also find a description of the book.

Figure 4.20 The book page offers bibliographic information for Audiobooks, including the narrator, length, and book description.

102

iTunes Music Store Compared with Audible.com

The content of the audiobooks in the iTunes Music Store comes from Audible.com. You can usually purchase the same items from Audible.com and drag the downloaded file into iTunes (as we mentioned in Chapter 2).

The files that are downloaded from Audible.com, however, are not as well-compressed as those in the iTunes Music Store. The songs in the iTunes Music Store are AAC files, so you'll be able to fit more on any limited-space drive or device. (For a better understanding of the AAC file format, see Chapter 2. Also, see "File Formats of Purchased Songs and Audiobooks" later in this chapter.)

On the other hand, Audible.com has a $15-per-month subscription plan that allows you to download one book each month. If the books you wish to purchase cost more than $15, this might be a more economical route.

✔ Tips

- Because of their length, audiobooks have a special feature: They remember where you paused them, so you can return to that spot when you're ready to continue listening. This works whether you are listening on your iPod or within iTunes on your computer.

- We highly recommend that you use that Preview button before you buy. You want to be quite sure that the vocal quality of the reader doesn't get on your nerves.

- The audiobooks you purchase at the store are *almost* identical in format to the songs you purchase there: They can be burned to CD or put on an iPod, but they currently can't be shared using iTunes network sharing capabilities. (We cover CD burning in Chapter 6, iPods in Chapter 7, and sharing in Chapter 8.)

- Most audiobooks are divided into chapters. While iTunes shows no visible indication of these chapters, you can jump to the next chapter by holding down the Shift and Ctrl keys while pressing the right arrow key on Windows, or the Shift and Command keys while pressing the right arrow key on a Mac. (Do the same with the left arrow key to go to the beginning of the current chapter, or to the beginning of the previous chapter if you're already at the beginning of a chapter.) Jumping in this way works only if the audiobook is playing—at least as of this writing.

- If you use QuickTime Player to open the file that's downloaded when you buy an audiobook, you'll typically see a chapter menu (a pop-up menu on the right side of the playback controls), from which you can select a chapter to play.

Saving Links

As you navigate through the store, you'll encounter all sorts of interesting pages and songs that you might want to revisit later. Or you may want your friend to hear a new single from an artist you've recently discovered. iTunes provides two simple methods for saving links (called *deep links*) to most anything in the store: via a shortcut (or alias), and by copying a URL.

To save a shortcut or alias to your desktop:

◆ Click any clickable element in the store (a link to a page in the store or a song in a song list), and drag it to your desktop (**Figure 4.21**).

When you release the mouse button, a pointer file—called an *alias* on the Mac, or a *shortcut* in Windows—is created on your desktop (**Figure 4.22**). You can click this at any time to return to the page to which the link pointed, or the page on which you found the song.

Figure 4.21 Drag any link or song from the store to your desktop...

Figure 4.22 ...to create a shortcut (Windows) or alias (Mac). Clicking the shortcut or alias will get you back to that page or song.

Figure 4.23 Right-click (Windows) or Control-click (Mac) on almost any link or song and you'll see Copy iTunes Music Store URL. Select this, and then you'll be able to paste it in an email message or document.

Web Page Authoring with iTunes Music Store Links

Do you want to create a Web page with deep links to your favorite items in the iTunes Music Store?

Apple's iTunes Link Maker, (http://phobos.apple.com/WebObjects/MZSearch.woa/wa/itmsLinkMaker) is a Web page from which you can search the store. You select from the results of this search, and the Link Maker then generates the necessary HTML code for embedding the link to the selected item (be it a song, an album, or an artist).

If viewers of your Web page have iTunes and click a link on the page, they will be taken directly to the right place in the store. iTunes Link Maker also provides the code for putting a Download iTunes button on your page, so those viewers who don't have iTunes can get it easily.

To copy the URL of an item:

1. Right-click (Windows) or Control-click (Mac) a graphic or text link, or a song in a song list.

2. Select Copy iTunes Music Store URL (**Figure 4.23**).

   The address is copied to the Clipboard so you can paste it into most any other application that will let you paste in text. For example, you can paste it into an email message or an instant message session to share it with a friend. ("Listen to this song, dude!")

✔ Tips

- The URL that's copied begins with http://. This means that when you click this URL, your operating system opens a Web browser, which in turn opens iTunes. However, if you replace the http:// with itms://, iTunes opens directly. This is a bit faster, and doesn't open a Web browser if one isn't already open.

- If you link to a song, you'll find that the page opens with the song selected, so you just need to press Return (Mac) or Enter (Windows) to play it. Other methods, like pressing the space bar, will also usually work.

- Unfortunately, there *are* links that you can't copy or drag to your desktop. Some that we've found include links to an artist's video, and to exclusive tracks on an artist page. (Don't ask us why you can't copy the URL for these items.)

Chapter 4

Getting an Account

Before you can purchase any of the songs, albums, or audiobooks that you've located, you'll need to create an Apple account, unless you already have an Apple account or —with the introduction of iTunes 4.2—an AOL account. (You already have an Apple ID if you've shopped at the online Apple store, if you've bought photos through iPhoto, or if you have a .Mac account.). If you do have an existing Apple or AOL account, you'll need to set it up for iTunes Music Store purchasing.

Figure 4.24 Click the Sign In button to start the process of creating an account.

To create an account if you don't already have an Apple ID or an AOL screen name:

1. In the upper right corner of the Music Store window, click the Account Sign In button (**Figure 4.24**)

    A Sign In window appears (**Figure 4.25**).

2. Click Create New Account.

3. Proceed through the three screens that appear.

    These will be labeled Step 1, Step 2, and Step 3. You'll need to agree to the "Terms and Conditions" for the Store on the first screen; fill in identifying information (**Figure 4.26**) on the second; and provide credit card information on the third.

    When you finish entering your information, you'll see a screen with a message that says you're ready to buy music from the iTunes Music Store.

Figure 4.25 In the Sign In window, click Create New Account if you have no existing Apple or AOL account. (If you do have an account, enter your Apple ID or AOL screen name and password and click Sign In.)

Figure 4.26 If you're creating an Apple account from scratch, you'll see this screen, where you enter identifying information. (Additional screens ask you to agree to Terms and Conditions, and to fill in credit card information.)

GETTING AN ACCOUNT

106

To set up an existing Apple or AOL account to make purchases in the iTunes Music Store:

1. Click the Account Sign In button (refer to Figure 4.24).

2. Enter your Apple ID or AOL screen name and password, and click Sign In.

3. Proceed through the screens that appear. This will include one page on which you'll have to agree to the "Terms and Conditions" for the Store. If Apple doesn't already have credit card information associated with your account, you'll also need to fill in a form with your credit card information.

   When you finish entering your information, you'll see a screen with a message that says you're ready to buy music from the iTunes Music Store.

✔ Tips

- It's a good idea to put some serious thought into your password, because if somebody else guesses it, they can buy lots of music on your credit card.

- One important note: You can buy from the iTunes Music Store only if you have a credit card with a U.S. billing address.

- You can wait until you're ready to buy something before you set up your account. The first time you click a Buy or Add button (to add something to your Shopping cart), a Sign In window (almost identical to the one shown in Figure 4.26) will appear. You'll need to go through all the steps for creating an account after Step 1.

Chapter 4

Signing In and Out of the Store

Once you have an Apple or AOL account that's set up for the iTunes Music Store, you'll be able to sign in to the store to make purchases. You'll also want to know how to sign out, to be sure that nobody else downloads songs on your computer, running up hefty charges on your credit card.

To sign in:

1. Click the Account Sign In button (**Figure 4.27**).
2. If you are signing in with an AOL screen name, click the AOL radio button; otherwise make sure the radio button with the Apple icon next to it is selected (**Figure 4.28**).
3. Enter your Apple ID or AOL screen name and password.
4. Click Sign In.
   Your Apple ID or AOL screen name appears as the label of the button that was the Sign In button.

To sign out:

1. Click your account name in the location you clicked to sign in (**Figure 4.29**).
   A window appears, giving you the options of viewing your account or signing out.
2. Click Sign Out (**Figure 4.30**).

✔ Tips

- Quitting or exiting iTunes also signs you out.
- Remember that your password is case sensitive. If your Caps Lock key is on, you'll see a warning in the window in which you enter your password.

Figure 4.27 Click the Sign In button.

Figure 4.28 Enter your Apple ID or AOL screen name and password and click Sign In.

Figure 4.29 To sign out of the store, first click your account name, then type your password.

Figure 4.30 Click Sign Out to disable purchasing. Once you're signed out, you can still browse the store, but you'll need to sign in again to make additional purchases.

Select if you want to download songs instantly.

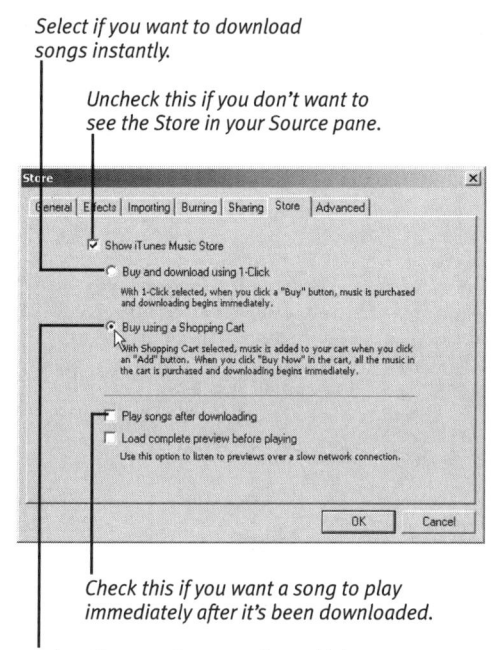

Uncheck this if you don't want to see the Store in your Source pane.

Check this if you want a song to play immediately after it's been downloaded.

Select if you prefer to pay for multiple songs at the end of your shopping session.

Figure 4.31 The Store tab of the iTunes Preferences window.

Setting iTunes Purchasing Preferences

Before you start spending your money at the iTunes Music Store, take the time to set up the settings in the Preferences window that will shape your shopping experience.

To set purchasing preferences:

1. From the Edit menu (Windows) or iTunes menu (Mac), select Preferences.

2. Click the Store tab.

3. Make choices (**Figure 4.31**):

   The most important of these is whether you want to use 1-Click shopping or a Shopping Cart. Choose 1-Click if you like the idea of immediate gratification—it lets you buy songs with a single click of your mouse. Choose Shopping Cart if you want to gather up a number of items before making a purchase; this option is better if you're trying to control impulse buying, or if you have a slow Internet connection. Your choice of 1-Click or Shopping Cart impacts whether you will see Buy buttons or Add buttons throughout the Store.

   You can also opt to have songs play automatically after downloading (another feature for those who demand instant gratification).

   If you don't want to be tempted at all by the Store, click to deselect Show iTunes Music Store; this way it won't show up in your list of Sources.

✔ Tip

- We explain the "Load complete preview before playing," option you see in Figure 4.31 in the section "Previewing Songs," earlier in this chapter.

109

Chapter 4

1-Click Purchasing

Even though it's called 1-Click shopping, it may require more than a single click.

To buy songs if using 1-Click:

1. Click the Buy button (**Figure 4.32**) for the item you wish to buy.

   (This may be a Buy Song, a Buy Album, or a Buy Book button.)

2. If a sign-in window appears, fill in your information and click Buy.

   Another window appears, asking if you're sure you want to buy and download your book, song, or album.

3. Click Buy (**Figure 4.33**).

   iTunes downloads the item(s) to your computer. The Status display shows the progress of the download (**Figure 4.34**).

   If you have money in your account from a gift certificate or allowance (see the next two sections in this chapter), the amount of your purchase is subtracted from your account.

   If you don't have money in your account (or not enough money), the appropriate amount is charged to your credit card.

   Once downloaded, the purchased item appears both in your Purchased Music playlist (**Figure 4.35**) and in your library. In most cases, album or book cover artwork is downloaded as well, and appears in the Artwork pane.

Figure 4.32 Ready to part with your hard-earned cash? Click the Buy button. (This button may actually say Buy Song, Buy Album, Buy Book, or Buy All Songs, depending on your selection.)

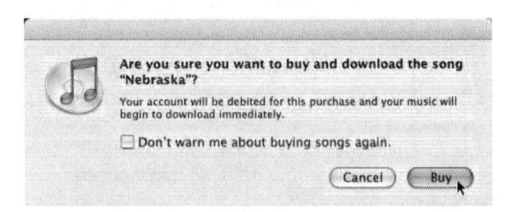

Figure 4.33 iTunes asks you if you're sure you want to make the purchase.

Figure 4.34 The Status display shows the progress of the download. If you have a dial-up Internet connection, this might take several minutes.

110

Shopping at the iTunes Music Store

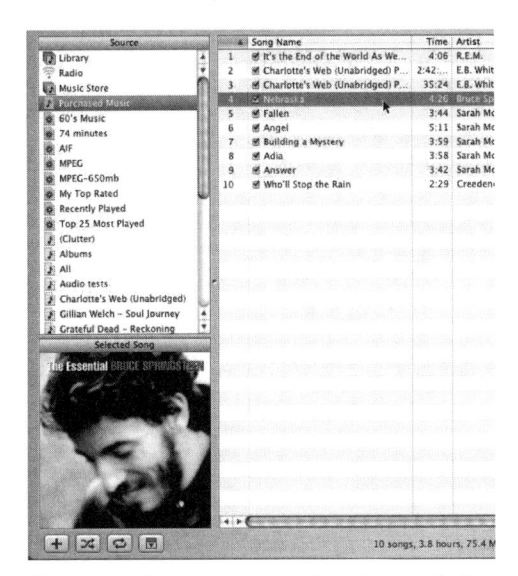

Figure 4.35 All songs you've purchased appear in the Purchased Music playlist.

✔ Tips

- Some audiobooks download in multiple parts; for these, the progress bar shows the progress of each part (not the whole book).

- In the screen that asks if you're sure about your purchase (refer to Figure 4.33), you can check an option to have iTunes skip the warning in the future. Unless you wish to throw caution to the wind, don't check this. If you do check it, however, you can undo your action; see "Managing Your Account" at the end of this chapter.

What Can You Do With Purchased Songs and Audiobooks?

While the iTunes Music Store will let you download an almost unlimited number of items, Apple does place restrictions on how and where you listen to the files you've purchased. You can play your purchased music on up to three different computers (Macs or PCs), as long as they're *authorized* (see Chapter 8 for more information on authorizing). You can, however, transfer your purchased items to an unlimited number of iPods. And while you can burn an individual song to as many audio CDs as you want, you're prevented from burning the same playlist with a purchased song more than ten times. (See Chapter 5 for more about playlists, and Chapter 6 for more about burning CDs.)

These restrictions are enforced via FairPlay, a Digital Rights Management (DRM) technology that Apple uses.

1-CLICK PURCHASING

111

Chapter 4

Shopping Cart Purchasing

It's not much more difficult to use the shopping cart.

To buy songs if using the Shopping Cart:

1. Click the Add button (**Figure 4.36**) for each item you want to add.

    The first time you click an Add button in a session, you may see a sign-in screen, similar to that in Figure 4.28. Fill in your info and click Add to Cart.

2. When you're done adding all the items you want to purchase, click Shopping Cart in the Source pane (**Figure 4.37**).

3. If you have second thoughts about some of the items, click the Remove button(s) for the items you've decided you no longer want.

4. When the list shows the items you want to buy, click Buy Now.

5. When asked if you're sure you want to buy and download the items in your shopping cart, click Buy.

    All items in your shopping cart are downloaded. You'll find them in your Purchased Music playlist (refer to Figure 4.35).

Figure 4.36 Click an Add button to add an item to your shopping cart.

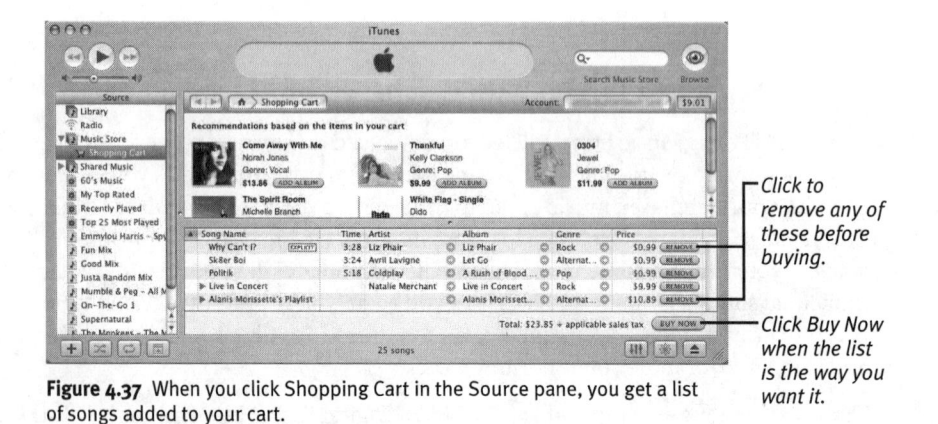

Figure 4.37 When you click Shopping Cart in the Source pane, you get a list of songs added to your cart.

112

✔ Tips

- If you put something in your shopping cart on one computer and then sign in using the same account on another computer, your shopping cart will contain the items that you placed in it earlier.

- If you purchased a song but it didn't download (this can happen if you quit iTunes before you finish downloading), iTunes should automatically restart that download the next time you open iTunes. If it doesn't, go to the Advanced menu and choose Check for Purchased Music. (You'll have to enter your account information.) If there are songs you've purchased but not downloaded, they should download immediately.

- If you accidentally delete a purchased song, Apple's not going to replace it for you. Be careful about deleting songs from your library!

File Formats of Purchased Songs and Audiobooks

When you buy music and audiobooks from the iTunes Music Store, the files you download are AAC-compressed MPEG-4 files.

You may recall from Chapter 2 that AAC is a highly efficient audio compressor, even more efficient than the popular MP3. AAC is the default compressor that iTunes uses to encode music when you import songs from an audio CD.

Audio files from the iTunes Music Store, however, aren't the same as the audio files you create when you import songs from a CD. Files from the store carry a file extension of .m4p or .m4b (the former is for music, the latter is for books) and are restricted, as we describe in the sidebar "What Can You Do with Purchased Songs and Audiobooks?" The songs that you import from your own CDs carry a file extension of .m4a, and are free of any kind of copy protection.

Chapter 4

Giving Gift Certificates

Stuck for an idea for a birthday or holiday present? An iTunes Gift Certificate may be just what you're looking for: easy for you to buy and flexible enough to fit just about anybody. The quickest and most efficient way to get this done is to have the gift certificate sent via email, so we provides steps for doing so. (But see the first tip on the facing page if you'd rather send a paper gift certificate.)

To give an email gift certificate:

1. Click the Gift Certificates link on the home page or a genre page (**Figure 4.38**).

2. On the iTunes Gift Certificate page, click the Email button (**Figure 4.39**).

3. Fill in the form that appears and click Continue (**Figure 4.40**).

4. You'll see a window asking you to sign in to buy. Enter your Apple ID or AOL screen name (if it's not already there) and password; then click Continue.

5. On the "Confirm your purchase" page, click Buy (**Figure 4.41**).

   A screen appears with a message that the gift certificate was sent.

Figure 4.38 Click the Gift Certificates link to start the process of buying a gift certificate.

Figure 4.39 Click the Email button, assuming you want to send an electronic gift certificate.

Figure 4.40 Click Continue when you're done filling in the form.

114

Figure 4.41 Click Buy to confirm that you really want to make this purchase.

Music Store Customer Service

Have you run into problems with your account? From iTunes's Help menu, choose Music Store Customer Service. (you'll need to provide an Apple ID, even if you're signed into the Store). This is the place to get answers to various questions about your account: The pages provide a good deal of information, and you can also send an email query.

✔ Tips

- If you'd rather send a paper gift certificate, click the U.S. Mail button rather than the Email button on the iTunes Gift Certificate page (refer to Figure 4.39). Your Web browser opens to the Apple Store, showing a page on which you can fill out a form to buy a Music Store Gift Certificate. Make sure to leave "U.S. Postal Service" selected, fill out the form, and click Continue. (If you want to hand-deliver the gift certificate, specify your address as the mailing address.) From here you'll continue with an online purchase, similar to the process at many other online stores.

- You don't have to use iTunes to purchase an iTunes Music Store gift certificate. You can also go directly to the Apple Store, http://store.apple.com, to buy email or paper gift certificates. This allows someone who doesn't have a system modern enough to run iTunes (your mother, perhaps) to buy someone (you, perhaps) an iTunes Music Store gift certificate. You should be able to find a link to buy an iTunes Music Store Gift Certificate on the Apple Store home page. (As of this writing, the link was there, which is a good thing, because the Apple Store search function doesn't find it.)

- Whichever source you use to buy a gift certificate, you'll at some point come across a Terms and Conditions section. It's a good idea to read this, as it covers topics such as expiration dates.

- Sending a gift certificate is like sending cash, so it's very important that you get the email address of your recipient right, if sending via email. If you err, you may send a gift certificate to someone you don't even know.

Chapter 4

Redeeming Gift Certificates

If you're lucky, some kind soul may send you an iTunes Gift Certificate. With just a few clicks, you can load up on songs like a kid in a candy store until you've used up your gift certificate. But even if you haven't received one, you might like to know what the experience is like for the recipients of *your* gifts.

To redeem an iTunes Gift Certificate:

1. In your email program, find and open the gift certificate email that was sent to you from the iTunes Music Store (**Figure 4.42**).

2. In the body of the email message, click the Redeem Now button.

3. You will follow one of two paths:
   ▲ If you aren't already signed in at the Store, you'll see a Sign In window. Enter your Apple ID or AOL screen name and password if you have one, and click Redeem Gift Certificate. If you don't already have an Apple or AOL account, click Create Account, and follow the process outlined in "Getting an Account," earlier in this chapter.
   ▲ If you *are* signed in at the Store, you'll see a window that asks if you want to redeem your gift certificate; click Redeem Gift Certificate (**Figure 4.43**).

Regardless of the path you follow, the Gift Certificate Redemption page appears, letting you know that you've successfully redeemed your iTunes Music Store Gift Certificate. This page has a very obvious arrow, pointing to the amount that has been credited to your account (**Figure 4.44**).

Click when ready to redeem the gift certificate.

Figure 4.42 If you're the recipient of a gift certificate, Apple will send you an email like this.

Figure 4.43 Click Redeem Gift Certificate.

Figure 4.44 Once you've successfully redeemed the gift certificate, iTunes lets you know and shows the amount you have left in your account.

116

✔ Tips

- If you don't see a Redeem Now button in the email message, you may see a URL starting with itmss://; double-click this URL or copy it into a browser. You'll then follow the same process described in Step 3.

- Did you receive a *paper* gift certificate for the iTunes Music Store? If so, use the same method described in the sidebar "No HTML Email?"(You'll just have to type in the number, rather than paste it in, at the Redeem a Gift Certificate page.)

No HTML Email?

Apple uses *HTML* email—email that's formatted with text and graphics, similar to a Web page—to send you iTunes Music Store updates and gift certificates. If you're using an email program that can't read HTML, or if you have that option turned off, you may not be able to click the button to redeem your gift certificate. But you're not out of luck. Refer to the following steps to redeem your gift certificate:

1. Copy the number of the gift certificate in the email.
2. At the iTunes Music Store, click the Gift Certificates link on the home or genre page (refer to Figure 4.38).
3. Click Redeem Now (**Figure 4.45**).
4. At the Redeem an iTunes Gift Certificate page, paste in the number you copied from the email, read the Terms and Conditions, and then click Redeem (**Figure 4.46**).

The Gift Certificate Redemption page appears, letting you know how much money you have to spend at the iTunes Music Store (refer to Figure 4.44).

Figure 4.45 Click Redeem.

Figure 4.46 Enter the number of your gift certificate on this page.

Giving a Music Allowance

Got kids? Allowances are a great feature of the Music Store, allowing your children (or others) to make purchases in the store without requiring access to your credit card. You can set up an account for your child that is automatically credited on the first of each month with an amount of your choosing—between $10 and $200.

To set up an iTunes allowance:

1. At the iTunes Music Store home or genre page, click Allowance (refer to Figure 4.38).

2. Fill in the form fields on the page that appears and click Buy Now (**Figure 4.47**).

3. When a window appears asking you for your account name and password, provide them and then click Setup.

   If you had previously signed in, your account name will be automatically filled in.

4. If you selected "Create an Apple Account for recipient" (refer to Figure 4.47), you will be presented with a Create an Apple Account page. Fill in the information here and click Create (**Figure 4.48**).

   Notice that you are not required to enter credit card information to create this account.

continues on next page

Figure 4.47 After you click Allowance on the home page or a genre page, you'll see this screen. Fill in the information requested and click Buy Now.

Figure 4.48 If the recipient of your iTunes allowance doesn't already have an Apple ID (that you know about), you'll have to fill out this form to create an account for him or her.

Chapter 4

5. On the "Confirm your purchase" page, assuming that you are sure about giving at least this first installment, click Buy (**Figure 4.49**).

A page appears saying that the allowance has been successfully set up, the specified amount has been deposited in the recipient's account, and the next installment will be on the first of the following month.

The recipient will receive an email message telling them that they've been given an allowance. If they didn't previously have an account, the message includes the Apple ID and password you provided. When they sign in, they will (at most) have to agree to Terms and Conditions but they won't have to provide any additional information. Their iTunes window will show the amount in their account that's available to spend just as it does for gift certificates (**Figure 4.50**).

✔ Tips

- You can cancel an allowance; see the next page.
- If your child has an existing AOL account rather than an existing Apple account, you can enter their AOL screen name even if the page on which you set up an allowance refers to an Apple ID (as is the case as of this writing).
- Don't panic if an allowance doesn't show up immediately. We've seen it take over 15 minutes from the time the recipient receives the email to the time the allowance becomes available to them in the store.

Figure 4.49 When you're ready to purchase the first allowance installment, click Buy. (See next page if you need to cancel the allowance.)

Figure 4.50 When the recipient of your allowance signs in, they'll see that they have money in their account.

120

Figure 4.51 The Apple Account Information page confirms your billing address, credit card information, and computer authorizations, and tells you the names of those to whom you have given an allowance.

Managing Your Account

Let's say you've got a new credit card and you need to update your personal information so you can continue to buy music through iTunes. Or maybe you want to make sure your teenagers aren't downloading hundreds of dollars worth of Eminem songs on the family computer. Luckily, iTunes provides a page for you to manage various aspects of your account.

To view your account information:

1. Once you've signed in, click your account name in the button at the top right of the iTunes window.

2. In the window that appears, enter your password and click View Account.

    You'll see your Account Information page (**Figure 4.51**).

continues on next page

Chapter 4

3. On this page, you can:
    - ▲ Click Edit Account Info to open the Edit Apple Account page, where you can make changes to the basic information you entered when you originally set up your account (refer to Figure 4.26).
    - ▲ Click Edit Credit Card to open the Edit Credit Card Information page.
    - ▲ Click Purchase History to open the Purchase History page (**Figure 4.52**), where you'll see your most recent purchase, as well as any previous purchases. If you want to see more detailed information about any single purchase, click an arrow icon. Click Done to return to the Purchase History page.
    - ▲ Click Manage Allowances to open the Edit Allowances page (**Figure 4.53**), where you can cancel an allowance by clicking the Remove button. The amount currently in the recipient's account remains there, but no future installments will be made to their account.
    - ▲ Click Gift Certificates or Setup Allowance to buy a gift certificate or set up an allowance.
    - ▲ Click Reset Warnings if you have previously told iTunes not to warn you before buying (refer to Figure 4.33, for example), and you have now decided that you do want that warning.

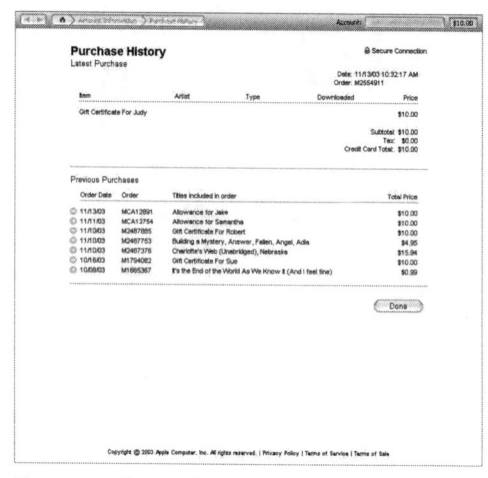

Figure 4.52 The Purchase History page can offer a sobering dose of reality. Have you really downloaded that many songs?

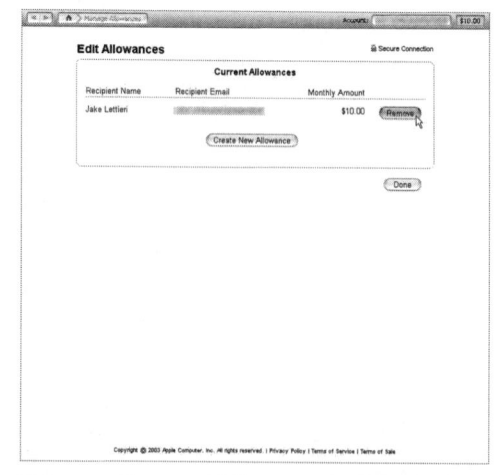

Figure 4.53 Has your child been naughty? The Manage Allowances page lets you cancel somebody's allowance.

ORGANIZING YOUR LIBRARY

When you first start using iTunes, you're probably too busy importing CDs, downloading music, and playing songs to think about organizing it all. But as you start adding more and more music to your iTunes library, things can quickly get out of hand. With hundreds or thousands of songs available, it's just too hard to keep track of what's there or to decide which songs you feel like listening to.

This chapter discusses those features of iTunes that will help you keep control over your ever-growing collection of music The core of the chapter is devoted to *playlists*, iTunes's primary method of letting you group your songs into categories that *you* define.

We'll cover both regular playlists, which you create manually, and *Smart Playlists*, which are created automatically based on pre-defined criteria that you set.

You'll find, however, that the more information that is associated with your songs, the more easily you or iTunes can group songs in order to create playlists. So we'll start the chapter with techniques for editing the information associated with your songs.

At the end of this chapter, we'll explain how iTunes organizes files on your hard drive.

About Song Information

Many of the songs in your library already have information associated with them, such as the song title, artist, album, and file size. You've seen this information populating the columns in the song list.

How does this information get there? When you import songs from an audio CD, information for that specific CD is automatically downloaded from the CDDB (Compact Disc Database), the online music database, as long as you're connected to the Internet. When you purchase music from the iTunes Music Store, the songs you download to your computer arrive complete with information and album artwork. And most MP3 files that you obtain from other sources contain special tags that contain information about the songs (see the sidebar "About ID3 Tags").

The basic information that comes with most files includes song name, artist, album, and track number. Genre, year, and disc number are often included as well. Occasionally you'll see a composer or grouping listing provided. (The latter is used most often to indicate that a track is part of a larger piece, and is most commonly included with classical music.)

When you first add a song to your iTunes library, the two other types of information that you *won't* likely find are comments and BPM (which stands for beats per minute).

✔ Tip

- If basic information about a song is missing (or if you accidentally edit information), you can tell iTunes to try to get the data from the CDDB. To do this, select the song, and from the Advanced menu choose Get CD Track Names.

About ID3 Tags

ID3 tags, which contain song information, are found only in MP3 files. When you insert an audio CD into your CD drive, iTunes accesses CDDB, the online database that contains song information; if iTunes imports as MP3, this data is placed in the file as an ID3 tag. (iTunes also places the CDDB data in AAC files, which can contain information much like ID3 tags, although what's in an AAC file is technically not an ID3 tag.)

Early versions of ID3 stored limited types of information (only artist, song name, album, year, genre, comments, and track number) and also restricted the maximum number of characters for each type of information to 30. The current implementation is much more flexible and supports all the information types that iTunes does. However, iTunes can read any version of ID3 tags through the current version (ID3 2.4.0).

You may find that you need to change the version of the ID3 tags in your MP3 file—for instance, if you have an older MP3 CD player that can't handle newer (version 2) ID3 tags. In this case, you would select the MP3 song, and from the Advanced menu, choose Convert ID3 Tags. A window appears in which you can change the version of the ID3 tags in your MP3 file. In this window, you can also select Reverse Unicode, something you may want to try if your song information contains odd or illegible characters. For Mac users, this window also offers options to switch between the ASCII (American Standard Code for Information Interchange) and ISO (International Organization for Standardization) Latin-1—use one of these options if you know you need one or the other of these character sets.

Organizing your library

Figure 5.1 From the File menu, choose Get Info if you want to edit the information for one or more selected songs.

Editing Song Information

You can edit any of the information associated with your songs. Take advantage of this fact to correct data or fill in missing info. In particular, you can populate the Comments field with all sorts of keywords that will help you or iTunes locate songs in order to organize them.

Ways to edit song information:

◆ Select the song(s) in the song list (see the sidebar "Selecting Songs" later in this chapter). Then, from the File menu, choose Get Info (**Figure 5.1**); or right-click (Windows) or Control-click (Mac) and choose Get Info from the contextual menu.

If you've selected a single song, edit the information on the Info tab (**Figure 5.2**) of the information window for that song. If you've selected multiple songs, the Multiple Song Information window (**Figure 5.3**) has fields in which you can edit or enter information that's common to all the songs.

Figure 5.2 If you're editing the information for a single song, the information window for the song appears. You edit on the Info tab.

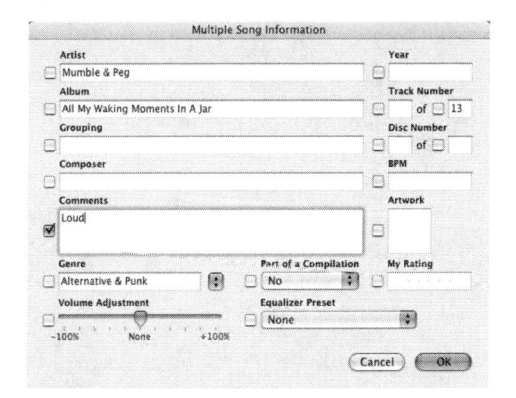

Figure 5.3 If you're editing information about multiple songs at one time, the Multiple Song Information window appears. Changes you make here apply to all the songs you selected.

125

- Click to select a song in the song list. Then click *once* in the column you'd like to edit for that song and type (**Figure 5.4**).

    Typing directly in the song list like this works only for some columns: Album, Artist, Comment, Composer, Genre, and Grouping.

This text has been clicked on and is now editable.

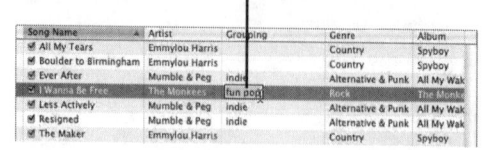

Figure 5.4 You can also click and edit information directly in the song list.

✔ Tips

- In the information window for a single song, click the Next or Previous button (refer to Figure 5.2) to edit the information about the next or previous song in the song list.

- When you edit the text for Album, Artist, Composer, or Genre directly in the song list (as in Figure 5.4), iTunes types ahead to match the first name (alphabetically) in your library that matches what you've typed thus far. Press Return (Mac) or Enter (Windows) to accept what iTunes has typed for you. Or just keep typing if it hasn't typed the right thing.

- When you edit song information, iTunes may, depending on the preferences you've set, make changes to the files and folders on your hard drive that contain the songs. To understand more about what happens on your hard drive, see "How iTunes Organizes Files on Your Hard Drive," later in this chapter.

Selecting Songs

Since a preliminary step for many organizing tasks is selecting songs, we'll go over the various methods for selecting them:

- Click a song to select it.

- Shift-click to select multiple contiguous songs (that is, songs that are next to each other in your library).

- Command-click to select multiple songs that are not contiguous.

- From the Edit menu, choose Select All to select all the songs currently in the song list.

- To select the currently playing (or most recently played) song, choose File > Show Current Song. (Remember from Chapter 3 that the selection does not necessarily correspond to the current song.)

- To select the song above or below the selected song, click the up or down arrow on your keyboard.

- To add to the selected song(s), hold down the Shift key and click the up arrow or down arrow key.

Organizing your library

Figure 5.5 Click in the My Rating column to assign a rating.

Figure 5.6 Or choose a rating from the contextual menu that appears when you Control-click (Mac) or right-click (Windows) on a song.

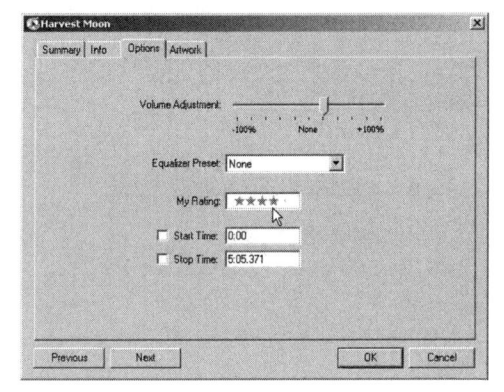

Figure 5.7 Or rate the song on the Options tab of the information window for the song.

Rating Songs

One additional piece of information that iTunes can store about a song is your personal rating of it. Song ratings come in handy when you want to sort your library in order of rating—or when you want to create a playlist of your favorite songs. You can rate songs between 1 and 5 stars. iTunes provides a variety of ways to do this, either one song at a time, or as a group.

Ways to rate a single song:

◆ In the My Rating column, click at the position of the number of stars you want to assign (**Figure 5.5**).

◆ Right-click (Windows) or Control-click (Mac) in any column of the song you want to rate, choose My Rating, and then choose the number of stars you want to assign (**Figure 5.6**).

◆ Open the information window for the song (choose File > Get Info), and on the Options tab, assign a rating by clicking at the position of the number of stars you want to assign; in other words, to assign a four-star rating, click the fourth star (**Figure 5.7**).

127

Chapter 5

♦ To rate the current song (the one with the speaker icon next to it), click and hold on the iTunes icon in the Dock (Mac; **Figure 5.8**) or right-click the iTunes icon in the system tray (Windows; **Figure 5.9**); then choose the number of stars from the My Rating submenu.

To assign the same rating to multiple songs:

♦ Select the songs, choose File > Get Info, and in the Multiple Song Information window, click in the My Rating field (**Figure 5.10**).

✔ Tips

- In the My Rating column or in the rating fields in the information windows, you'll find that once you press the mouse button down, you can drag to change the number of stars assigned.

- The My Rating column may not be visible; see Chapter 3 for details about hiding, showing, and moving columns.

- It's great that you don't have to painstakingly rate each song in your iTunes library one by one. Do you adore every track on *Abbey Road*? If all the songs on the album are in a playlist, select the playlist in the Source pane; if not, use the browse or search feature to show them all in the song list. Then select them all, choose File > Get Info, and give all the songs on the album five stars.

Figure 5.8 Mac users can rate the currently playing song by clicking and holding on the iTunes menu in the Dock, choosing My Ratings, and selecting the desired star rating. (This is useful when iTunes is providing background music and is not the frontmost application.)

Figure 5.9 Windows users can rate the currently playing song by right-clicking the iTunes icon in the system tray, choosing My Ratings, and selecting the appropriate number of stars.

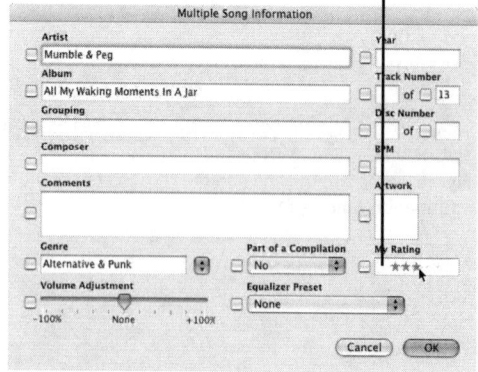

Figure 5.10 If you select more than one song and choose Get Info, this Multiple Song Information window appears, letting you rate all the selected songs at once.

Organizing your library

About Playlists

Playlists—customized lists of songs—are a great way to group songs, whether for playback in iTunes, for creating audio CDs, for transferring to an iPod, or for sharing with others over a network.

It's important to understand that playlists are merely *pointers* to songs in your library, not copies of the songs themselves. Songs in playlists don't take up any additional space on your hard disk. A single song can be in as many playlists as you want. And if you delete a song from a playlist, it remains in your library. (On the other hand, if you delete a song from your library, it *does* get removed from any playlists that it's in.)

There are two kinds of playlists in iTunes: regular ones (which we'll generally refer to simply as *playlists*) and *Smart Playlists*. Both show up as sources in your Source pane, though each has a different icon (**Figure 5.11**). You add songs to regular playlists manually. For Smart Playlists, you set up criteria defining the kinds of songs that you want, and iTunes automatically adds any songs that meet those criteria.

Anything you can do to the list of songs in your library, you can do to the set of songs in a playlist. As long as the playlist is the selected source, you can use the Browser to limit the songs that appear in the song list, to search the playlist, or to sort it in any of the ways covered in Chapter 3. You'll find this useful when you have very long playlists.

✔ Tip

- You won't see a Browse button in the iTunes window when a playlist is selected as the Source. To show the Browser, you'll have to use the menu option (Edit > Show Browser) or its keyboard equivalent (Ctrl-B in Windows; Command-B on the Mac).

These are Smart Playlists.

These are regular playlists.

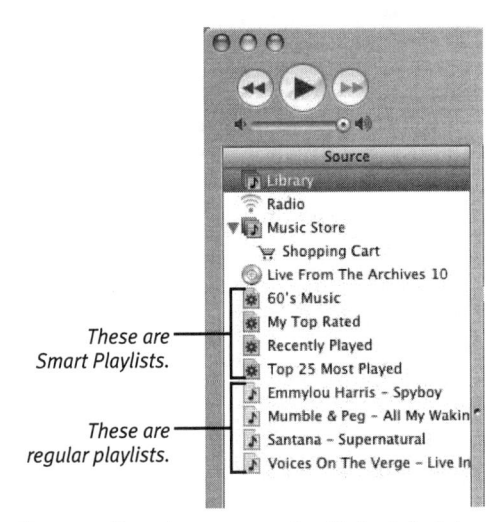

Figure 5.11 iTunes lets you create two kinds of playlists: Smart Playlists and the regular kind. Both help you organize your music collection.

Playlist Ideas

There are as many reasons to make playlists as there are CDs in your library. As a matter of fact, many people create a playlist whenever they import songs from a favorite CD; then they can click the playlist for that CD in their Source pane anytime they want to listen to it. Or would you rather group songs by artist? If you like to listen nonstop to Elvis Costello, for example, just find all his songs and put them in a playlist. Think also about creating different playlists for different tasks, such as working, playing, cooking, exercising, or going to sleep. Or consider putting together playlists to match the tastes of different friends or family members that may visit. You can create playlists of your favorite songs or songs by a single artist or songs about a certain topic. The possibilities are endless.

129

Creating a Playlist and Adding Songs to It

We'll start with regular playlists, the kind to which you add songs manually.

To create a playlist:

1. Click the button with the plus sign (+) in the lower left of the iTunes window (**Figure 5.12**), or choose File > New Playlist.

   A new playlist is added with the name "untitled playlist" highlighted (**Figure 5.13**).

2. Type to edit the playlist name (**Figure 5.14**).

Figure 5.12 To create a new playlist, click the plus-sign (+) button.

Figure 5.13 A new, untitled playlist appears.

Figure 5.14 You should edit the name of the playlist so it describes what you will put in it.

Importing Musicmatch Playlists

If you're a former Musicmatch Jukebox user, and you've imported into iTunes all your MP3s ripped by Musicmatch Jukebox, you may also want to import the playlists you created there.

Musicmatch Jukebox doesn't store your playlists in the My Music folder on your PC, as you might expect. By default, it stores them in C:\Program Files\MUSICMATCH\MUSICMATCHJukebox\Playlist\Default.

The playlists created by Musicmatch Jukebox are .m3u files, which iTunes can easily handle. Just drag an .m3u file to the Source pane (or add it by choosing Import from the File menu). This creates a new iTunes playlist. If the songs aren't already in your library, it adds them (assuming the song files are where the playlist said they are). If the songs are already in your library, the new playlist points to the ones already in your library.

Organizing your library

Figure 5.15 To put songs in a playlist, drag them from the song list to the playlist.

To add songs to a playlist:

1. In the Source pane, click the name of the source that contains the song(s) you want to add.

    The source can be your library, your radio, an audio CD, or another playlist.

2. If the number of songs in the selected source is very large, you may want to limit the number of songs showing in the song list.

    Use whatever method works best for you—browse, search, or simply sort—to ensure that the songs you want to add are visible in the song list.

3. Select the songs you want to add.

4. Drag the songs from the song list to the playlist (**Figure 5.15**).

✔ Tips

- You may find it convenient to use the keyboard shortcut Command-N (Mac) or Ctrl-N (Windows) to create a new empty playlist.

- After creating your first untitled playlist, each subsequent untitled playlist you create since you opened iTunes will be numbered sequentially (that is, untitled playlist 2, untitled playlist 3, and so on).

Including Streams in Your Playlists

A reminder: You can add streams (whether from iTunes radio or other sources) to your playlists, too. It may seem odd to put streams in a playlist: After all, while you often group songs in playlists so that they'll play one after another, iTunes will never play the item after a stream in a song list—the stream will play until you actively choose another item to play. You also can't burn a CD containing a stream, or copy a stream to your iPod. However, adding a stream to a playlist offers the convenience of having it in an easily accessible and logical location. Do you want to have a ready source for anything and everything bluegrass-related? Create a bluegrass playlist, and make sure to include that bluegrass stream.

CREATING A PLAYLIST AND ADDING SONGS TO IT

131

Ways to create a playlist and add songs to it at the same time:

- Select the songs and then choose File > New Playlist from Selection (**Figure 5.16**).

- Drag selected songs from the song list to the empty area at the bottom of your Source list (**Figure 5.17**).

If the selected songs are all from the same album or by the same artist, or both, iTunes names the playlist by artist name, album name, or both. (For example, if all the songs happen to be by Emmylou Harris, the resulting playlist will be called "Emmylou Harris.") Otherwise, the newly created playlist will be named "untitled playlist."

To import songs from a CD and create a playlist at the same time:

- Insert a CD, select some or all of the songs, and drag the selected songs from the song list to the empty area at the bottom of your Source list (**Figure 5.18**).

The songs are imported and a playlist containing the imported songs is created. The playlist is automatically named according to the artist and album (or just the album, if the songs are by different artists).

✔ Tips

- (Mac only) You can select songs from your library or a playlist, and then Shift-click the plus-sign button to both create a new playlist and add the selected songs to it.

- To create a playlist, you can also select any item(s) from the Browser (genre name, artist name, or album name) and then drag the item(s) to the empty area at the bottom of your Source pane. The new playlist will contain all songs from the selected genre(s), artist(s), or album(s).

- If you drag a single song to the Source pane below the existing sources, iTunes creates a new playlist containing only that song, with a name identical to the song name.

Figure 5.16 If songs are selected, you can choose File > New Playlist From Selection to create a playlist that contains the selected songs.

Figure 5.17 You can also drag selected songs to the area below existing playlists to create a new playlist containing those songs.

Figure 5.18 If you insert a CD and drag selected songs to the area below your playlists, iTunes creates a playlist containing the selected songs.

Creating a Smart Playlist

Smart Playlists are playlists that iTunes automatically builds based on criteria you set. As long as the playlist exists, iTunes can continue to add to it whenever a song meets the specified criteria. For example, if you like old blues songs, you can create a Smart Playlist that consists of all songs in the blues genre recorded between 1920 and 1950. Are you a longtime Nick Lowe fan? Create a Smart Playlist with Nick Lowe as the specified artist, and iTunes will update it every time you add new Nick Lowe songs to your library.

To create a Smart Playlist:

1. From the File menu, choose New Smart Playlist (**Figure 5.19**) to open the Smart Playlist window.

2. If there is a specific condition you want iTunes to match, select a type of information—such as Artist, Genre, or Time—from the leftmost pop-up menu at the top of the window, then specify your criteria by choosing from the second pop-up menu (**Figure 5.20**) and filling in a value or values (**Figure 5.21**).

   Once you've done this, you'll find you've created a nice little sentence that describes what you're looking for.

   continues on next page

Figure 5.19 Choose New Smart Playlist to show the Smart Playlist window.

Pick the type of information here.

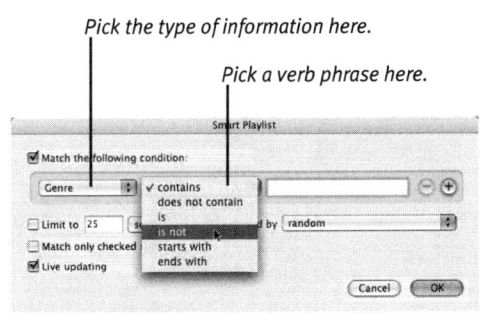

Pick a verb phrase here.

Figure 5.20 After you choose the type of information you want iTunes to look at, specify a verb phrase...

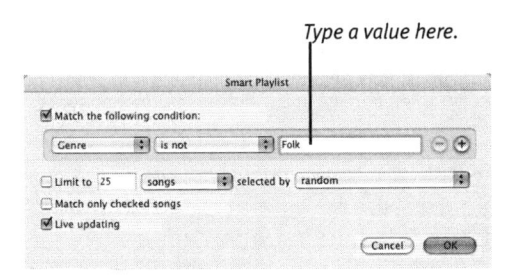

Type a value here.

Figure 5.21 ...and a value. Here, we're making sure that no folk songs make their way onto this playlist.

Chapter 5

3. If you'd like to specify additional conditions, click the plus-sign button to add a new line (**Figure 5.22**) and then repeat step 2.

   Once you have more than one condition, the first line reads, "Match all of the following conditions." The word *all*, however, appears in a pop-up menu and can be changed to *any*. This allows you to specify, for example, that you want any songs for which the artist is The Who or Pete Townshend.

4. Uncheck the "Match the following condition" check box if you don't want to specify any conditions.

5. If you want iTunes to limit the amount of music (whether by song length, number of songs, or disk space used), select the second check box and specify how you would like it limited (**Figure 5.23**).

6. If you've unchecked songs in your library, you may want to check "Match only checked songs" (refer to Figure 5.23).

7. If you want iTunes to continually add to the playlist, leave Live Updating checked.

8. Click OK.

   The new playlist shows in your Source pane. It is selected and editable.

9. Type a new name for the playlist, if desired (**Figure 5.24**).

   If you've set criteria that match any songs in your current collection, those songs are added to the playlist. If you have left Live Updating checked, iTunes continues to add to the playlist as you add new songs to your library, edit song information, or play songs.

Click to add a condition after this one.

Click to delete the condition in this row.

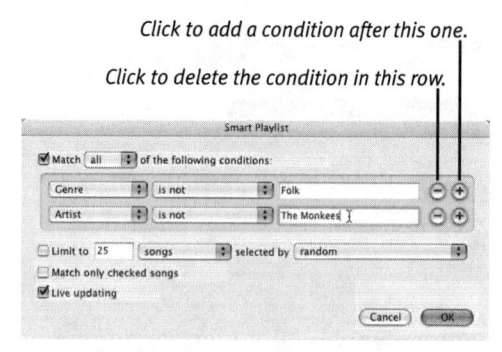

Figure 5.22 Click the plus-sign buttons to add a new row for specifying a condition, and the minus-sign buttons to remove the condition in that row. Here, we've already added a second condition—no Monkees, either.

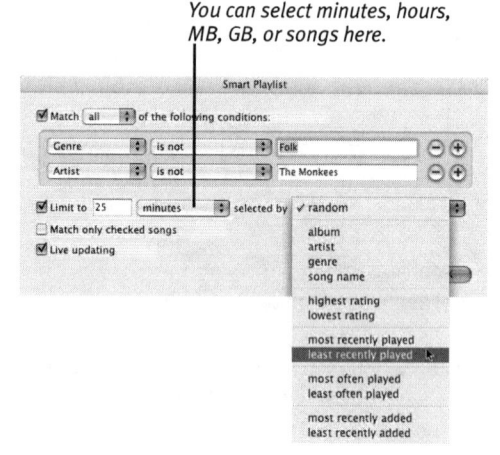

You can select minutes, hours, MB, GB, or songs here.

Figure 5.23 Specify limitations on time, file size, or number of songs here. You can have iTunes pick randomly or by the top songs (alphabetically, numerically, or temporally) in a variety of information types.

Figure 5.24 Type a name for the Smart Playlist.

Organizing your library

To edit a Smart Playlist:

1. Select the Smart Playlist in the Source pane.

2. From the File menu, choose Get Info (or its keyboard equivalent: Command-I for Mac, Ctrl-I for Windows).

3. In the Smart Playlist window, make changes and click OK (refer to Figures 5.20 through 5.23).

✔ **Tips**

- A quick way to create a new Smart Playlist is to hold down the Option key (Mac) or the Shift key (Windows) so that the icon on the Add Playlist button changes to a Smart Playlist icon (gears); click it to create a new Smart Playlist.

- If you make a choice other than random for the "selected by" pop-up menu (refer to Figure 5.23), iTunes selects the top songs from a sort of your library by that attribute. (For example, if you choose album, you are likely to get only albums that start with the letters at the beginning of the alphabet.)

- As you fill in the fields in the Smart Playlist window, iTunes types ahead to match the first name (alphabetically) in your library that matches what you've typed so far.

- If you rely on play count to help you organize your library, but someone else uses your library and the play count no longer reflects how many times *you* played the song—maybe drunken guests at your holiday party played "Jingle Bell Rock" 25 times—you may want to reset the play count for that song to 0. To do so, select the song, Control-click (Mac) or right-click (Windows), and choose Reset Play Count.

continues on next page

- iTunes may do some intelligent naming of your Smart Playlists. If you specify a single textual criterion as your Smart Playlist criteria (for example, the artist Elton John), the playlist name will be the same as the value you choose—in this case, Elton John. Otherwise, it will be named "untitled playlist," followed by a number, to indicate how many untitled playlists have been created.

- You'll typically want to set time or space limitations for a playlist when you plan to burn a CD or move songs to a limited-space device. (See Chapters 6 and 7 for more details.)

- (Mac only) You can Option-click a Smart Playlist to edit it.

> **Smart Playlist Ideas**
>
> You'll get some ideas for Smart Playlists by looking at the ones that come with iTunes (60's Music, My Top Rated, Recently Played, and Top 25 Most Played). Here are some others:
>
> ♦ If you accidentally delete your Purchased Music playlist, you could regenerate the same list by building a Smart Playlist that looks for "Kind is Protected AAC."
>
> ♦ If you tend to sit in front of your computer for too long, make a Smart Playlist that you "Limit to 90 minutes selected by random"; when the music stops, it's time to take a break. Then just delete all the songs in the playlist, and iTunes will pick a new set of random songs. (This assumes you've left Live Updating checked.)
>
> ♦ Create a Smart Playlist of the radio streams you like to listen to: Specify "Time is greater than 300000" (which translates to 3 days, 11 hours, 20 minutes, and 0 seconds); iTunes will choose files that are continuous.
>
> ♦ Want to know which songs you haven't played recently? Try "Last Play is not in the last 6 months" (or whatever time period you'd like).
>
> ♦ You can have a Recently Added section (just like in the iTunes Music Store). To do this, "Limit to 25 songs selected by most recently added."

Organizing your library

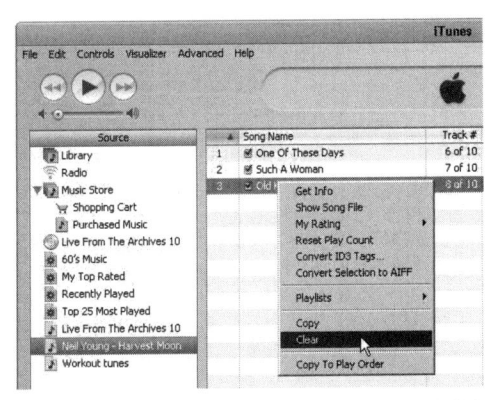

Figure 5.25 To delete a song from a playlist, Control-click (Mac) or right-click to access this contextual menu, then choose Clear.

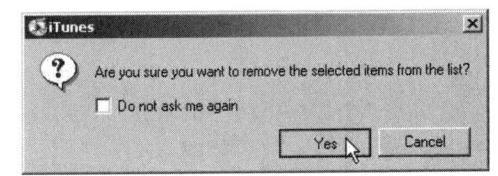

Figure 5.26 iTunes asks if you're sure you want to remove the items from your playlist.

Deleting Song Files from Your Hard Drive

Songs in your iTunes Music folder (a folder that we discuss in greater detail later in this chapter) can be deleted when you delete them from your library (refer to Figure 5.27). Songs that aren't stored in this folder have to be manually dragged to the Trash or Recycle Bin if you don't want them taking up space on your hard drive.

If you inadvertently trash a song file (with the Mac Finder or Windows Explorer) for a song that is still listed in your library, nothing happens until you try to play that song. When you try to play the song, iTunes puts an exclamation point in the column to the left of Song Name, tells you that it couldn't find the file, and gives you a chance to locate it.

Deleting Songs

It's not always about *adding* songs to iTunes. Eventually, you'll want to *delete* some songs from playlists, too—perhaps you dragged the wrong song to a playlist, or maybe you want to subtly change the focus of particular playlists. And as part of your general housekeeping, you may want to delete songs from your iTunes library. Remember, deleting a song from a playlist doesn't actually delete the song from iTunes. Deleting a song from your iTunes library, on the other hand, is far more permanent; so proceed with caution.

To delete songs from a playlist:

1. Do one of the following:
   ▲ Select the song(s) you want to delete, and press the Delete key.
   ▲ Select the song(s) you want to delete, and from the Edit menu choose Clear.
   ▲ Control-click (Mac) or right-click (Windows) the song you want to delete, and choose Clear from the contextual menu that appears (**Figure 5.25**).

2. If iTunes asks whether you're sure you want to delete the selected items from the list (**Figure 5.26**), click Yes.

DELETING SONGS

137

Chapter 5

To delete songs from the library:

1. Complete steps 1 and 2 from the previous task, selecting the song(s) from your library rather than from a playlist.

2. If the file for the song is stored in your iTunes Music folder (see "How iTunes Organizes Files on Your Hard Drive" later in this chapter), you are asked whether you want to move the files to the Trash or Recycle Bin (**Figure 5.27**). Click Yes, as long as you won't ever want the song in your library again. Click No if you want the song removed from your library, but you still want its file to remain on your hard disk.

   Songs deleted from your library are also deleted from any playlists they're in.

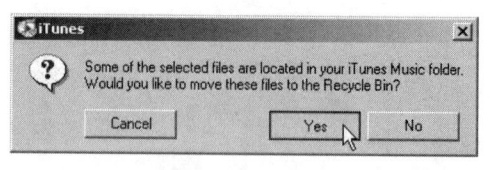

Figure 5.27 When removing from the library, rather than a playlist, iTunes asks if you want to delete the file from your hard drive, too. (This occurs only if the file is stored in your iTunes Music folder.)

✔ Tips

- If, when deleting a song from a playlist, you also want it deleted from the library, hold down the Option key (Mac) or Shift key (Windows) while you press Delete or choose Edit > Clear.

- If you don't want to see any warnings, hold down the Command key (Mac) or Ctrl key (Windows) when you delete.

- Mac users can drag the song(s) from the playlist to the Trash icon on the Dock. In our tests, we were unable to drag songs to the Windows Recycle Bin.

Finding Out Which Playlists a Song Is In

Before you delete a song from your library, you may want to see the playlists that contain it. Control-click (Mac) or right-click (Windows) the song, and in the contextual menu that appears select Playlists (**Figure 5.28**). You'll see the playlists (other than the one you're currently looking at) that contain this same song. If Playlists isn't a choice in the contextual menu, then the song isn't in any playlists.

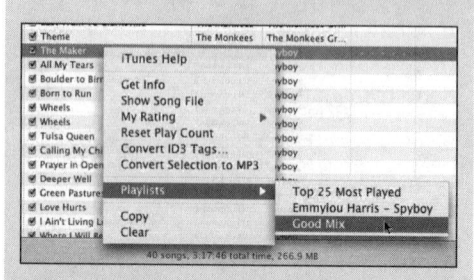

Figure 5.28 Before you remove a song from your library, you might want to check to see what other playlists it's part of. (Windows users right-click and Mac users Control-click on the song to see this contextual menu.)

DELETING SONGS

138

Organizing your library

Click here.

Figure 5.29 To change the order of songs in a playlist, start by clicking the column head on the left so that the songs are not sorted by any other column.

Figure 5.30 Shuffle mode has to be turned off; click the Shuffle button so it's not highlighted blue.

This indicator line shows that if you release the mouse button now, the selected song will become the 14th song in the list.

Figure 5.31 Drag a song up or down to reposition it.

Reordering the Songs in a Playlist

In many ways, working with the songs in a playlist is much like working with them in the library: You can browse, search, and sort. One key difference, however, is that you can reorder songs in a playlist any way you want. This is especially useful when you're creating a playlist that you plan to burn to CD.

To reorder songs in a playlist:

1. With the playlist selected, click the empty column head of the leftmost column (**Figure 5.29**) of the song list.

2. If the Shuffle button is highlighted blue (indicating that Shuffle mode is on), click it to turn it off (**Figure 5.30**).

3. Click any song and drag up or down in the list.

4. Release your mouse button when the indicator line appears in the position you would like the song to be (**Figure 5.31**).

5. Repeat steps 3 and 4 until your songs are in the order you want them to play.

✓ Tips

- If you click another column head (which re-sorts the songs in the playlist according to that column), you can always get your preferred order back by clicking the column head of that leftmost column.

- If you click the Shuffle button to let iTunes randomly reorder the songs in the playlist, you can see the new order as long as the songs are sorted by the leftmost column.

- If you like the way iTunes has shuffled your songs, you can set the current order as your preferred order: Control-click (Mac) or right-click (Windows) anywhere in the song list, and in the contextual menu that appears choose Copy to Play Order.

139

Chapter 5

Organizing Multiple Playlists

As you create more playlists and the number of songs in those playlists grows, you may find that you need to reorganize them in various ways: merging two playlists into one, or taking selected songs out of one playlist and putting them into another. One convenient touch is that you can see each playlist in its own window.

To view a playlist in its own window:

◆ Double-click the Playlist icon (**Figure 5.32**).
  A new iTunes window opens, showing only a Detail pane (**Figure 5.33**).

To merge playlists:

◆ Drag one playlist from the Source pane to the window for the other playlist (**Figure 5.34**).

To copy selected songs from one playlist window to another:

◆ Open the playlists in their own windows, select the songs you would like to copy in one playlist window, and drag to the other playlist window (**Figure 5.35**).

✔ **Tips**

■ To open a playlist in its own window, you can also click the white space to the right of the playlist name in the Source pane. It won't work to click the text itself, however; doing so allows you to edit the playlist name.

■ If you don't need to see what's in your playlists when you merge them, simply drag one playlist in the Source pane on top of the other one in the Source pane.

■ You can't manually add to a Smart Playlist, but you can copy songs from one of them to a regular playlist.

Figure 5.32 In the Source pane, double-click a Playlist icon...

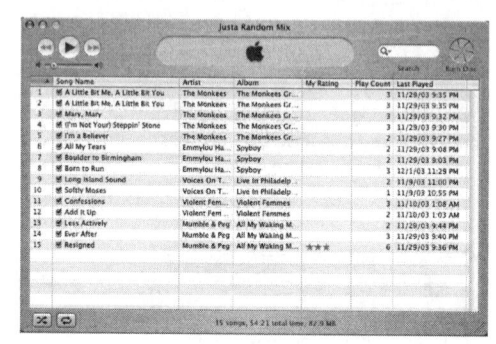

Figure 5.33 ...to open the playlist in its own window. (Notice that there's just a Detail pane; no Source pane.)

Figure 5.34 You can drag a whole playlist to another playlist's window.

Figure 5.35 You can also drag selected songs from one window to another.

Deleting Playlists

Eventually, you may want to remove some of your playlists, particularly once you start reorganizing them. Think carefully before deleting a playlist, as there's no way to undo the action.

Ways to delete a playlist:

◆ Select the playlist in the Source pane and press the Delete key.

◆ Select the playlist in the Source pane, and from the Edit menu, choose Clear.

◆ Control-click (Mac) or Right-click (Windows) on the playlist in the Source pane and choose Clear (**Figure 5.36**).

If you have any songs in the playlist, you'll be asked if you really want to remove the playlist (**Figure 5.37**). Click Yes.

Figure 5.36 You can delete a playlist by selecting it and Control-clicking (Mac) or right-clicking (Windows) and then choosing Clear.

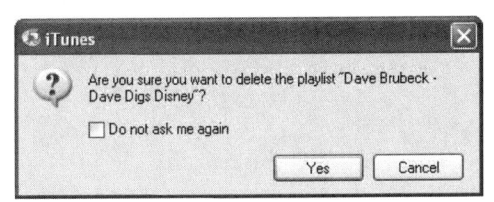

Figure 5.37 If you try to delete a playlist, iTunes asks if you're sure. Click Yes unless you've had second thoughts.

Chapter 5

To delete a playlist and all the songs it contains from your library:

◆ Hold down the Shift key (Windows) or Option key (Mac), and use either of the first two methods listed on the previous page for deleting a playlist.

You'll be asked if you want to delete the playlist and all contents from your music library (**Figure 5.38**). If you click Yes and the file is stored in your iTunes Music folder (see "How iTunes Organizes Files on Your Hard Drive" later in this chapter), you will then be asked if you want to move the contents to the Trash (Mac) or Recycle Bin (Windows).

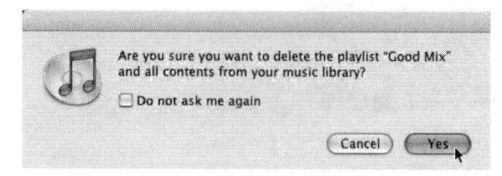

Figure 5.38 If you hold down the Shift key (Windows) or Option key (Mac) and choose Edit > Clear, iTunes asks if you really want to remove both the playlist and its contents from your library.

✔ Tips

- (Mac only) To delete a playlist, you can also drag it from the Source pane to the Trash icon in your Dock.

- (Windows only) To delete the songs in the playlist from your library when you delete the playlist, you can also hold down the Shift key while you right-click and choose Clear from the contextual menu.

- If you'd rather not see the warnings shown in Figure 5.37 or 5.38, hold down the Ctrl key (Windows) or Command key (Mac) when you delete.

- You can't select multiple playlists in the Source pane, so you can't delete more than one playlist at a time.

Exporting and Importing Song Lists

Do you want to store data about your songs in an external file? Maybe you want to send your friends a list of your extensive Grateful Dead bootleg recordings. Or maybe you're just geeky enough to want to analyze your collection to figure out the average length of your songs, or to produce a graph showing how your collection is distributed by year.

Regardless of what's currently in the song list—say, the contents of a playlist or the results of searching or browsing—you can have iTunes produce either a tab-delimited text file or an XML file containing all the information about the songs appearing in the list. You can also have iTunes export an XML file of your entire library.

You can open the exported files in various other applications, such as spreadsheet programs like Microsoft Excel, or database applications like FileMaker Pro.

You can reimport either type of file into iTunes as long as you don't alter the file's structure. This means you can share the list with another iTunes user (as long as that user has the same music in their library) or simply use it as a record of your iTunes library. Keep in mind that when you export a song list or your library, you export only data about the songs, not the songs themselves.

Chapter 5

To export a song list:

1. From the File menu, choose Export Song List (**Figure 5.39**).

   You can also Control-click (Mac) or right-click (Windows) a playlist or your library in the Source pane and choose Export Song List from the contextual menu.

2. In most cases, you'll want to save a text file. In Windows, from the "Save as type" menu, choose Text files (**Figure 5.40**); on a Mac, from the Format menu, choose Plain Text or Text.

   See the sidebar "Why XML?" if you're curious about the XML option.

3. If you like, provide a new name and location for the file.

4. Click Save.

   You can export the file (whether saved as text or XML) back into iTunes (see below). If you saved it as text, you can open it in a spreadsheet or other application that reads tab-delimited data (**Figure 5.41**).

Figure 5.39 Choose Export Song List to create a file containing all the information about your songs.

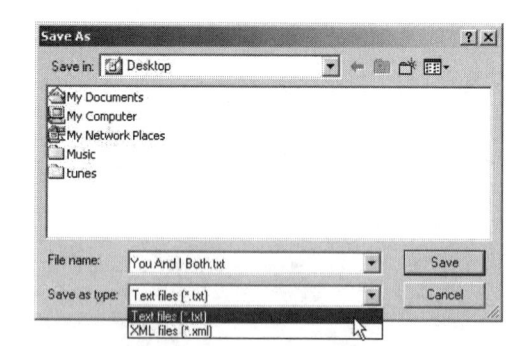

Figure 5.40 Most users will want to export iTunes data in a text file, which produces tab-delimited text.

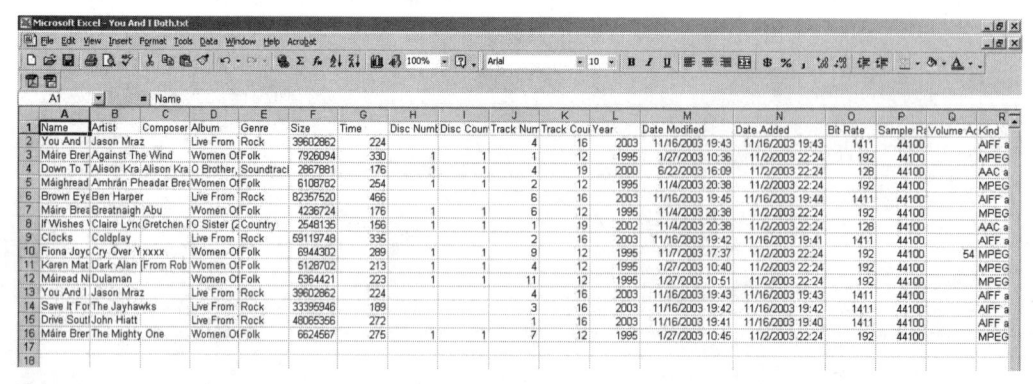

Figure 5.41 An exported song list can be opened in a variety of applications; here we show a tab-delimited text file in Excel.

144

Organizing your library

Figure 5.42 Choose File > Import to open a previously exported song list.

To export data for your entire library:

1. From the File menu, choose Export library.

2. If you want, provide a new name and location for the file and click Save.

   The file is exported as XML. It can be imported in another copy of iTunes or can be read by another application. (See the "Why XML?" sidebar.)

To import a song list:

1. From the File menu choose Import (**Figure 5.42**).

2. Locate the file and click Open (Windows) or Choose (Mac).

   A new playlist appears with the same name as the file you imported.

   A new playlist is created even if the song list you exported was not a playlist or a portion of a playlist.

✔ Tips

- When you export a song list, the file created contains all the information about the songs, even data that's in hidden columns.

- You can also choose selected lines of a song list and copy them. (From the Edit menu, choose Copy.) In this case, only data from visible columns is copied. You can then paste the selected lines directly into any application that will accept pasted text. (This operation works quite well in a spreadsheet.)

- Exporting in Unicode text (a Mac-only choice) is appropriate in the case where you have text in double-byte characters, such as those used in Asian languages.

Why XML?

When iTunes exports a song as XML, the file contains not just the information about the songs, but also information about how the data is structured. This means that a program that knows nothing about iTunes can read the file, make sense of it, and do something with it. How do you know whether you need to create an XML file? You're either a programmer, or you know that the application that needs to read the data requires XML.

145

How iTunes Organizes Files on Your Hard Drive

iTunes designates a special folder that it refers to as the *iTunes Music folder*. When you first install iTunes, this folder is named "iTunes Music." For Mac users, this special folder resides by default in the iTunes folder that is located in the Music folder of your home folder. In Windows, the default location of the iTunes Music folder is My Documents\My Music\iTunes. You'll see the path to this folder listed on the Advanced tab of the Preferences window (**Figure 5.43**); you can, however, identify a different folder as your iTunes Music folder, as we'll discuss later in this chapter.

What files are in your iTunes Music folder?

The files iTunes automatically places in the iTunes Music folder are those for songs that you import from CD or that you buy from the iTunes Music Store.

If you have "Copy files to iTunes music folder when adding to library" checked (refer to Figure 5.43), any song files you add to your library from your hard drive are also added to this folder.

Additionally, if you are a Mac user, and you told iTunes to Find Files when you first launched (see Chapter 1, Figure 1.18), your pre-iTunes music files were all copied there.

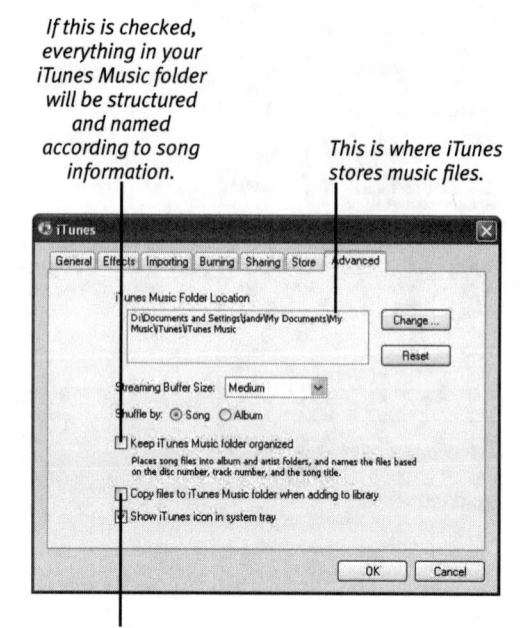

If this is checked, everything in your iTunes Music folder will be structured and named according to song information.

This is where iTunes stores music files.

If this is checked, iTunes copies all songs you move into your library from your hard drive to the folder listed above.

Figure 5.43 The Advanced tab of the Preferences window lists the location of the iTunes Music folder, which is where iTunes stores many, if not all, of the files for the music in your library.

Organizing your library

What's the folder structure?

Within your iTunes Music folder, iTunes organizes files in a simple artist-album-song hierarchy; that is, every song imported from CD or purchased from the iTunes Music Store goes into a folder named for an album (or "Unknown Album" if the album can't be determined), and almost every one of these album folders is located in a folder named for an artist (or "Unknown Artist" if the artist can't be determined). **Figure 5.44** shows how this looks in the file system.

Artist folders

Album folders. (Album folders are stored within Artist folders.)

Song files. (Song files are stored within Album folders.)

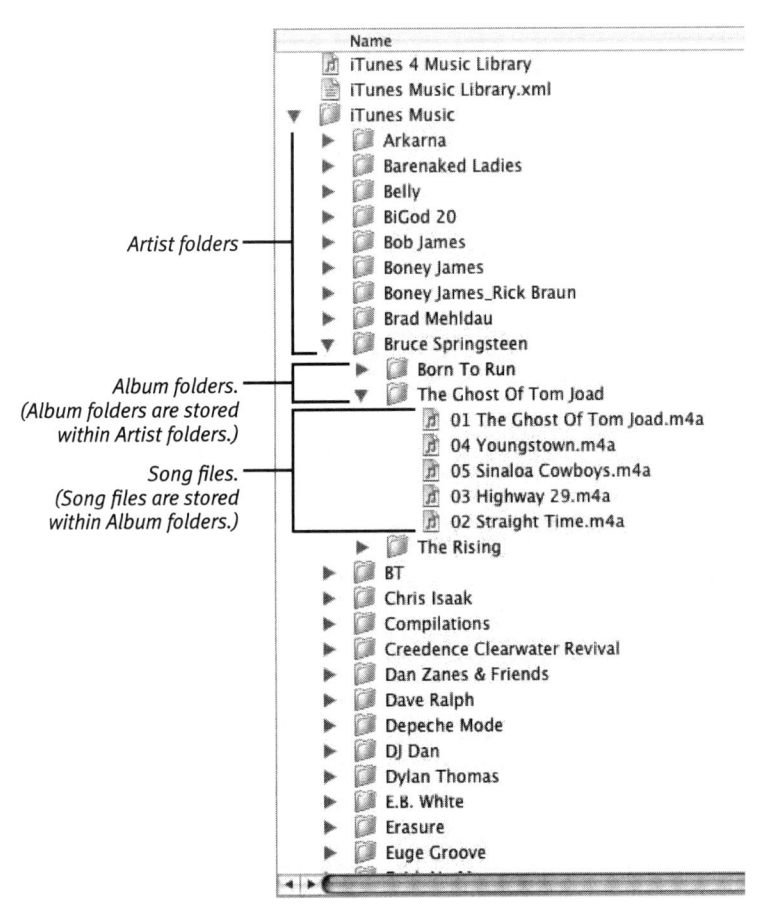

Name
iTunes 4 Music Library
iTunes Music Library.xml
▼ iTunes Music
▶ Arkarna
▶ Barenaked Ladies
▶ Belly
▶ BiGod 20
▶ Bob James
▶ Boney James
▶ Boney James_Rick Braun
▶ Brad Mehldau
▼ Bruce Springsteen
▶ Born To Run
▼ The Ghost Of Tom Joad
01 The Ghost Of Tom Joad.m4a
04 Youngstown.m4a
05 Sinaloa Cowboys.m4a
03 Highway 29.m4a
02 Straight Time.m4a
▶ The Rising
▶ BT
▶ Chris Isaak
▶ Compilations
▶ Creedence Clearwater Revival
▶ Dan Zanes & Friends
▶ Dave Ralph
▶ Depeche Mode
▶ DJ Dan
▶ Dylan Thomas
▶ E.B. White
▶ Erasure
▶ Euge Groove

Figure 5.44 Here's an example of how iTunes structures the iTunes Music folder.

HOW ITUNES ORGANIZES FILES

147

Songs added from your hard drive are placed in the iTunes Music folder in the same way, assuming that you've checked "Copy files to iTunes music folder when adding to library."

To achieve all this, iTunes depends primarily on the artist and album information you see and can edit (as described at the beginning of this chapter). iTunes also uses the song name information to determine the names of song files.

If you edit song name, album, or artist information in iTunes (as covered earlier in this chapter), and you've checked "Keep iTunes Music folder organized" (refer to Figure 5.43), you may change the names and/or the structure of what's stored on your hard drive. For examples, see the sidebar "Implications of Keeping Your Music Folder Organized."

Implications of Keeping Your Music Folder Organized

If you have selected the "Keep iTunes Music folder organized" check box, iTunes renames files and folders and moves song files around so that the songs are in folders that match what's listed for artist and album and so that the song files have names that match what's listed for song name. (This affects only files and folders that are in your iTunes Music folder.) Some examples:

- If you edit a song's artist info (for example, adding a middle initial or listing only last name) or album info (perhaps adding a subtitle), iTunes creates a new folder and moves the song file (and possibly other folders) around accordingly.

- If you add an MP3 or AAC file to your library, and you've checked "Copy files to iTunes music folder when adding to library," iTunes renames the copied version of the file (if necessary) to match the song name embedded in the file. (The song name is stored in the ID3 tag for an MP3 file and in the equivalent of the ID3 tag for an AAC file.) iTunes may also create folders to match what's listed for album and artist.

- If you drag an entire folder of music into iTunes and you've checked "Copy files to iTunes Music folder when adding to library," the copied version of the folder may be completely restructured the way iTunes thinks it should be, which may not be the way it was. Note, however, that the original folder remains untouched (assuming that the original folder was not inside your iTunes Music folder.)

✔ Tips

- One exception to the artist-album-song hierarchy occurs in the case of a song that is checked as part of a compilation (refer to the bottom right of the window shown in Figure 5.2); in this case the song is placed in its correct album folder, but that album folder is placed in a folder called Compilations that resides alongside the artist folders. (In other words, whatever is listed as artist is ignored for purposes of hard drive organization when a song is part of a compilation.)

- If you've left "Keep iTunes Music folder organized" unchecked and then decide to check it, upon closing the Preferences window iTunes will ask if you want to organize your library. If you click Yes, it will create folders and move files as necessary within the iTunes Music folder so that everything resides in the preferred hierarchy. The program will not touch anything outside of the designated iTunes Music folder.

- If you're ever curious about where a particular song resides on your hard drive, you can select it and choose Get Info from the File menu; the location appears at the bottom of the Summary tab. Alternatively, you can select the song and choose Show Song File from the File menu.

Choosing a New iTunes Music Folder

If you want iTunes to start using a new folder to store all music files—perhaps because you've added a new, bigger hard drive to your computer that you want to start using to store your music—you can tell the program to change the iTunes Music folder.

To choose a new iTunes Music folder:

1. Open the Advanced tab of the Preferences window.

   Notice the current location of your Music folder. By default, it's in Home/Music/iTunes/iTunes Music (Mac) or My Documents\My Music\iTunes\iTunes Music folder (Windows).

2. Click the Change button (**Figure 5.45**).

3. Locate the new folder you want to use, and click Choose (Mac) or OK (Windows).

   The new location is listed as the iTunes Music Folder location (**Figure 5.46**).

   The files for songs you import from CD or download from the iTunes Music Store in the future will be put in this new location. In addition, songs added from your hard drive in the future will be placed here, assuming you've checked "Copy files to iTunes Music folder when adding to library."

   The files for the songs that were previously in your library stay where they are.

Figure 5.45 Click Change if you want iTunes to store song files in a new folder.

Figure 5.46 Notice the new location for the iTunes music folder.

Moving Your Song Files to Another Location

As your library grows or as your computer system changes (or both), you may decide that you need to move your collection of song files from one physical location to another. To move the files in your iTunes library to a different physical location, you should first specify the new iTunes Music folder location (as described in the previous section), and then consolidate your library (as described in this section).

iTunes copies all the files in your library to the new iTunes Music folder and structures them in its preferred artist-album hierarchy.

Organizing your library

Figure 5.47 From the Advanced menu, choose Consolidate library when you want to move all your song files into your iTunes Music folder.

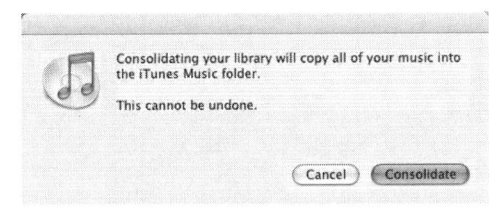

Figure 5.48 Click Consolidate as long as you're sure you want everything moved to your iTunes folder.

Path before consolidation.

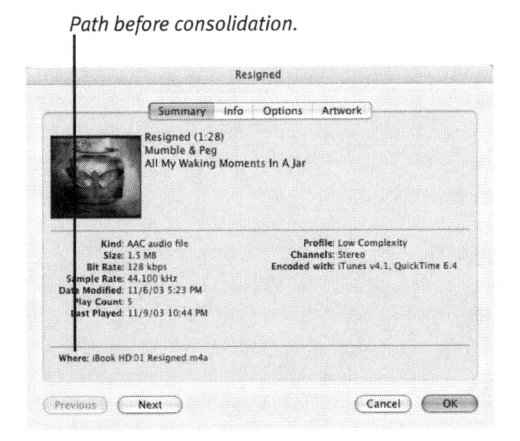

Figure 5.49 The Summary tab in the information window for a song before consolidation.

Path after consolidation.

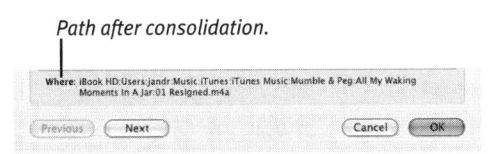

Figure 5.50 The Summary tab after consolidation.

Consolidating Songs on Your Hard Drive

It's possible that the music files in your iTunes library are scattered all over your hard drive, perhaps even on multiple hard drives. This is most likely to happen if you have had "Copy files to iTunes Music folder when adding to library" unchecked in your iTunes preferences, or if you've changed the location of your iTunes library. If you'd like to keep all your music in one place —especially handy if you want to back up your music—you can tell iTunes to gather everything up into your iTunes Music folder.

To move all your music files into your iTunes Music folder:

◆ From the Advanced menu, choose Consolidate library (**Figure 5.47**).

iTunes shows a window giving you a chance to change your mind (**Figure 5.48**).

If you click Yes, any files not in your designated iTunes Music folder are moved there and placed in an artist-album hierarchical structure, based on the information iTunes stores about the songs.

Figure 5.49 shows the location of a song file as it is displayed in the information window before consolidation.

Figure 5.50 shows the location of the same song file after consolidation. Notice that the folder structure has changed considerably, and that the file name has changed to match the song name in iTunes.

✔ Tip

■ If "Keep iTunes Music folder organized" is unchecked (refer to Figure 5.46) when you consolidate your library, iTunes moves song files into album and artist folders that match the album and artist information associated with the song, but it *doesn't* rename the files to match the song names in your iTunes library.

151

6

BURNING CDS AND OTHER DISKS

One of the coolest things you can do with iTunes is to *burn,* or create, your own CDs. You can create your own greatest hits compilation of your favorite songs, burn it to a CD, and then listen to that CD anywhere—take it to a party, or listen to it in your car. Unlike the commercial CDs you purchase, the CDs you burn contain only the music *you* want. It's downright liberating.

iTunes makes this process extremely easy. Essentially, you add the songs you want to a playlist, and then click the Burn Disc button. Of course, as is the case with most iTunes features, there are various options you should know about, and techniques that will ensure a smoother process.

In this chapter, we'll start by covering how to determine whether you have a CD burner that works with iTunes, and we'll give you some pointers to help you decide what type of CD to burn. Then we'll provide instructions for preparing to burn the different types of CDs—and then actually burning them.

We end the chapter with a bunch of tips that apply to all the different kinds of CDs you may want to burn with iTunes.

Checking for a Supported Burner

If you want to burn a CD, you'll need a CD burner that iTunes supports. If you have a Mac with a built-in CD burner (like the SuperDrive), you're set to go. If you're using a PC, or if you're using a third-party external CD burner with your Mac, you'll need to check to make sure your burner is compatible with iTunes.

To check to see if you have a supported burner:

1. From the iTunes menu (Mac) or the Edit menu (Windows) choose Preferences to open the Preferences window.
2. Click the Burning tab.
3. Look at the top line, labeled CD Burner (**Figure 6.1**).

   If a device is listed, you have a supported burner connected.

   If a pop-up menu appears for CD Burner, you have multiple supported burners; select the one you'd like to use.

   If a burner is listed, but the text is italicized, iTunes is telling you that you previously had a supported burner connected, but that device is no longer connected.

   If no burner is listed, then you don't have any burner connected that iTunes can use.

A supported burner shows here.

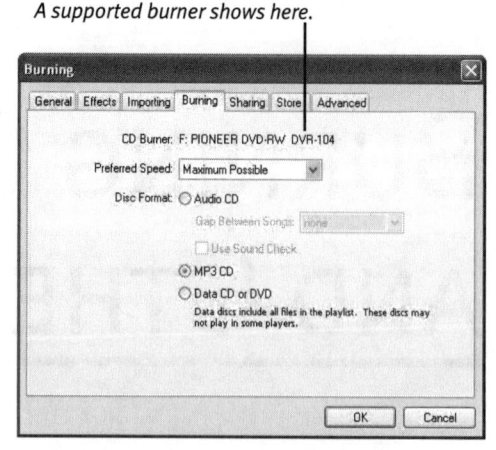

Figure 6.1 A device listed for CD Burner on the Burning tab of the Preferences window is supported by iTunes. (If this listing appears in italics, it means that the burner is no longer connected. If you see a pop-up menu where a device is normally listed, then you have a choice of burners.)

Burning CDs and Other Disks

✔ Tips

- If you have an external burner connected that you believe should work, but iTunes doesn't recognize it, try turning the burner off and then on again.

- (Windows) If you have a burner connected that you believe iTunes should support, but iTunes doesn't recognize it (even when you turn the burner off and then on), reinstall iTunes. If that doesn't work, go to www.gearsoftware.com/support/index.cfm and download and install the latest Windows GEAR driver set. (GEAR Software provides the software that Apple licenses for iTunes CD burning.)

In the Market for a CD Burner?

If you don't already have a CD burner, and are looking to buy one to use with iTunes, you may want to know which products to choose from. Unfortunately, as of this writing, Apple does not have an up-to-date list available online.

Mac users can get a list of devices that worked with iTunes 3 at http://docs.info.apple.com/article.html?artnum=75451; it's highly likely that these will work with the current version of iTunes, though some may no longer be on the market. Mac users can also check www.apple.com/macosx/upgrade/storage.html, which lists Mac OS X–compatible storage devices; though not iTunes specific, these should work with iTunes because it's actually OS X system software that does the burning, rather than something internal to iTunes.

Windows users can go to www.gearsoftware.com/support/tables/tables.cfm, choose the Windows platform, and then look for devices compatible with the GEAR.wrks Toolkit product (which is the software that Apple licenses for CD burning).

155

Deciding on a CD Format

You have a choice of three types of CDs that you can burn with iTunes, depending on what you ultimately want to do with that CD.

- **Audio CD.** This is a CD that plays in audio CD players (the kind that's part of your stereo system). When iTunes burns an audio CD, it converts songs in the selected playlist to an uncompressed format; the audio data is virtually identical in structure to that on commercial audio CDs, as well as to that in uncompressed AIFF and WAV files. The sound quality, however, may not be quite as good as on the original CD from which you ripped the songs; see the sidebar "About CD-Quality Audio."

- **MP3 CD.** This is a CD that will play only in MP3-enabled audio CD players. While many newer CD players have this feature, you can't count on it; thus, this choice is appropriate only when you are creating CDs to play on specific devices that you know can play MP3 CDs. The major advantage to an MP3 CD is the amount of music that will fit on it: You can fit about 10 hours on an MP3 CD versus the slightly more than 1 hour that will fit on an audio CD.

- **Data disc.** This type of disc is not designed to play in any audio CD player. Instead, it's a CD-ROM or a DVD-ROM designed to be read by a computer; the song files burned to a data disc remain in their initial format. A song file on a data disc is just like a file on a computer hard drive; you can open and play it with any application that can handle files of that format, iTunes included. Data discs provide a good method for backing up your song collection or for copying songs from one computer to another.

✔ **Tip**

- If you know that you want to burn an audio CD and you're anxious to get going, skip to the section "Burning Audio CDs" later in this chapter. iTunes is set up by default to do this reasonably well. The text on the pages between here and there merely explains your many options and may help you avoid problems.

What Type of Blank Discs Should I Buy?

It's usually best to buy name-brand discs, such as Sony, TDK, or Memorex. These almost always work, whereas the off-brands that you can sometimes find for bargain prices have a higher incidence of failed burns.

If you're trying to decide between CD-R (CD-Recordable) and CD-RW (CD-Rewritable) discs, know that both may work, but CD-R discs are likely to play in more audio CD players. CD-R discs are cheaper, anyway. On the other hand, you can erase and reuse CD-RWs, so you may want to try them, especially if you're just experimenting with making CDs.

When shopping, you may find both 74-minute (650 MB) and 80-minute (700 MB) blank CDs (though 74-minute discs are becoming harder to find). Either is fine; the latter will let you burn slightly more music to the CD.

If you plan to archive songs to DVD, you also have a choice of DVD-R or DVD-RW. Since the DVDs created in iTunes only play back on a computer, you don't need to be concerned with playback in audio players (as with CDs); feel free to use DVD-R or DVD-RW discs.

About CD-Quality Audio

Have you heard the term *CD-quality sound*? This is actually a euphemism for audio that is encoded at 44.1 kHz, the rate for the songs on an audio CD.

When you burn an audio CD with iTunes, the files that you copy to the CD are encoded at 44.1 kHz, too. Does this mean you get audio quality as good as that of commercial audio CDs? Not necessarily.

Recall that the files you've imported ("ripped") from CD have been compressed as AAC (or maybe MP3), unless you've changed your importing preferences to AIFF or WAV. No matter how good a job is done during compression, some audio data is lost; the file is just not as good as it originally was. When converted back to a CD audio file, the resulting file is as large as the original, but doesn't have all the data or all the quality of the original.

While most people can't hear the difference between a cleanly compressed AAC or MP3 file and the original uncompressed file, it may matter to you. If it does, the trick is to import as AIFF or WAV (see Chapter 2), and then burn an audio CD (not an MP3 CD). The imported files are much larger than if you had imported as AAC or MP3, but you'll have true CD-quality audio on the audio CD you burn from those files.

Preparing to Burn Audio CDs

Before you can burn any audio CDs, you'll want to set your preferences appropriately, and you'll also need a playlist to burn.

To prepare to burn an audio CD:

1. In iTunes, open the Preferences window.

2. On the Burning tab (**Figure 6.2**), make sure Audio CD is selected.

3. If you want to alter the amount of silence between songs, select from the Gap Between Songs pop-up menu.

   The 2-second default is usually fine, however, and is often what you'll find on commercial audio CDs.

4. Select Use Sound Check if you want iTunes to raise the volume of songs that are considerably more quiet than the rest of the songs or to lower the volume of songs that are much louder than the rest.

5. Click OK to close the Preferences window.

6. If you don't already have a playlist created containing the songs you want to burn, create such a playlist.

   These can be in any format. You don't want to include streams, however.

7. Make sure all the songs are checked.

8. Check at the bottom of the iTunes window (**Figure 6.3**) to see how many minutes of audio you have, and make sure you have a blank CD for each 74 or 80 minutes (depending on which type of blank CDs you've purchased) you want to burn.

   When determining how many minutes of audio you have in your playlist, you'll also need to account for the amount of time in the gaps between songs, though 2 minutes per CD is usually a safe estimate. See the sidebar "Watch the Gap" for more information.

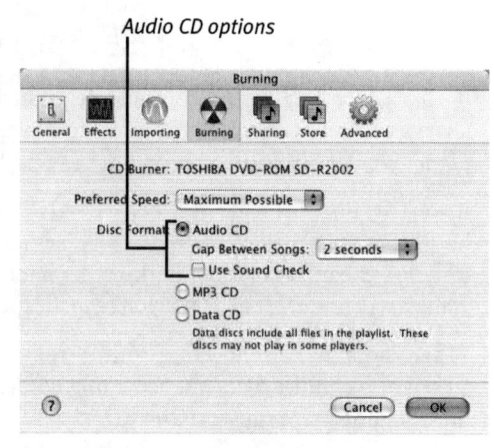

Figure 6.2 iTunes's default burning preferences are usually fine for burning audio CDs. Just make sure Audio CD is selected. You can also change the amount of silence between songs and specify whether you want iTunes to have all the songs on the CD play at approximately the same volume.

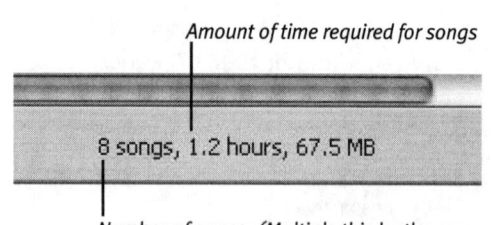

Figure 6.3 To determine the number of minutes for which you need to provide CD space, take the time required for the actual songs and add to it the amount required to account for the gap.

Burning CDs and Other Disks

A Smart Playlist for Creating an Audio CD

A Smart Playlist, such as that in **Figure 6.4**, can help you quickly put together a playlist for creating a single audio CD. In the Smart Playlist window, specify "Limit to 72 minutes" if you're using 74-minute discs or "limit to 78 minutes" if you're using 80-minute discs. To pick the music you want on this CD, try setting different conditions (such as "Comment contains party music"), selecting by different criteria (such as "selected by highest rating"), or limiting the playlist to a specific musical genre, like folk or blues.

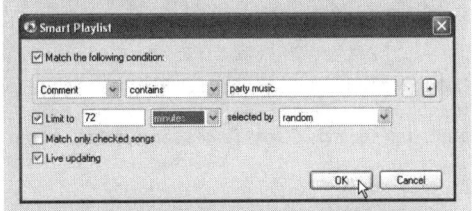

Figure 6.4 Here's an example of a Smart Playlist that will provide a playlist ready to burn to a single 74-minute, blank CD.

✔ Tips

- Use Sound Check is a good option to pick if you don't want to startle your listeners. For example, if you're creating an audio CD that veers from a quiet Nick Drake ballad to a raucous Screamin' Jay Hawkins song, you'll definitely want to enable this option.

- If you click the text at the bottom of the window, iTunes toggles between showing the time in hours or minutes (for example, 1.1 hours) and showing it in an hours:minutes:seconds format (for example, 1:10:36).

- iTunes doesn't list times over an hour in minutes. So 74 minutes is listed as 1:14:00 or 1.2 hours, and 80 minutes is listed as 1:20:00 or 1.3 hours.

- If iTunes lists the length of a playlist in days (rather than hours or minutes), you probably don't want to be burning it to CDs!

- If you've purchased an audiobook that's split into multiple items, you'll probably want the gap between "songs" to be set to 0.

- If you want to burn music that you've purchased from the iTunes Music Store, you must first be authorized to listen to it. See Chapter 8 for more information on authorization issues.

Watch the Gap

When you're checking to see how many songs you can fit on a CD, you need to account for the "gap between songs", which you set on the Burning tab of the Preferences window (refer to Figure 6.2). This is the amount of silence that iTunes automatically places in between the songs you burn to audio CD. To estimate how much additional time those silences are adding to your playlist's length, take the number of songs and multiply by the number of seconds set as the gap between songs in the Preferences window. This gives you a number in seconds, which you can then divide by 60 to determine how many minutes you should add to the figure shown at the bottom of your iTunes window listing the amount of time in your playlist. (If this all feels like too much work, use the 2-minute figure we mentioned earlier as a safe estimate for most CDs.)

159

PREPARING TO BURN AUDIO CDs

Chapter 6

Burning Audio CDs

There's nothing quite so satisfying as burning your own audio CD. The process is simple, and requires little input from you. Feel free to wander away to fix a snack once the CD burning commences.

To burn one or more audio CDs:

1. Follow the steps in "Preparing to Burn Audio CDs" in order to set your preferences appropriately and prepare a playlist.

2. Make sure the correct playlist is selected in your Source pane.

3. Click Burn Disc (**Figure 6.5**).

4. If directed in the Status display to insert a blank CD, do so.

    If you had previously inserted a blank CD, iTunes won't ask you to do so now.

5. If you have more audio (including gap silence) than will fit on the CD you've inserted, iTunes offers to create multiple CDs with the playlist split across them (**Figure 6.6**). Click Audio CDs to do this.

6. When the Status display tells you to click Burn Disc to start (**Figure 6.7**), click Burn Disc again.

    The Status display provides information about the burning process, including an estimate of how much longer the burn will take.

    If the playlist requires more than one CD, iTunes prompts you to insert another blank disc when it's ready for it.

    When the entire playlist has been burned, iTunes emits a "ding" sound and mounts the CD, just as if you had just inserted any commercial audio CD.

7. Eject the CD and try it out in an audio CD player.

    If the CD doesn't play, try some of the suggestions we provide at the end of this chapter and repeat the steps for burning.

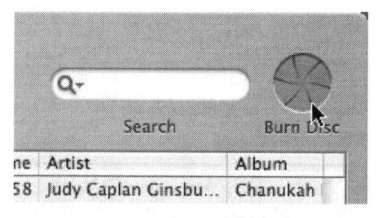

Figure 6.5 When you're ready to burn, click Burn Disc.

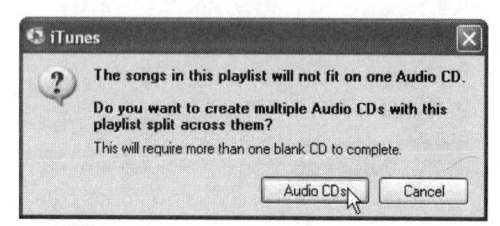

Figure 6.6 If you have more audio than will fit on one CD, iTunes gives you the option of creating multiple CDs.

Figure 6.7 iTunes tells you to click Burn Disc again. (Do it quickly; if burning a single CD, you only have about ten seconds before iTunes cancels the burn.)

Printing a Song List

Want to print a song list that shows the songs on your CD, so you can insert it in the CD case? Select the playlist from which you've burned the CD, and show only the columns you want to print. (See "Hiding and Showing Columns" in Chapter 3.) Next select all the items in the song list and copy them (Edit > Copy); then paste into a spreadsheet application (like Excel), tweak the formatting, and print. You can also paste into other types of applications, even word processors, but you may have to do more work to tweak the format if you want straight columns.

- If iTunes tells you it can't find the disc burner, but you're sure it's there and has been recognized by iTunes before, try quitting iTunes and reopening it.

- If iTunes reports errors at any time during the burning process, you may want to try some of the suggestions we provide at the end of this chapter.

Burning Limits on Purchased Music

If you've purchased music from the iTunes Music Store, you may encounter a few minor restrictions when it comes to burning.

The more likely restriction you'll come across is one that limits to ten the number of times you can burn a playlist containing purchased music. After the tenth burn, all you need to do is change the playlist slightly—repositioning just one song counts—and you'll be able to burn that playlist ten more times.

Another restriction is one you'll face only if you purchase music on a computer that you don't normally purchase from, and then try to burn from that computer. (This probably pertains to only a small percentage of you.) You can burn only songs that you're authorized to play. The first computer you ever purchase from is automatically authorized to play your purchased songs, but you'll need to actively authorize computers you purchase from subsequently. If you try to burn a playlist containing a song that you're not authorized to play, iTunes will refuse to burn. You'll need to remove the song from the playlist, or authorize the computer before you try again. (iTunes prompts you for authorization if you try to play the song; see Chapter 8.)

✔ Tips

- Once iTunes displays the message telling you to click Burn Disc to start, you have only about 10 seconds to do so, or iTunes kicks the disk out, assuming that you've changed your mind. You'll need to reinsert the disc and start again from step 2. (For some unexplainable reason, if your playlist requires multiple discs, iTunes gives you plenty of time; we've waited many minutes, and it never kicks out the disc.)

- When iTunes displays the message telling you to click Burn Disc to start (refer to Figure 6.7), it also shows the total time that will be recorded on the disc you have inserted; this includes the time for gaps between songs.

- After you click Burn Disc the first time, iTunes unchecks and dims any items that can't be burned. These are usually streams and items for which it can't find the audio file. In the case where multiple CDs will be burned, iTunes also unchecks and dims those that won't fit on the first CD.

- If you're listening to music while iTunes is burning, you can click the little right-pointing arrow on the left side of the Status display to cycle between showing the status of the burn, information about the current song, and the mini graphic equalizer.

- Wondering how long it's going to take for your audio CD to burn? If you know the speed rating for your drive, divide the number of minutes of audio by that number to approximate how long it will take to burn the actual data. (For example, 72 minutes of music burned on a 24x CD burner will take 3 minutes; 80 minutes of music burned on a 4x CD burner will take 20 minutes.) Then add a couple of minutes for initializing the disc before writing the songs and for finalizing the disc after writing the songs.

Chapter 6

Preparing to Burn an MP3 CD

To create an MP3 CD, you'll need to have a playlist containing MP3-encoded songs, and you'll need to set your burning preferences appropriately. Remember, MP3 CDs differ significantly from audio CDs. Although you can fit ten times as many songs on an MP3 CD, it can only be played on MP3-enabled audio CD players.

To prepare to burn an MP3 CD:

1. Create a playlist that contains only MP3 files and that's less than 700 MB if you're using 80-minute media (**Figure 6.8**) or less than 650 MB if you are using 74-minute media.

   If you're not sure if the files you want to include are MP3, or if you need to convert songs to MP3, refer to the next section.

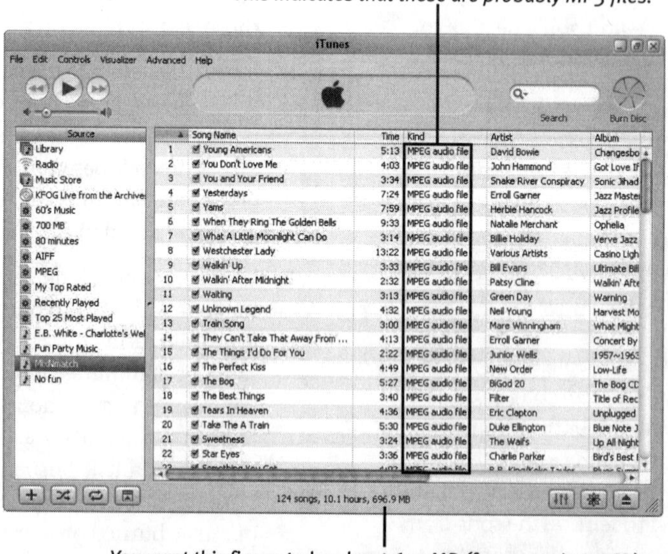

This indicates that these are probably MP3 files.

You want this figure to be about 650 MB (for a 74-minute CD) or 700 MB (for an 80-minute CD) if all the audio in the list is MP3.

Figure 6.8 To create an MP3 CD, you want a playlist that contains only MP3 songs and that's less than 700 MB. (Make it less than 650 MB if using 74-minute CDs.)

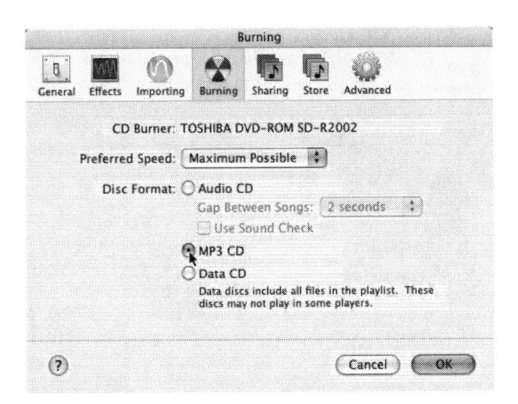

Figure 6.9 MP3 CD must be selected on the Burning tab of the Preferences window if you want to create an MP3 CD.

Check the bottom of your iTunes window to determine the amount of data in the playlist.

2. Make sure all the songs in the playlist are checked.

3. Open the Preferences window and on the Burning tab, select MP3 CD (**Figure 6.9**).

4. Click OK to close the Preferences window.

✔ Tips

- With the current version of iTunes, it's very important to limit your playlist to the amount of data that will fit on the CD, since iTunes won't split songs between multiple MP3 CDs (as it does for audio CDs and data discs).

- You can't include items purchased from the iTunes Music Store on an MP3 CD. What you can do, however, is burn purchased items to an audio CD, then import from the CD as MP3. Once the songs are reimported this way, you can burn to MP3. (The downside is that the songs have been compressed once using AAC, and then will be compressed again using MP3; this results in some quality loss.)

- Files you purchase from Audible.com may be MP3 files, but they can't be burned to an MP3 CD.

A Smart Playlist for Creating an MP3 CD

To create a Smart Playlist with enough music for an MP3 CD, make choices in the Smart Playlist window. Start with "Kind contains MPEG audio file," and "Limit to 700 MB selected by random" or selected in whatever way you prefer. (Limit it to 650 MB if you are using 74-minute discs.)

This playlist, however, may contain other forms of MPEG audio, if you happen to have them in your library; this might be the case if you've added old audio files from your computer hard disk. (See the next page if you want to confirm that these are MP3 files.)

Chapter 6

Making Sure Songs Are MP3s

It's a good idea to make sure all the songs you want to burn to an MP3 CD are actually *in* the MP3 format before you start burning your CD. If you want to include a song that's not an MP3, you'll need to convert it first.

To see if a song is in an MP3 format :

- If a song is listed in the Kind column as "MPEG audio file" (refer to Figure 6.8), select it and from the File menu choose Get Info. On the right side of the window it lists the format (**Figure 6.10**). "MPEG-1, Layer 3" or "MPEG-2, Layer 3" is what you want to see.

   If a song is listed in the Kind column as anything other than "MPEG audio file," it's not an MP3 file that can be burned to an MP3 CD.

To convert songs to MP3 format:

1. In the Importing tab of the Preferences window, choose MP3 Encoder in the Import Using pop-up menu (**Figure 6.11**), and then click OK to close the Preferences window.

2. In the song list, select the songs you want to convert to MP3.

Shows format. MPEG-1, Layer 3 means that it's an MP3 file. (So does MPEG-2, Layer 3.)

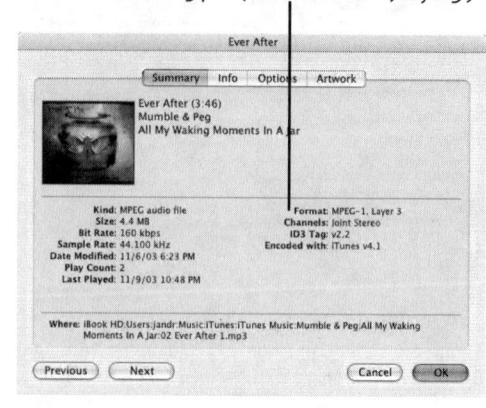

Figure 6.10 The only way to be sure that a song is MP3 is to get information on the song (File > Get Info).

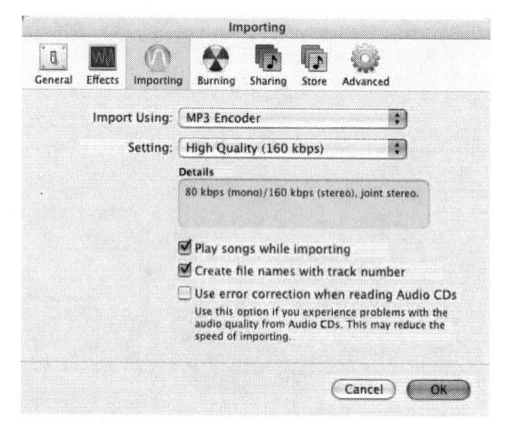

Figure 6.11 If you want to convert songs to MP3, you'll need to change your Importing preferences. (Yes, even though you're not importing.) Go to the Importing tab of the Preferences window, select MP3, and pick a setting: 160 usually provides a good compromise between quality and amount of music you can fit on a CD. (**See Table 6.1**.)

Burning CDs and Other Disks

Figure 6.12 Choose Convert Selection to MP3 to convert all selected songs to MP3. (You won't find this menu item unless you've first changed your importing settings.)

3. From the Advanced menu, choose Convert Selection to MP3 (**Figure 6.12**). iTunes converts the selected songs.

4. Delete the non-MP3 versions from the playlist.

✔ Tips

- MP3 *streams* (which can't be burned to an MP3 CD) are listed in the Kind column as "MPEG audio stream"; make sure the Kind column is wide enough so you can see if the last word is *file* or *stream*.

- When you select MP3 as your encoder, you can also select from the Setting pop-up menu (refer to Figure 6.11). See "Changing How Songs Are Encoded on Import" in Chapter 2 if you want to better understand what your Setting options are. Refer to Table 6.1 if you want to know how your bit-rate setting (the *kbps* figure) affects the number of hours of audio you can fit on the CD.

Table 6.1

How much audio fits on an MP3 CD		
BIT RATE	NUMBER OF HOURS ON 74-MINUTE CD	NUMBER OF HOURS ON 80-MINUTE CD
128 kbps	11.5	12.4
160 kbps	9.2	9.9
192 kbps	7.7	8.3

MAKING SURE SONGS ARE MP3S

165

Chapter 6

Burning an MP3 CD

Finally, you're ready to burn an MP3 CD. The process differs only slightly from burning an audio CD.

To burn an MP3 CD:

1. Follow the steps for preparing to burn an MP3 CD as described previously in this chapter.

2. Make sure the playlist is selected, and all the songs you want to burn are checked.

3. Click the Burn Disc button (**Figure 6.13**).

    The Status display tells you to click Burn Disc to start (refer to Figure 6.7 earlier in this chapter).

4. If directed in the Status display to insert a blank CD, do so.

    If you had previously inserted a blank CD, iTunes won't ask you to do so now.

5. Click Burn Disc again.

    iTunes unchecks any items that you left in the playlist that aren't MP3 files (**Figure 6.14**) and proceeds to burn the disc.

Figure 6.13 To create an MP3 CD from a playlist full of MP3-encoded songs, insert a blank CD and click Burn Disc.

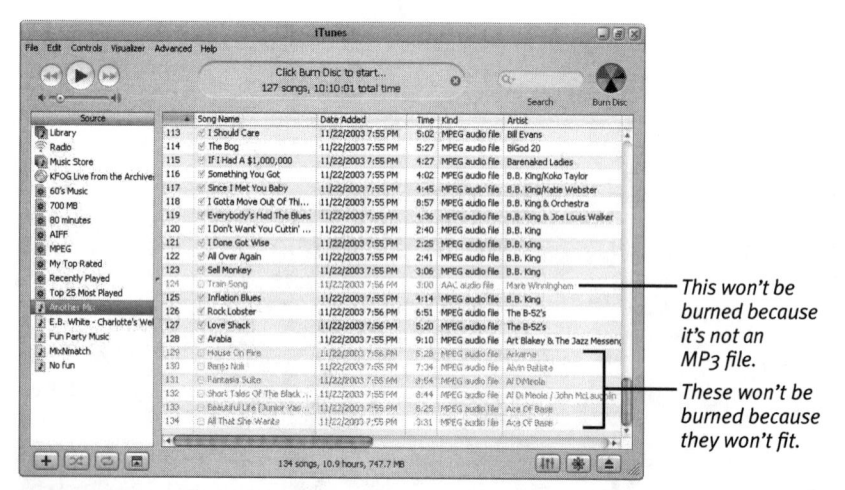

Figure 6.14 iTunes dims and unchecks the songs that won't be burned. (Of course, this won't happen to you if you've carefully prepared the playlist in the first place.)

This won't be burned because it's not an MP3 file.

These won't be burned because they won't fit.

166

Burning CDs and Other Disks

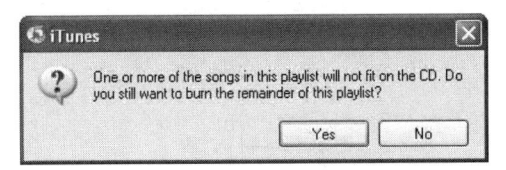

Figure 6.15 If you have too much data to burn, iTunes shows this message. It means that iTunes will burn only the songs in the song list that will fit on the blank CD you're inserted.

6. Take out the CD when it's done and test it by playing it in an MP3-enabled audio CD player.

   If it doesn't play correctly, read "Tips for Successful Burning" at the end of this chapter and try again.

✔ Tips

- If you wait more than about 10 seconds after iTunes prompts you to click Burn Disc, iTunes kicks out the disc. You'll have to start again at step 3.

- If the selected playlist has more data than can fit on the CD, iTunes tells you (after the first time you click Burn Disc) that one or more of the songs won't fit (**Figure 6.15**). Click Yes to go on, or No if you'd rather remove items from your playlist and start again. (According to iTunes Help, however, iTunes is supposed to split playlists between multiple MP3 CDs. Perhaps by the time you read this, iTunes will be able to do as Help says, and you'll see a window similar to that shown in Figure 6.6.)

BURNING AN MP3 CD

167

Chapter 6

Creating a Data CD or DVD for Archiving Purposes

We recommend creating a data disc (CD or DVD) so that you'll have a backup copy of some or all of your songs. This way, if something disastrous happens to your hard drive or you get a new computer, you won't have to re-rip all your audio CDs. Perhaps even more important, you'll have a backup of all your purchased music (as Apple won't replace purchased music).

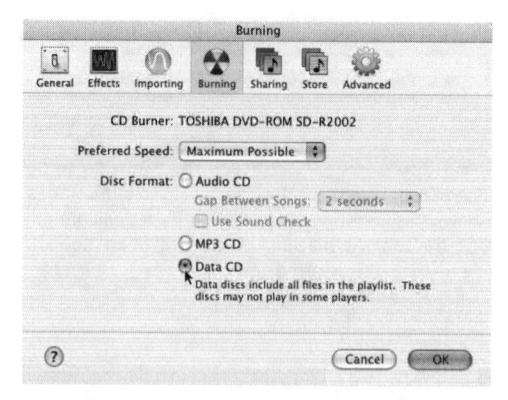

Figure 6.16 When you want to copy all your song files to a CD-ROM or a DVD-ROM for archiving purposes, select Data CD on the Burning tab of the Preferences window.

To archive songs in a playlist to a CD-ROM or DVD-ROM:

1. Open the Preferences window, and on the Burning tab, select Data CD as the disc format (**Figure 6.16**).

    This applies whether you intend to burn to a CD or a DVD.

2. Click OK to close the Preferences window.

3. Make sure the playlist you want to archive is selected in the Source pane.

    This playlist can contain all types of song files (**Figure 6.17**). It can even point to all the songs in your library. (See the sidebar "A System for Backing Up Your Whole Library" for more info on creating a playlist for your entire library.)

4. Click Burn Disc.

5. If directed in the Status display to insert a blank disc, insert your blank CD or DVD.

    In the case of a DVD, iTunes asks if you're sure that you want to create a data DVD. Click Data DVD to continue.

6. If you have more data than can fit on the CD or DVD you've inserted, iTunes asks if you want to create multiple data discs with the playlist split across them (**Figure 6.18**). Click Data Discs to continue.

Figure 6.17 For a data disc, the playlist you intend to burn can contain all types of audio files.

Figure 6.18 If you have more data than will fit on a single disc, you'll see this message.

168

Burning CDs and Other Disks

Figure 6.19 If you need to put files from a data disc back into your iTunes library, you can just drag the icon for the data disc to your library (or to any playlist).

The Status display tells you to click Burn Disc to start (refer to Figure 6.7 earlier in this chapter).

7. Click Burn Disc for the second time.

   In the song list, iTunes unchecks and dims any files it can't find, as well as any streams. If more than one disc will be required, iTunes also unchecks and dims the songs that won't fit on the first CD.

   The Status display provides information about the burning process, including an estimate of how much longer the burn will take.

   If the playlist requires more than one CD, it will prompt you to insert another when it's ready for it, and will then prompt you to click Burn Disc again.

   You end up with one or more CD-ROMs or DVD-ROMs, each with a name matching the name of the playlist. Each disc contains copies of all the audio files represented in the playlist, as well as an XML file with information about the songs on that disc.

To copy files from a data disc back into an iTunes library:

1. Insert the data disc.

   The data disc appears in the iTunes Source pane.

2. Do one of the following:
   ▲ Drag the entry for the data disc in the Source pane to the library or to a playlist (**Figure 6.19**).
   ▲ Click the entry for the data disc, and drag selected songs from the song list to the library or to a playlist.

   iTunes copies the files to your iTunes Music folder and adds the songs to your library (and to the playlist to which you dragged, if any).

169

✔ Tips

- As with other types of discs, once iTunes displays the message telling you to click Burn Disc to start, you have only about 10 seconds to do so, or iTunes will kick out the disk. (However, as with burning an audio CD, if your playlist requires multiple discs, iTunes give you plenty of time to click the Burn Disc button.)

- To copy files from a data disc back into iTunes, you could also drag song files from Windows Explorer or the Finder into the iTunes window—but not all song information will necessarily come with the songs. (It's only when you do the copy entirely from within iTunes that it reads the XML file containing song information; this is especially important for files other than AAC and MP3 files.)

A System for Backing Up Your Whole Library

If you want to make sure you always have a backup of all the items in your iTunes library, try this system.

First, back up your whole library in its current state. To do this, you'll need to create a playlist that contains all the songs in your library. One way to create such a playlist is to select your library in the Source pane, select all the items in it, and then choose File > New Playlist From Selection; give the resulting playlist a name like "Full Library" and burn that playlist. (Figure that this process will take roughly 5 minutes per CD with a 24x CD burner. Remember that iTunes reports the amount of data in a playlist at the bottom of the window, and that a CD can hold 650 MB or 700 MB.)

Once you've got your full library burned, you can do incremental backups on a regular basis, burning a CD that contains only those songs you've added since your last backup. One way to do this is to create a Smart Playlist that has the condition "Date Added is after," with a value matching the date of your last backup (**Figure 6.20**). You'll need to edit this playlist after each full backup to change the date value to that of the latest backup.

Change this date to the date of your last backup.

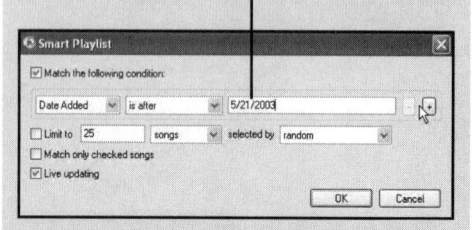

Figure 6.20 This Smart Playlist keeps track of all songs added since a particular date.

Burning CDs and Other Disks

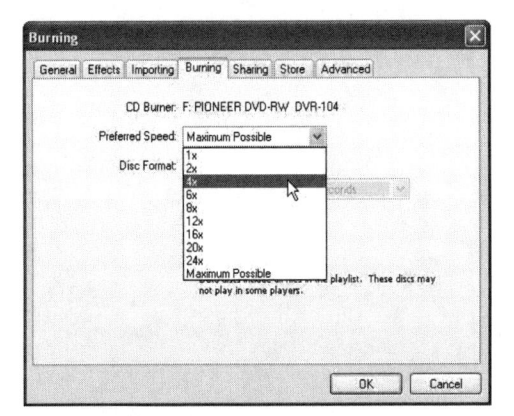

Figure 6.21 Some drives don't burn well at their maximum possible speed, so you should try lowering the preferred speed.

Tips for Successful Burning

If you've spent any time burning CDs, you know that the process isn't always foolproof. It's not uncommon to wind up with a few CD "drink coasters" after some failed burning attempts. But worry not. There are a number of things you can try if you don't successfully burn a CD the first time.

To improve your chances of a successful burn:

◆ Change the speed at which iTunes burns. It normally tries to burn at the maximum speed of the drive and/or blank disc. Sometimes this is just too fast to do a good job, and you'll need to tell the system to slow down. To do so, go to the Burning tab of the Preferences window, and from the Preferred Speed pop-up menu (**Figure 6.21**), select a lower burn speed. (We recommend first trying 2x, which is slower than the majority of drives out there today; if that works, try higher speeds on subsequent burns, until you reach a point where burning doesn't work again. If even 2x doesn't work, try 1x.)

◆ If you're using CD-RW blank discs, try switching to CD-R blanks.

◆ Change your computer's sleep timing preferences so that your computer won't go to sleep during the burn.

◆ Turn off programs that may interrupt the burning process; such programs include screensavers and antivirus programs.

171

- Defragment your hard disk. A fragmented hard disk is one that has files and parts of files dispersed all over the disc, which means that during a burn the system may not find the pieces it needs when it needs them. (Symantec's Norton Utilities is one application that includes a defragmenting tool.)

- Determine whether there's a problem with your CD burner that needs repairing. (For example, try to burn a CD with the software that came with the burner to make sure it's not a problem with the burner rather than iTunes.)

- Check with the manufacturer of your burner to make sure the burner has the latest firmware. (Most manufacturers will provide information about firmware updates on their Web site, in a support area.)

- (Windows) If you have two internal burners (maybe a DVD burner and a CD burner), try disconnecting one.

- If you're burning an MP3 CD and you find it doesn't work in an older MP3 CD player, it may be because that player can't handle the newer version of the ID3 tags in the files. Choose Advanced > Convert ID3 Tags, and in the window that appears, choose v1.0 or v1.1; then burn again.

General Care of Discs

CD and DVD discs are somewhat fragile, so you should handle them with care, both before and after burning. Most of the following tips are common sense, but it can't hurt to be reminded, right?

- Do your best to keep your hands (and the hands of small, messy children) off the disc, especially the underside (meaning the side that has no manufacturer's imprint).

- Keep your discs dust-free. Before you burn, make sure your blank disc has no dust on it. (The best thing to do is blow off any dust with compressed air.)

- Don't write on a disc with anything but a felt-tip pen; and write only on the top side.

- Keep discs out of direct sunlight.

USING ITUNES WITH YOUR IPOD

The iPod is an amazing portable music player. It is, admittedly, more expensive than other MP3 players, but when you compare it to any of those other devices, it blows them away. It's small, light, sleek, and very easy to use; it just feels *good* in your hand. It can store songs and audiobooks in a variety of formats (not just MP3). The iPod's internal hard disk, which currently maxes out at 40 GB, makes it easy to carry around many thousands of songs or hundreds of audiobooks in your pocket. You can store other stuff on your iPod, too, such as contact info, calendars, and notes. And because the iPod doubles as a portable FireWire hard drive, you can use it to transfer or back up large files.

We could write a whole book about the iPod, but we don't have to: If you want to know *everything* about the iPod, check out Christopher Breen's excellent *Secrets of the iPod* (Peachpit Press, 2004).

This chapter isn't designed to teach you how to use your iPod; rather, we'll stick to iPod topics that relate to its use with iTunes: establishing a relationship between your iPod and iTunes, moving songs from your iTunes library to the iPod, the various buttons and controls you use in iTunes to make changes to your iPod, and the few things you can do on your iPod that impact your iTunes library. We'll end the chapter with a brief summary of how iTunes works with other MP3 players.

Introducing the iPod mini

As we were finishing this book, Apple announced the *iPod mini*—a smaller, sleeker, more colorful iPod. This model sports a 4-gigabyte hard drive, stores up to 1000 songs, and will be priced at $249 when it releases in February 2004. We're assuming that when the mini is released, it will function identically to its big sibling, and that the material in this chapter will apply to both iPod models.

Making Sure You Have the Latest Version of iPod Software

To make sure you can take advantage of all your iPod's bells and whistles, you want your iPod to have the most current version of iPod software that it will allow. At this writing, the current version for the third-generation iPod (the one featuring a Dock Connector port) is 2.1. For older iPods, which use a FireWire cable instead of a docking connection, version 1.3 is the latest version you can use.

To check which version you have:

◆ Using your iPod's scroll wheel, navigate through the iPod menu and choose About.

   The version number appears in the About menu (**Figure 7.1**).

   If you don't have the latest version, you should update.

To update to the latest version:

1. Visit the iPod Download page at www.apple.com/ipod/download/ and download to your computer the iPod Software Update appropriate for your computer and iPod.

2. Run the downloaded installer.

3. Connect your iPod to your computer.

   You'll be prompted to update your iPod's software (**Figure 7.2**). Follow the onscreen instructions.

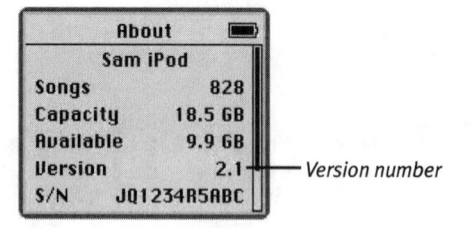

Figure 7.1 You can check on your iPod to see the version number.

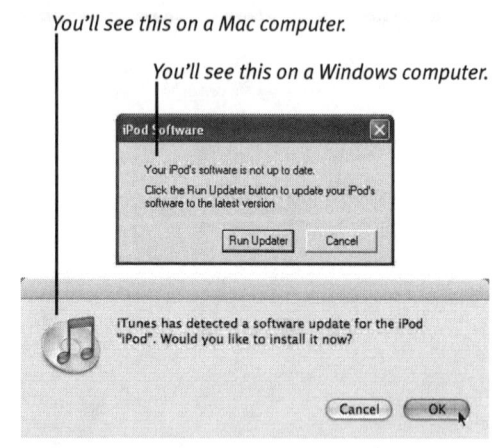

Figure 7.2 When you connect your iPod after installing the Updater on your computer, you'll see this window. (The Windows and Mac versions are slightly different.)

✔ Tips

- A software installer comes on the CD that's bundled with your iPod. We recommend, however, that you get the software from the Web site instead, because it's likely to be more current.

- For older, nondockable iPods, you need at least version 1.3 if you want to be able to put AAC files on your iPod. (All songs and audiobooks that you download from the iTunes Music Store are in AAC format.)

Connecting Your iPod to a PC for the First Time

Got a brand new iPod? An iPod, straight out of the box, is formatted for use on a Mac. Or do you have an iPod that previously had been used on a Mac? After installing the current version of the iPod software on your Windows system and restarting with your iPod connected, you'll see a message that the iPod is not readable and that it needs to be formatted for use on a PC (**Figure 7.3**). If you click Update, the iPod Software Updater opens. Click Restore and then follow the onscreen instructions to reformat the iPod's hard drive; this ensures that your iPod will play nicely with your PC. (Warning: This also erases the contents of your iPod, something you only have to worry about if it previously had been used on a Mac.)

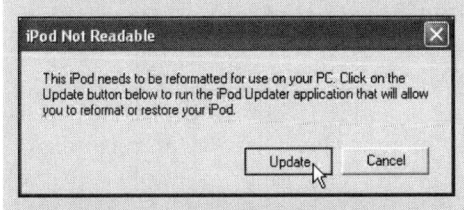

Figure 7.3 If you have an iPod that's never been used on a Windows system and connect it to a Windows computer, you'll see this window. You must update if you want to use the iPod on your Windows computer.

Setting Up Your iPod with iTunes

The first time you connect your iPod to your computer (assuming all software is up-to-date) or immediately following most iPod software updates or formatting, iTunes automatically launches (if it's not already open) and displays a screen where you specify how you want iTunes and the iPod to interact.

To set up your iPod for use with iTunes:

1. Connect your iPod to your computer.
2. In the iPod Setup Assistant window that appears (**Figure 7.4**), enter a name for your iPod.

    This is the name that will appear in the iTunes Source pane when the iPod is connected.

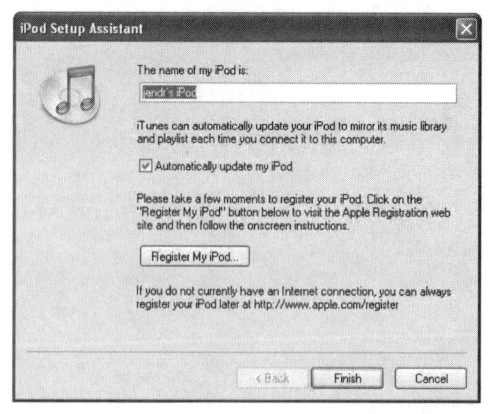

Figure 7.4 This window allows you to initially define how your iPod should be updated.

Notes for Windows Audible.com or Musicmatch Users with an iPod

When you install iTunes, it effectively disables any interaction between an iPod and other applications, most notably AudibleManager (the tool you use to download Audible.com files) and Musicmatch Jukebox. All transfers to your iPod are handled solely by iTunes.

With Audible.com, in particular, this is—we hate to admit it—a substantial drawback to using iTunes. Why? Using iTunes requires more steps: You must first use AudibleManager to download an audiobook file and then locate the file and add it to your iTunes library. Once the file is in the iTunes library, you must then update your iPod (via an automatic or manual update) to get the audiobook on the iPod. If iTunes wasn't installed, you'd simply use AudibleManager to download and then directly transfer the file to the iPod.

Not only that, but AudibleManager can be set to automatically download periodical content once published *and* transfer it to a connected iPod. If you have a New York Times subscription, for example, you can set AudibleManager so that every morning it automatically downloads the day's issue and puts it on your iPod; when you're ready to leave for your daily commute in the morning, just eject the iPod, put it in your pocket, and head out the door, knowing how much more informative your commute will be. (With iTunes installed, AudibleManager can still do the automatic download every morning, but you'll need to manually move the downloaded file into iTunes and then update your iPod.)

There's a hint of good news at the Audible.com Web site, however. A note acknowledges the drawbacks to the multistep process and hints that Apple and Audible may very well come up with a more palatable solution.

Using iTunes with Your iPod

3. Leave "Automatically update my iPod" checked if you want iTunes to put everything in its library onto your iPod.

   Uncheck this item if you'd rather pick and choose what to put on your iPod.

4. Register your iPod if you like.

5. Click Finish (Windows) or Done (Mac) to close the window.

   If you left "Automatically update my iPod" checked, iTunes updates your iPod, adding your current iTunes library and its playlists to the iPod. (See "About Automatic Updating" later in this chapter.)

   If you unchecked "Automatically update my iPod," you'll see the iPod selected in the Source pane and an empty song list; you can manually add songs and playlists to your iPod. (See "Manually Updating Your iPod" later in this chapter.)

   In either case, you'll notice that the bottom of your iTunes window has some additions: a storage indicator (showing how much data is stored on the iPod and how much room is left), an iPod Options button, and an iPod Eject button (**Figure 7.5**).

✔ Tip

- Your choice of automatic updating (or not) is not permanent, nor is it actually an all-or-nothing proposition. See "Changing iPod Updating Preferences" later in this chapter.

Shows how full the iPod is   *iPod Options button*

iPod Eject button

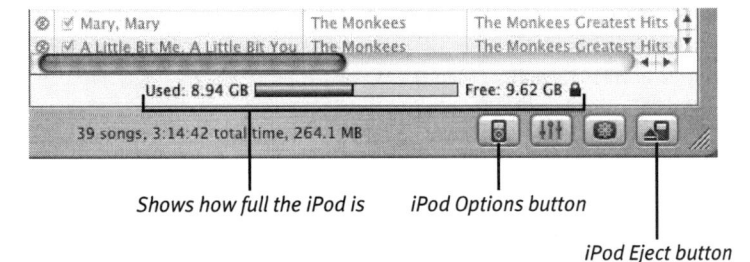

Figure 7.5 When an iPod is connected, the bottom of your iTunes window appears slightly different.

177

Chapter 7

Ejecting an iPod

Don't ever unplug your iPod from your computer unless you've first ejected it. If you're transferring data to your iPod when you unplug it, for example, you could corrupt the iPod's hard drive, which means you'd have to reformat the tiny device. Apple gives you a slew of one-step methods for ejecting your iPod. Choose the one that suits you best!

Ways to eject your iPod:

♦ Select the iPod in the Source pane, and click the iPod Eject button (refer to Figure 7.5).

♦ Control-click (Mac) or right-click (Windows) the entry for the iPod in the Source pane, and choose the Eject item from the contextual menu that appears (**Figure 7.6**).

♦ Select the iPod in the Source pane, and from the Controls menu choose the Eject item (**Figure 7.7**).

♦ (Mac only) Drag the iPod icon from the Desktop to the Trash.

♦ (Mac only) Choose the Eject item from the menu that appears when you click and hold on the iTunes icon in the Dock.

♦ (Windows only) Use the Safely Remove Hardware icon in the system tray.

♦ (Windows only) Choose the Eject item in the menu that appears when you click the iTunes icon in the system tray.

Once you eject it, the iPod disappears from the Source list. It also no longer appears as an icon on the Desktop (Mac) or in My Computer (Windows). The iPod shows a message: "OK to Disconnect."

✔ Tip

■ To remount your iPod after ejecting, you can disconnect it and reconnect it, or you can quit iTunes and then re-open it.

Figure 7.6 To eject an iPod, Control-click (Mac) or Right-click (Windows) to show this contextual menu, and choose Eject iPod.

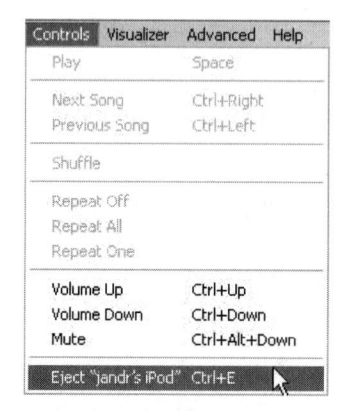

Figure 7.7 If the iPod is selected, you'll also find an item to eject your iPod in the Controls menu.

Figure 7.8 Click the iPod Options button if you want to change your updating preferences.

Changing iPod Updating Preferences

As we mentioned earlier, you can always change the way you want your iPod updated.

If you've set your iPod for automatic updating, you may change your mind if the size of your library grows and you can no longer fit all your songs on the iPod. You can tell iTunes to automatically update only specific playlists, or you can switch to manual updating.

On the other hand, if you have your iPod set for manual updating, you may at some point decide that you'd prefer the mindlessness of automatic updating; or perhaps you want some features that are enabled only with automatic updating (such as On-The-Go playlists and the ability to transfer song ratings from your iPod to your iTunes library, both of which are covered later in this chapter). You can tell iTunes to automatically copy all songs from your library or to copy only selected playlists.

The preferences you set for your iPod are stored on the iPod itself. This means that if you connect your iPod to a different computer, the copy of iTunes on *that* computer will recognize the preferences you've set for your iPod.

To change iPod updating preferences:

1. Select the iPod in the Source list.

2. Click the iPod Options button at the bottom right of the iTunes window (**Figure 7.8**).
   You can also Control-click (Mac) or right-click (Windows) the iPod icon in your Source pane; from the contextual menu that appears, choose iPod Options.

continues on next page

What Types of Files Can Be Transferred to an iPod?

Luckily, the majority of files in your iTunes library can be copied to your iPod without a hitch. This includes WAV, AIFF, MP3, AAC (including the protected ones purchased from the iTunes Music Store), and Audible (.aa) files.

The file types that *won't* be copied to an iPod include anything that iTunes recognizes as a QuickTime file (including MIDI and Karaoke), as well as some older, more obscure formats, such as SoundDesigner 2 and System 7 Sound.

Also, MPEG Layer I and Layer II files—both the MPEG 1 and MPEG 2 versions—won't be transferred to an iPod. (As you'll see in the next chapter, this is even more restrictive than what iTunes sharing allows.)

Remember, as we mentioned in Chapter 2, that you can convert files to MP3, AAC, WAV, or AIFF. Use this option if it's important to copy a song that's in a nonsupported format.

Finally (and unsurprisingly), any item in your library that's a stream or a pointer to something on the Internet—in other words, anything that doesn't have a file on your hard disk—won't be transferred.

Chapter 7

3. In the iPod Preferences window that appears (**Figure 7.9**), specify how you want iTunes to update your iPod:

   ▲ If you want iTunes to update your iPod so it has almost all the same songs and exactly the same playlists as you have in iTunes, select "Automatically update all songs and playlists." (We say *almost* because of a few potential exceptions; see step 4 below and also the sidebar "What Types of Files Can Be Transferred to an iPod?" later in this chapter.)

   ▲ If you want iTunes to put only specific playlists from your collection onto the iPod, select "Automatically update selected playlists only," and then click to put checkmarks next to those playlists you want updated. It's important to understand that after the update, your iPod will contain only the selected playlists; songs not in those playlists will be erased from the iPod.

   ▲ If you want to drag individual songs or playlists to your iPod and not have anything automatically added or erased, choose "Manually manage songs and playlists."

4. If you've selected one of the Automatic choices, you can check "Only update checked songs," so that any unchecked songs will *not* be transferred.

5. Click OK.

   If you have chosen either of the automatic updating choices, as soon as you click OK iTunes starts the update. (See "About Automatic Updating" later in this chapter.)

   If you've chosen manual updating, all files and playlists that had been on your iPod previously will be there, viewable in the song list; you'll be able to add to or remove from those lists. (See "Manually Updating Your iPod" later in this chapter.)

If you select this, you need to check the playlists you want iTunes to copy to the iPod. Songs not in the selected playlists won't be copied and will be erased from the iPod.

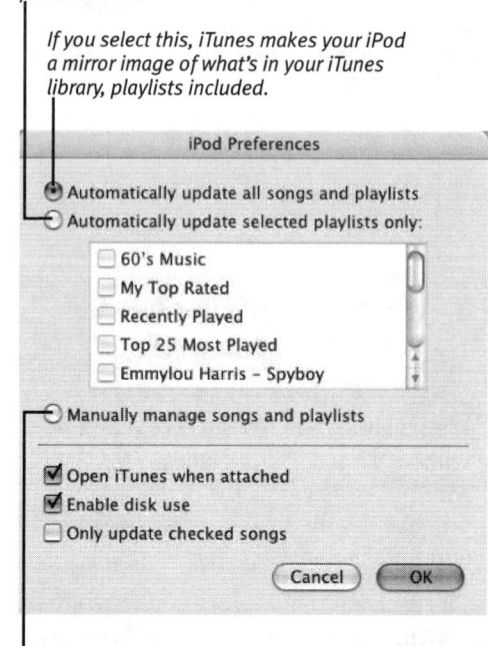

If you select this, iTunes makes your iPod a mirror image of what's in your iTunes library, playlists included.

If you select this, you'll be able to drag individual songs or playlists to your iPod.

Figure 7.9 The iPod Preferences window.

✔ Tips

- An additional reason to switch to manual updating is if you want to copy songs from multiple iTunes libraries to your iPod; see the sidebar "Copying Music from Multiple Libraries to Your iPod" later in this chapter.

- If iTunes doesn't recognize your iPod, try quitting iTunes and reopening it.

About Automatic Updating

Automatic updating occurs immediately after you've specified an Automatic Updating choice either in the initial set up window (refer to Figure 7.4) or in the iPod Preferences window (refer to Figure 7.9). Thereafter, the updating occurs every time you connect your iPod to your computer.

As iTunes updates the iPod, copying songs to it, you'll see continual updating of the storage information at the bottom of the window; a song list showing the songs that will be copied to the iPod, with an icon for each song in the far left column that disappears as the song is copied; and progress information in the Status display (**Figure 7.10**).

Shows status of update

These icons indicate songs that still need to be copied.

Click here if you can't wait for the update to finish.

This icon indicates that you can't change the contents of the iPod yourself; it's set for automatic updating.

Figure 7.10 The iTunes window during an automatic update. Note that all the songs in the iPod library are dimmed while the update takes place.

181

Chapter 7

When the update is complete, the Status display tells you so (**Figure 7.11**). You can eject and then disconnect the iPod at this point, if you like.

If you don't disconnect, you can scroll through the song list using the vertical scroll bar, but you can't do much of anything else—you can't browse, search, or sort columns, nor can you click on any songs to play them. (Of course, since all the songs were copied from your iTunes library, you can still play them from your iTunes library or playlists.)

✔ **Tips**

- Can't wait for updating to finish? (Gotta run, gotta take the iPod *now*!) You can click the little *x* icon on the right side of the Status display (refer to Figure 7.10); remove the iPod as soon as it tells you it's OK to disconnect. You'll have, on the iPod, as many files as iTunes was able to copy before you interrupted it. When you reconnect, copying will continue where it left off.

- If files for songs in your iTunes library are missing, a window appears saying that some of the songs were not copied to the iPod (**Figure 7.13**). (The past tense is inaccurate since it actually reports this before it does the update.) You can dismiss this window by clicking OK. If you don't want to be notified in this way, check "Do not warn me again."

- If you've got songs in your library that can't be played on an iPod because they're not a valid file format, you'll see a window similar to the one in Figure 7.13, indicating that the files couldn't be copied because they couldn't be played.

All you can do is scroll to see the entire list of songs in your library.

Notice that these items are still grayed out, indicating that you can't select them or play them.

Figure 7.11 The iTunes window after an automatic update. The Status display tells us that the update is complete.

What If You Change Your Library After an Automatic Update?

After your iPod has been automatically updated, you may continue to make changes to your iTunes library or playlists while the device is still connected. Before you disconnect the iPod, however, you should update the iPod to reflect these latest changes, using either of the following methods:

♦ From the File menu, select the Update Songs item (**Figure 7.12**).

♦ Control-click or right-click the iPod icon in the Source pane and, in the contextual menu that appears, choose Update Songs.

Figure 7.12 If you change your library when the iPod is connected, you should choose the Update Songs item from the File menu to ensure that your changes are reflected on the iPod.

ABOUT AUTOMATIC UPDATING

182

Using iTunes with Your iPod

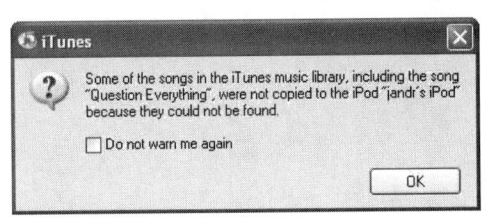

Figure 7.13 This window pops up to warn you that not all the songs in your library will be copied to your iPod (in this case, because the files can't be found). Similar windows appear if you have songs that are in the wrong format or songs that the computer you're on isn't authorized to play.

The Monogamous iPod

An iPod set for automatic updating wants to have a relationship with only one computer. If you connect to a second computer, you'll see a window (**Figure 7.14**) announcing that your iPod is linked to another iTunes library and giving you the option of changing the link to this second computer's iTunes library. *Don't* agree to this unless you're willing to have what's currently on your iPod erased and replaced with the contents of the Library to which you're about to link. If you want your iPod to "play the field" (that is, to receive songs from more than one computer), see the sidebar "Copying Music from Multiple Libraries to Your iPod" on the next page of this chapter.

- Items purchased in the iTunes Music Store or at Audible.com will transfer to your iPod and play just fine, assuming that the Mac or PC you're using is authorized to play those items. If you're not authorized to play them, you'll see a window similar to that in Figure 7.13, but it will say that the files couldn't be transferred because you weren't authorized to play them. (See Chapter 8 for more on authorization issues.)

- If you've got more data in your library than can fit on your iPod, iTunes simply tells you it can't do the update. This is a good time to either prune your library or change your iPod updating preferences.

- (Mac only) You can temporarily disable auto-updating so no update occurs when you connect your iPod. Immediately after you connect your iPod, hold down the Command and Option keys until the iPod appears in your Source pane. The iPod will mount without updating, and you can then change your preferences if you wish. (You might want to switch to manual updating, for example, if you've substantially changed your playlists in iTunes since your last update, but you would rather leave your iPod mostly as it was.)

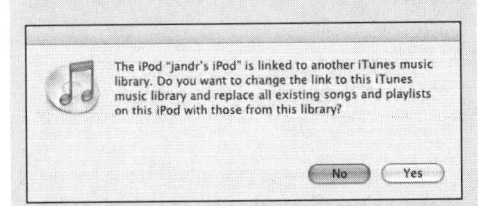

Figure 7.14 iTunes displays this window if an iPod set to do automatic updating is connected to a computer other than the one it was updated from previously.

ABOUT AUTOMATIC UPDATING

183

Manually Updating Your iPod

If you've set your iPod preferences to indicate that you don't want iTunes to automatically update your iPod (either in the window shown in Figure 7.4 or in the one in Figure 7.9), you'll have just about complete control over what's on your iPod.

To view the playlists on your iPod:

1. Click the disclosure triangle to the left of the entry for the iPod in your Source pane so that it points down.

   The playlists on your iPod are shown in the Source pane (**Figure 7.15**), indented directly below the listing for the iPod itself.

2. Click the name of any of the iPod's playlists to see its contents.

Figure 7.15 When you've specified manual updating mode, the playlists on the iPod show beneath its entry in the Source pane.

Copying Music from Multiple Libraries to Your iPod

Do you have more than one iTunes library—one at home and one at work, for example? If you want to be able to add music from both your libraries, we suggest that you start by syncing your iPod with one computer using an automatic update; but *before* you eject the iPod, switch to manual updating (refer to Figure 7.9). When you plug your iPod into the second computer, you can drag new songs and playlists to it. From then on, as long as you keep your preferences set to manual updating, there should be no problem adding songs from any computer that's running iTunes.

If you're transferring songs from both Windows and Macintosh computers, you'll have to establish the initial connection on the Windows computer. This is because the iPod needs to be formatted for Windows; a Mac can read a Windows formatted disk, but not vice versa. (Please note: Apple says that you *shouldn't* share an iPod between computers of different platforms, but we can report that we've been doing it without problems. Your mileage may vary.)

Using iTunes with Your iPod

Figure 7.16 You can drag songs to an iPod library or playlists just as if it was an iTunes library or playlist.

Why Can't I Transfer Songs from my iPod to iTunes?

By this point, you're getting used to using iTunes to drag songs from a song list and move them into playlists at will. It seems only natural to be able to drag a song from your iPod library to an iTunes playlist. Sorry. You can't do it using iTunes. Apple, in order to discourage rampant illegal copying from one library to another using the iPod as the transfer mechanism, made it impossible to copy songs from an iPod to an iTunes library.

However, there are some ways around this design limitation. (We trust you've got a good—and legal— reason for copying from your iPod to a computer!)

For one thing, the files are actually stored in an invisible folder on your iPod. If you know how to show invisible (or *hidden*) files and folders, you'll be able to see the song files on the iPod in the Finder (Mac) or in Explorer (Windows).

There are also third-party tools available that you can use to transfer files from an iPod to a computer. We've found a number at www.ipodlounge.com/downloads.php.

To add and delete songs and playlists to and from your iPod:

◆ Use any of the methods covered in Chapter 5 for manipulating playlists. (**Figure 7.16** shows an example of dragging songs from an iTunes playlist to an iPod playlist.)

After you drag items to the iPod or its playlists, the Status display informs you that iTunes is updating the iPod.

The only thing you can't do with the playlists on your iPod is drag items from them to sources outside the iPod.

You also can't drag songs to the iPod or its playlists unless they're in formats that the iPod can handle. (See the sidebar "What Types of Files Can Be Transferred to an iPod?" earlier in this chapter.)

✔ Tip

- If you don't necessarily want songs in a playlist on your iPod, you can drag songs directly to the main icon for the iPod in the Source pane. Later you can use the iPod to put the songs in playlists; see "Creating Playlists for iTunes on Your iPod" later in this chapter.

MANUALLY UPDATING YOUR IPOD

185

Creating Playlists for iTunes on Your iPod

If you have one of the newer iPods (that is, the ones with a Dock Connector port), you can create playlists directly on your iPod that can later be transferred to iTunes. This is very handy if you suddenly have the time or find the inspiration to create a spontaneous song playlist when you're not near your computer.

The method for creating playlists on your iPod, however, is not completely intuitive. If you scroll to the bottom of the iPod's Playlists screen, you'll see an On-The-Go playlist (**Figure 7.17**). You add songs to this playlist using your iPod, and then transfer the playlist back to iTunes, *so long as your iPod is set for automatic updating.* You can create only one On-the-Go playlist on your iPod at a time. (Note: You'll need to be running iPod Software version 2.1 or later and iTunes 4.1 or later to transfer On-The-Go playlists to iTunes. If you have an older scroll-wheel or touch-wheel iPod without a Dock Connector, you're out of luck, unfortunately.)

Figure 7.17 An On-The-Go playlist is always in your iPod's Playlists menu. (To add a song to it, select the song and press down on the Select button for several seconds, until the selection blinks.)

Don't See Playlists on Your iPod?

If you can't seem to find any playlists on your iPod, your settings may not be set to show them. This is easy to fix. From your iPod menu, choose Settings. From the Settings menu, choose Main Menu. From the Main Menu, select Playlists. Press the Select button so the value is set to On.

Audiobooks on an iPod

If you're interested in listening to audiobooks on your iPod, you'll be happy to know the following:

- You can see chapter marks in audiobooks, whether purchased from the iTunes Music Store or Audible.com. When playing a book, tap the Select button to display the scrub audio control. You'll now see vertical lines inside the bar (**Figure 7.18**); these represent the chapters or sections of a book. You can use the Fast Forward or Rewind button to jump from chapter to chapter. (You can't see chapter marks when you look at the same items in iTunes—at least not as of version 4.2.)

- Your iPod remembers where you stopped listening to an audiobook, so when you next play that audiobook on your iPod, it continues where you left off. When you connect to iTunes, and play the book, it also picks up where you stopped on the iPod. Update the songs on your iPod before disconnecting, and the iPod will know how far you got in iTunes.

- If you own an iPod, you can get a free one-month subscription to Audible.com! Check out www.audible.com/ipod/.

Figure 7.18 You can see chapters on an audiobook playing on the iPod.

To add songs to the On-The-Go playlist on your iPod:

1. Select a song in the iPod's All Songs menu or one of its playlists.

2. Press down on the Select button for several seconds, until the selection blinks.

   If you check your On-The-Go playlist, you'll see that it contains the song(s) you've added.

✔ Tips

- You don't have to grow old while you laboriously add songs to your iPod's On-The-Go playlist, one by one. If you like, you can add entire lists of songs to an On-The-Go playlist at one time. On your iPods' Artists, Albums, Composers, Genres, or Playlists menus, you can scroll to an item, then press the Select button for several seconds to add all the songs from the selected artist, album, composer, genre, or playlist to the On-The-Go playlist.

- It's also easy to delete an On-The-Go playlist on your iPod. To do so, go to the On-The-Go playlist in your iPod's Playlists menu and press the Select button. In the On-The-Go menu, scroll to the bottom of the list, select Clear Playlist, and press the Select button; in the Clear menu, select Clear Playlist and press the Select button.

To transfer an On-the-Go playlist to iTunes:

◆ Simply connect your iPod to your computer.

After iTunes does its automatic updating, you'll see in your Source pane an On-The-Go 1 playlist (**Figure 7.19**). As with any playlist, you can add or delete songs, as well as edit song information (see Chapter 5 for more on manipulating playlists). If you do edit your On-The-Go playlist, you'll need to then update songs (an option in the File menu) to put the edited version back on your iPod.

After you disconnect your iPod, you'll find that its On-The-Go playlist is empty, but that the On-The-Go 1 playlist is now in your list of iPod playlists (**Figure 7.20**), and it contains the songs that used to be in your iPod's On-The-Go playlist.

Each time you repeat the process of adding to an On-The-Go playlist on your iPod and then connecting to your computer, you'll find an additional On-The-Go playlist in your Source pane. These are numbered sequentially (On-The-Go 2, On-The-Go 3, and so on, as in **Figure 7.21**) as long as you haven't deleted or renamed the previous ones.

✔ Tip

■ If you have specified "Automatically update selected playlists only", when you connect your iPod to your computer, it adds an On-The-Go 1, or On-The-Go 2 (or higher) to your list of playlists (as you would expect). Since this new playlist, however, couldn't possibly be in your list of selected playlists—it's brand new—iTunes is not going to copy it back to your iPod unless you open the iPod Preferences window and check this latest On-The-Go playlist to make it one of your selected playlists.

Figure 7.19 When you connect the iPod to your computer, the On-The-Go playlist is transferred to iTunes. *This contains pointers to the same songs that were in the On-The-Go playlist on the iPod.*

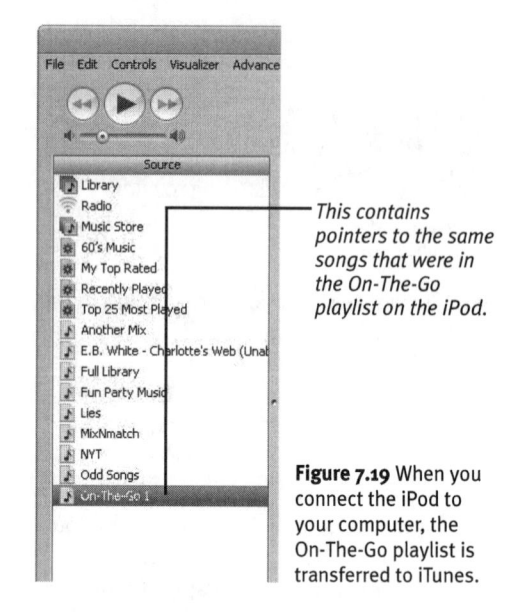

Figure 7.20 When you disconnect your iPod, the songs that used to be in the On-The-Go playlist are now in an On-The-Go 1 playlist.

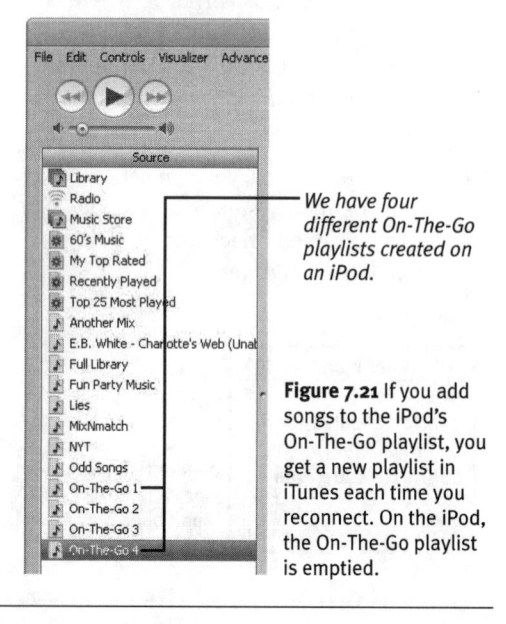

Figure 7.21 If you add songs to the iPod's On-The-Go playlist, you get a new playlist in iTunes each time you reconnect. On the iPod, the On-The-Go playlist is emptied. *We have four different On-The-Go playlists created on an iPod.*

Rating Songs for iTunes on Your iPod

There's another important task you can accomplish when you're on the road with your iPod: You can rate your songs. iTunes will transfer the rating to your library when it next does an automatic update. Take note, however: Rating songs is possible only on third-generation (Dock Connector) iPods.

To rate songs on your iPod:

1. When a song is playing (or paused), press the Select button twice.

   The screen changes to show gray bullets in place of the song progress bar.

2. Use the scroll wheel to turn the bullets into stars (**Figure 7.22**).

To transfer song ratings to iTunes:

◆ Connect your iPod (set to automatically update) to your computer.

   You'll find that the song now has the rating you applied on your iPod (**Figure 7.23**).

Figure 7.22 When a song is playing on your iPod, press the Select button twice to show the screen, then use the scroll wheel to rate a song.

Figure 7.23 The rating is transferred to your iTunes library during the next automatic update.

Chapter 7

About Other Portable MP3 Players

No devices work with iTunes quite as well as the iPod—not that that should be a surprise. But you can find several MP3 players that rival the iPod in function and cost, if not sex appeal. If you're using an alternative MP3 player, don't worry—with a little work, you can most likely still use it with iTunes. While iTunes offers some support for other MP3 players on the Mac, there's no direct support for other MP3 players in the Windows version of iTunes. But you still have several ways of getting songs from your Windows iTunes library to your MP3 player.

Transferring Songs from a Mac

On the Mac, most other MP3 players work just fine out of the box with iTunes. Once you connect one to your Mac, it appears in the Source pane (**Figure 7.24**). (If the device uses both internal and external memory, two entries may appear.) Two additional buttons may appear in the iTunes window: one that opens a window in which you pick Settings for the device, and another that you use to completely clear the contents of the device. (Some devices don't let you pick settings, so you'll see only the latter button.) You can see the device's songs in the song list, delete songs, and add songs to it by dragging MP3 songs from a library or playlist to the player's icon in the Source pane.

A few devices won't work unless you obtain additional software first. The Sony Clié (which is actually a Palm device that doubles as an MP3 player), for example, requires software called The Missing Sync, from Mark/Space. Others may require additional software that is available at the device vendor's Web site.

MP3 player is listed here.

Figure 7.24 When you connect an MP3 player (in this case, a Rio 550 MP3 player) to your Mac, iTunes recognizes the device, enabling you to drag songs and playlists to it.

Click to set options for the player.

Click to delete all the songs on the player.

Select songs located on your hard drive here.

Click to transfer to the device

Figure 7.25 Here, we've connected the Rio MP3 player to our PC. Because the Windows version of iTunes doesn't recognize non-iPod MP3 players, we're using the Rio Music Manager to select songs in the iTunes Music folder and transfer them to the Rio MP3 player. (Other MP3 players have similar software.)

Transferring Songs from a Windows Computer

In Windows, unfortunately, iTunes doesn't recognize any portable players other than the iPod.

You'll likely use the software that came with the device to grab song files from your hard drive. (To find the songs on your drive, you'll want to understand how and where iTunes stores files; see Chapter 5 for details.) An example of the software for one portable MP3 player is shown in **Figure 7.25**.

For devices that allow you to mount their memory as a disk (the Sony Clié, for one), you can drag files from the iTunes song list to the icon for the device's disk in Windows Explorer.

✔ Tip

- Don't let your computer go to sleep during a transfer to a portable MP3 Player.

Sharing Music Over a Network

8

iTunes lets you do more than just listen to your favorite songs. You can actually *share* your iTunes music library over a small local network. This might mean your home, a small business, or a segment of a large corporate network (otherwise known as a *subnet*). Sharing over a network is an easy way for family members or office mates to listen to your music collection.

The way iTunes sharing works is, in our opinion, an example of Apple software at its best. In most cases, on both Macintosh and Windows computers, no network configuration is needed. With other methods of sharing files on a network, somebody needs to do quite a bit of configuration work.

And, with iTunes sharing, you can share more than just the music *files*. Shared libraries show up in an iTunes song list, so the person accessing the share can browse, search, and sort the songs, as well as view the full range of information associated with each song (including comments). This is a lot more interesting than just sharing music files over a network!

In this chapter, we'll show you how to set up iTunes to share your music, how to access the shared libraries of other iTunes users, and how to authorize other computers to play your purchased songs. We'll end the chapter with a brief overview of firewall issues, the only thing that may complicate sharing via iTunes.

Making Your Music Available to Others

If you want to make your music available to others on your network, you need to enable sharing in iTunes.

To turn on sharing:

1. Open your Preferences window by selecting iTunes > Preferences (Mac) or Edit > Preferences (Windows); then click the Sharing tab.

2. In the Sharing tab, click to check "Share my music" (**Figure 8.1**).

3. If you want to share only selected playlists, select "Share selected playlists," and then check the playlists you want to share.

4. If you want to change the way your shared music is listed when it appears in someone else's Source pane, type the name you prefer in the "Shared name" field.

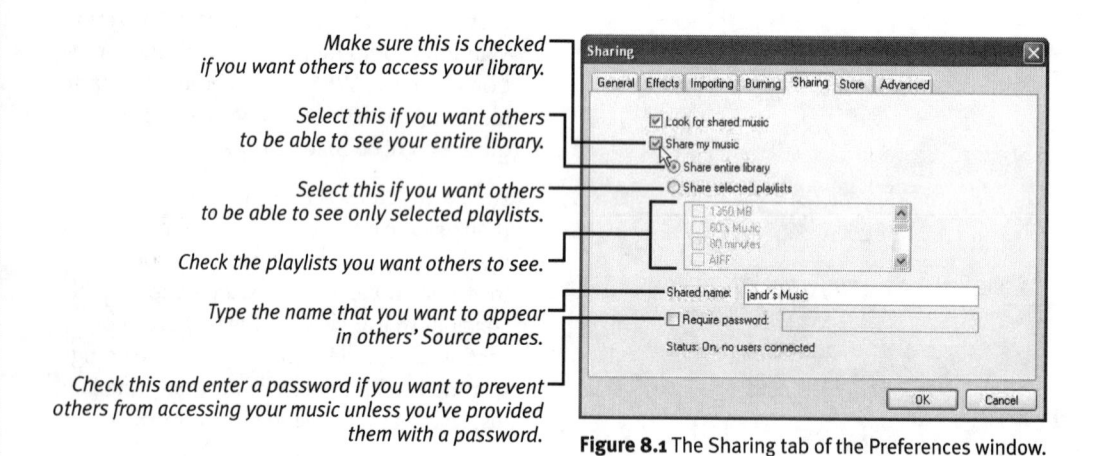

Make sure this is checked if you want others to access your library.

Select this if you want others to be able to see your entire library.

Select this if you want others to be able to see only selected playlists.

Check the playlists you want others to see.

Type the name that you want to appear in others' Source panes.

Check this and enter a password if you want to prevent others from accessing your music unless you've provided them with a password.

Figure 8.1 The Sharing tab of the Preferences window.

Sharing Music Over a Network

5. If you want people to have to type a password before they can connect to your library, select "Require password" and type a password.

6. Click OK to close the Preferences window and save your settings.

Once you turn on sharing, all computers on your local area network—or on your subnet if you're part of a large network—can see an item for your shared library in their iTunes Source pane. (See "Accessing Shared Libraries" next in this chapter.)

To turn off sharing:

◆ In your Preferences window, in the Sharing tab (refer to Figure 8.1), uncheck "Share my music."

✔ Tips

- If you want to know whether anyone is connected to your library, look at the bottom of the Preferences window's Sharing tab (refer to Figure 8.1).
- Only five computers can share your music at one time.
- You can't disconnect individual users or determine which users are connected.
- If you quit iTunes, all users are disconnected from your library, and your shared library disappears from their Source pane. (iTunes first warns you that you have connected users and asks if you want to quit; you can click No if you decide you don't want to quit, click Yes if you do want to quit, or do nothing if you want iTunes to automatically quit and disconnect those accessing your library after 20 seconds.)
- If you need to be able to determine if you're on the same subnet as another computer, check your TCP/IP settings; if the first three sets of numbers are the same (for example, 192.168.12.43 and 192.168.12.135), you're on the same subnet.

What Won't Be Shared

Not everything in your library will be accessible to others on your local network.

iTunes skips over songs purchased from the iTunes Music Store when playing songs via iTunes sharing, unless the computer is authorized to play music from the account under which the song was purchased. If you try to play a shared purchased song by double-clicking it, iTunes prompts you to authorize the computer. (See "Authorizing a Computer to Play Purchased Items" later in this chapter.)

Audiobooks purchased from the iTunes Music Store or Audible.com don't appear at all in a shared library (at least as of this writing), regardless of whether the computer accessing the share has been appropriately authorized. (The method for playing audiobooks is also covered in "Authorizing a Computer to Play Purchased Items" later in this chapter.)

Anything that iTunes considers a QuickTime movie file (including karaoke and MIDI files), as well as various obscure audio formats (such as Sound Designer and System 7 Sound), don't show up in a shared library, either (even though they work just fine when played in iTunes on the computer on which they reside).

Chapter 8

Accessing Shared Libraries

Turning on sharing so that others can access your music is nice, but iTunes is much more fun when you can access other users' shared music libraries.

To view shared libraries:

1. Look in your Source pane.

   Any shared libraries should already be visible. (The icon for a shared library is similar to that for your iTunes library and the Music Store, except that it's blue.)

   If there's one shared library on your network, you'll see it listed in your Source pane (**Figure 8.2**).

   If multiple people on your network are sharing, you'll see a Shared Music entry in your Source pane, with the different libraries listed below that (**Figure 8.3**).

2. If you don't see any shared libraries, and you know there are people on your local network who are sharing, open the Preferences window, and on the Sharing tab, make sure that "Look for shared music" is checked (**Figure 8.4**). (This is the default setting.)

This is the only shared library on this user's network.

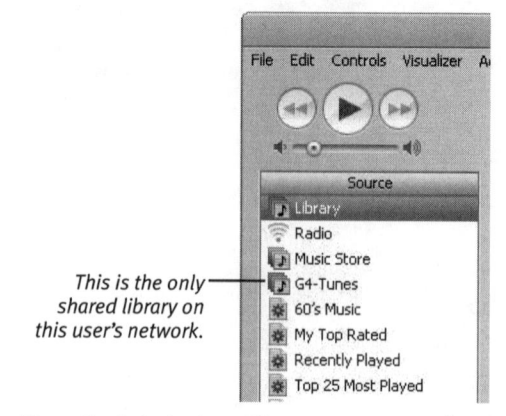

Figure 8.2 A single shared library on your network appears like this.

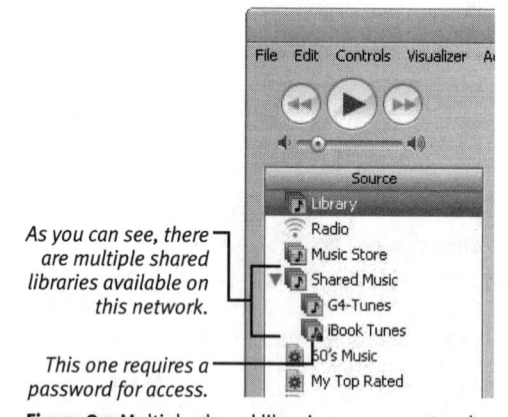

As you can see, there are multiple shared libraries available on this network.

This one requires a password for access.

Figure 8.3 Multiple shared libraries on your network make your iTunes experience much more exciting.

This needs to be checked to see others' shared libraries.

You don't have to share your music to see others' shared libraries. (But it would be a little selfish to not reciprocate if you're taking advantage of others' shared libraries, don't you think?)

Figure 8.4 If you see no shared libraries, make sure that your Sharing preferences are set to "Look for shared music."

196

Sharing Music Over a Network

Figure 8.5 When you try to connect, you may be asked for a password. The owner of the shared library will give this to you if they want you to have access.

Disclosure triangle

Figure 8.6 A disclosure triangle indicates that you've connected to a library with playlists. (The songs listed in the song list are all those that the owner of the shared library wants to share, and that are shareable.)

Figure 8.7 When you click the disclosure triangle, you see the playlists that the owner of the library has shared.

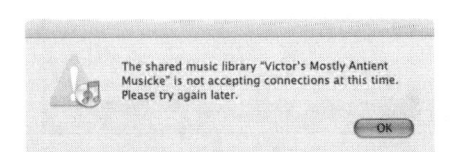

Figure 8.8 If you try to connect to a shared library but there are already five users connected (the maximum), you'll see a message like this.

To connect to a shared library:

1. Click the name of a shared library in the Source pane.

2. If the owner of the shared library has required a password, you are prompted to enter it (**Figure 8.5**). (Without the password you won't be able to get any further.)

   After a second or so, the songs in the shared library appear in your Detail pane. Assuming the shared library has playlists, a disclosure triangle appears to the left of the shared library entry (**Figure 8.6**).

   You can browse, search, or sort the shared library and play songs in it, just as you can with your own library.

To access playlists in a shared library:

1. Click the disclosure triangle next to a shared library entry in the Source pane to show the playlists in that library that are shared (**Figure 8.7**).

2. Click a playlist name to see what's in that playlist.

   You can also browse, search, and sort the playlists, and play songs from them. You can also open shared playlists in a separate window.

✔ Tips

- If there are already five users connected to a shared library when you click on it, a window appears telling you that the shared library is not accepting connections at this time (**Figure 8.8**).

- When you're browsing someone's shared iTunes library, you can select any song and get information about it (File > Get Info), but you can't change anything: you can't rate songs, edit information, or even access the artwork pane.

continues on next page

ACCESSING SHARED LIBRARIES

197

Chapter 8

- You *can* view and access streams that have been placed in a shared library or its playlists.

- You can't drag any songs from a shared library or its playlists to your own iTunes library.

- If the owner of a shared library requires a password, the icon for their library in the Source pane will have a have a tiny (*really* tiny) graphic of a locked icon (refer to figure 8.3).

- Sometimes, you'll have problems seeing or connecting to a shared library because of firewall issues. See the last section of this chapter for more information on firewalls and iTunes.

Who's Listening to My Stuff?

While iTunes 4.2 offers you the vicarious thrill of listening to other users' music over a network, there's one major flaw in this otherwise brilliant feature: You can't tell *who* is currently browsing or listening to songs in your library. If you quit iTunes while a user is connected to your library, you'll see a message informing that you that one or more users is connected. If you check the Sharing tab of your Preferences window, you can see how many users are connected. Apart from that, you have no idea which users are dipping into your music collection.

To get around this, try downloading iTunes Monitor 1.1 (`www.ebyss.net/pages/software.html`) a freeware application for Mac OS X.

When launched, iTunes Monitor displays a list of currently connected users (by hostname or IP address), and their current status, with a colored indicator (**Figure 8.9**). You can keep this window open so you don't have to keep opening the Preferences window to see how many users are connected to your library.

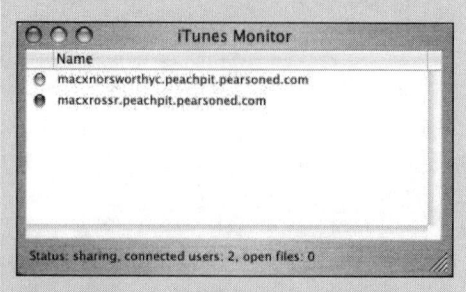

Figure 8.9 iTunes Monitor 1.1, a free download, lets you see who's connected to your iTunes library.

Sharing Music Over a Network

Figure 8.10 Click the Disconnect button at the lower right of the iTunes window to disconnect from a shared library.

Figure 8.11 Or from the Controls menu, choose the Disconnect item.

Figure 8.12 You can also use the contextual menu to disconnect.

Disconnecting from a Shared Library

Once you've clicked on a shared library in your Source pane, you stay connected to that library until you actively disconnect, or until the owner turns off sharing or quits iTunes. (Selecting your own iTunes library does *not* disconnect you from a shared library.)

Remember that a shared library maxes out at five connections at once. If you want to play nice and let somebody *else* use one of those five connections, be courteous and disconnect when you're finished listening to someone's music library.

To disconnect from a shared library:

1. In the Source pane, click the name of the library from which you want to disconnect.

2. Do one of the following:
   ▲ Click the Disconnect button in the lower-right corner of the iTunes window (**Figure 8.10**).
   ▲ From the Controls menu, choose the Disconnect item (**Figure 8.11**).
   ▲ Right-click (Windows) or Control-click (Mac) and select the Disconnect item (**Figure 8.12**).

   The disclosure triangle disappears, and your own library becomes selected in the Source pane.

   Somebody on the network is now free to take the connection you've given up.

Authorizing a Computer to Play Purchased Songs

If you've purchased songs using one computer, other computers accessing your shared library don't have access to that content unless you authorize them.

You can authorize up to two additional computers (besides your own) to play the music you have purchased using a particular account. Once you authorize a computer for an account, that computer is authorized to play *all* the music purchased with that account. (There is no per song authorization.)

Authorization, however, is not necessarily permanent; any computer you authorize can be deauthorized (see next section), allowing you to authorize yet another computer.

Figure 8.13 When you try to play a purchased song that hasn't been authorized for the computer you're trying to play from, this window appears. Enter the username and password for the account that was used to purchase the song.

To authorize another computer to play songs you've purchased from the iTunes Music Store:

1. Working at the computer you want to authorize, make sure it's connected to the Internet.

2. In iTunes, connect to your shared library, and try to play any one of your purchased songs. (Double-clicking the song will work, though you can use any other method of playing.)

   A window appears, requesting a password for the account under which the song was purchased (**Figure 8.13**).

3. Enter the password for the account you used to purchase the music.

4. Click Authorize.

   A window appears for a second or so, indicating that iTunes is accessing the Music Store; the song then begins playing.

   You have authorized the computer to play any songs purchased using your account.

Multiple Users on One Computer

If your computer has multiple users (that is, individuals that access the system with separate accounts), all users will have access to iTunes Music Store items purchased via an account that has been authorized for that computer. In other words, authorization is per computer, not per user account.

For Windows users, however, this is not the case with Audible.com purchases; each user account must be authorized separately. (Oddly enough, Mac users with separate accounts on the same computer, *can* access Audible.com content without multiple authorizations.)

Sharing Music Over a Network

✔ Tips

- It's a really bad idea to give your password to someone else so that they can enter it in the authorization window—unless you *really* trust that person. They'll have full access to your account and will be able to purchase songs, possibly running up quite a bill on your credit card.

- The window in which you enter your account name and password to authorize a computer (refer to Figure 8.13) contains a Preview button. If you click this button, the iTunes Music Store opens to the album page in the store that allows you to preview or purchase the song (just in case you'd rather not use one of your authorizations on this particular computer).

Authorizing a Computer to Play Audiobooks

Although you can't currently share audiobook content via iTunes sharing, it's still possible to authorize another computer to play the content. To do so, you'll need to copy the file for the audiobook to the computer you want to authorize. (You can do this by burning the file to a data CD or putting it on removable media, such as a Zip disk, and bringing the media to the computer you want to authorize. Or you can copy the file over a network, or email it.)

Once you've placed a copy of the file on that computer, drag it to your iTunes library, (**Figure 8.14**) or from the iTunes File menu choose Add to Library (Mac) or Add File to Library (Windows). (On a Mac, you can also double-click the file in the Finder to have iTunes try to open it.) A window appears in which you are requested to enter your user name and password (**Figure 8.15**); if you do as requested, the audiobook will be added to your library.

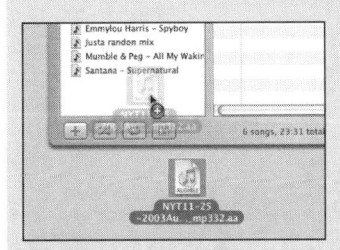

Figure 8.14 Once you copy an audiobook file to another computer, you can drag the file to your iTunes library.

Figure 8.15 iTunes prompts you for the account name and password if you haven't already authorized the computer to play content purchased by the owner of the audiobook. (You have to first copy the file to the computer; iTunes sharing won't work.)

Deauthorizing Computers for Your Account

You may decide you no longer want a particular computer to be authorized to play your purchased music. This may be because you are selling the computer, or simply because you need for another computer to have one of your three authorizations.

To deauthorize a computer:

1. Working at the computer you want to deauthorize, make sure you're connected to the Internet, then open iTunes.

2. From the Advanced menu, choose Deauthorize Computer (**Figure 8.16**).

   A window appears in which you can select Deauthorize Computer for Apple Account or Deauthorize Computer for Audible Account (**Figure 8.17**).

3. Select whichever type of account you want to deauthorize.

4. Click Finish (Windows) or OK (Mac).

5. In the Deauthorize Computer window that appears, provide your iTunes Music Store account information (**Figure 8.18**) or Audible User Name and password and click OK.

   A window appears for a few seconds indicating that iTunes is accessing the Music Store or Audible.com, and then you'll see a window indicating that the computer has been successfully deauthorized (**Figure 8.19**).

6. Click OK.

   You won't be able to use this computer to listen to songs purchased from your account unless you authorize it again.

Figure 8.16 From the Advanced menu, choose Deauthorize Computer.

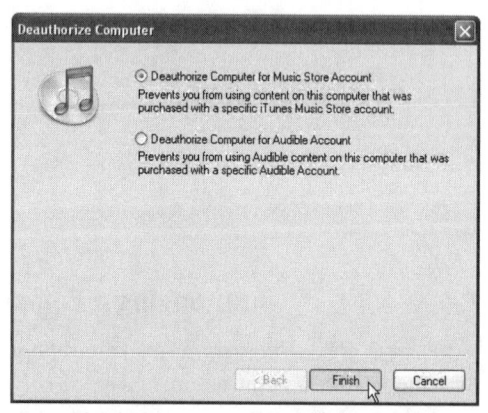

Figure 8.17 Select the type of account for which you want to deauthorize, and click Finish. (Or click OK on a Mac.)

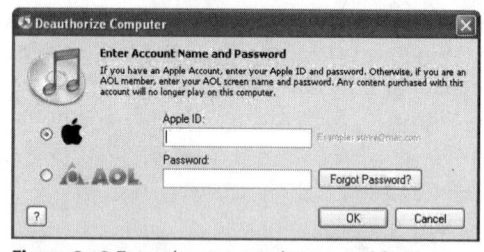

Figure 8.18 Enter the name and password for the account you want to deauthorize, and click OK.

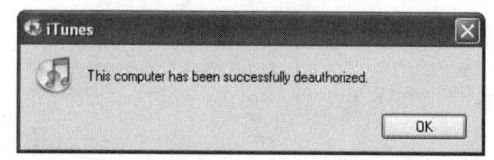

Figure 8.19 iTunes tells you that deauthorization was successful.

Dealing with Firewalls

Due to the increased incidence of bad behavior on the Internet (that is, by hackers accessing computers other than their own), it's a good idea to set up a *firewall*, a set of programs that protects your computer from unauthorized network access. This firewall, however, may prevent you from sharing your library with others.

If sharing is important to you, you can set up a port that will let iTunes traffic through, without unduly compromising your security.

This issue arises mainly with Windows computers, as Mac OS X is set up by default to let iTunes traffic through.

Figure 8.20 Mac OS X system preferences are usually set to allow iTunes traffic through the firewall.

To ensure that iTunes can get through your firewall (Mac):

- In the Sharing pane of your System Preferences, click the Firewall button and make sure iTunes Music Sharing is checked (**Figure 8.20**).

To let iTunes traffic through your firewall (Windows):

- You need to open up port 3689 for TCP traffic and port 5353 for UDP traffic.

  If you have a system administrator, pass this information on to them and let them do it.

  If it's all up to you, you're going to have know (or learn) how to configure your own firewall. XP users can read a tech note that Apple provides at http://docs.info.apple.com/article.html?artnum=93396. (**Figure 8.21** gives you an idea of the many windows you may have to pass through in order to do this on XP.)

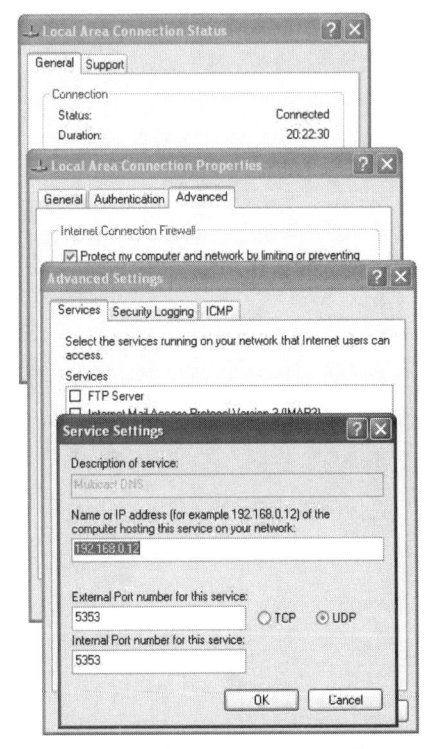

Figure 8.21 Windows XP users can configure their firewalls, too. Complete instructions can be found at http://docs.info.apple.com/article.html?artnum=93396.

✔ Tip

- After you configure your Firewall to let iTunes traffic through, sharing may still not work until you close iTunes and reopen it.

iTunes in Your iLife (Mac Only)

A

Apple designed its consumer-level media applications— iTunes. iPhoto, iMovie, iDVD, and the new GarageBand, collectively known as *iLife*—to work together. From an iTunes perspective, this means that you can use music from your iTunes library in a slideshow assembled in iPhoto, in a video made with iMovie, or in a DVD produced with iDVD. And, with GarageBand, you can export musical masterpieces you create directly to your iTunes library.

In this appendix, we'll briefly cover only the areas in which iTunes overlaps with each of these tools. For the most part, we'll be discussing the latest versions of these tools, those that are included in the iLife '04 package. If you bought a Mac after mid-January '04, you're in luck—the iLife '04 applications came pre-installed on your machine. Otherwise, you can purchase iLife '04 from the Apple store (http://store.apple.com) and in retail computer stores for $49.

A great resource for learning much, much more about all of these tools and how they all interact with each other is Jim Heid's *The Macintosh iLife '04* (Peachpit Press, April 2004).

Appendix A

iTunes and iPhoto 4

Using the photos you have in iPhoto, you can create a slideshow to share with friends and family. Of course, you'll want a soundtrack for that slideshow, and what better one to use than a song or playlist from your iTunes Library? iPhoto makes this easy.

To use an iTunes song in an iPhoto slideshow:

1. In iPhoto, click the Slideshow button (**Figure A.1**).

   The Slideshow window appears.

2. Click the Music tab at the top of the window, if not already selected.

3. In the Source pop-up menu, select iTunes Library.

   All the songs in your iTunes library appear in the song list below the pop-up menu (**Figure A.2**).

Slideshow button

Figure A.1 Click the Slideshow button in iPhoto to pick settings for a slideshow.

Click to play the selected song (or the first song in the list if none is selected, or the last song you played). The button changes to a Stop button, which you can click to stop the music from playing.

Click any column head to sort by that column.

When done specifying options (including a song to play, of course), click this so iPhoto will remember your settings.

Music tab

Choose a playlist from this pop-up menu. (Or select iTunes Library if you want a list of all songs in your library.)

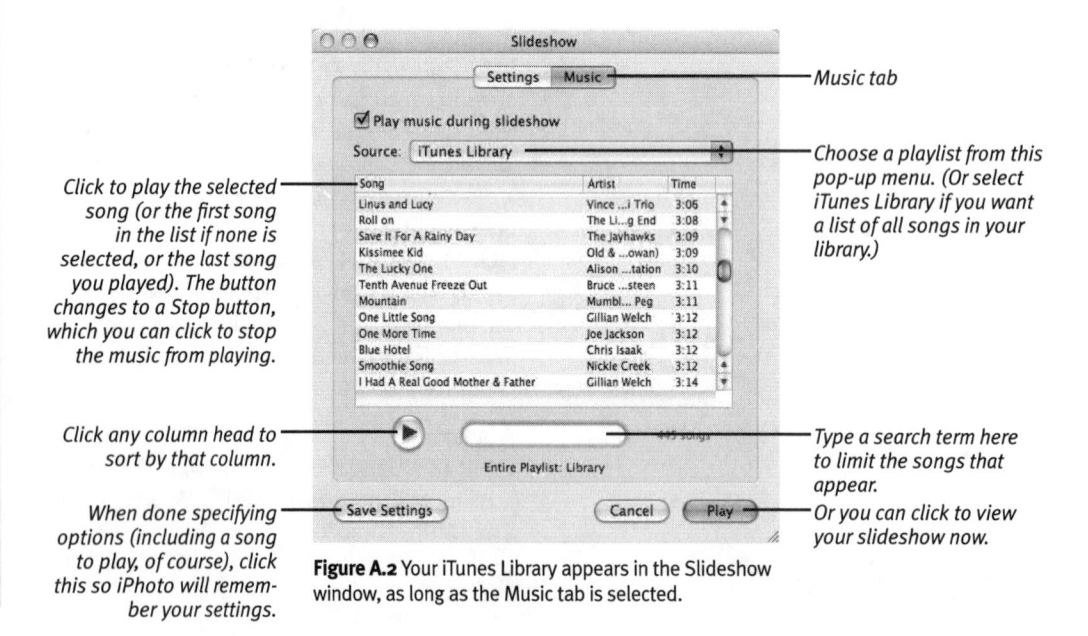

Type a search term here to limit the songs that appear.

Or you can click to view your slideshow now.

Figure A.2 Your iTunes Library appears in the Slideshow window, as long as the Music tab is selected.

Figure A.3 You can limit the songs that appear by selecting a single playlist.

4. From the list, select a song you want to use.

   To help locate the song you want, you can click column headings to sort by Song, Artist, or Time. In addition, you can reverse the order of the sort by clicking on the selected column head and you can reorder the columns by dragging the column heads.

   You can double-click a song or click the button with the triangle icon (not the button labeled *Play*) to listen to whatever you've selected, to make sure it's what you want.

   To narrow the number of songs showing, you can use a search function that operates much like iTunes's search function (though it searches only in the Song and Artist columns), or you can pick from any of your iTunes library's playlists (**Figure A.3**).

5. Click the Play button if you want to view your Slideshow with your iTunes music now; if not, click Save Settings.

✓ **Tip**

- If the song you select from your iTunes Library to put into an iPhoto slideshow is a purchased one, you'll find that if you export the slideshow as QuickTime, the resulting movie can be played successfully only on a computer that is authorized to play that music. If someone tries to play the slideshow movie on a different computer—perhaps because you've emailed it to them or copied it over a network—QuickTime will prompt them to open iTunes in order to authorize the computer. If they don't authorize the computer, the slideshow will play without the audio.

Appendix A

To use an iTunes playlist in an iPhoto slideshow:

1. In iTunes, create a playlist containing the songs you want to use, arranged in the order you'd like them to play in your slideshow. (See "Reordering the Songs in a Playlist " in Chapter 5 if you don't remember how to do this.)

2. Follow steps 1 and 2 on the previous page to open the Slideshow window to the Music pane.

3. Select a playlist from the Source pop-up menu (refer to Figure A.3).

4. If you click any individual song in the song list—perhaps to play it in order to remind yourself of the beat or the mood—make sure to re-select the playlist in the Source pop-up menu. (Otherwise, only the selected song will be used.)

5. Click the Play button if you want to view your Slideshow with your iTunes music now; if not, click Save Settings.

✔ **Tips**

- If you want to share an iPhoto slideshow with background music, you can export it as a QuickTime movie. Choose File > Export and then click the QuickTime tab. Make sure that "Add currently selected music to movie" is checked (**Figure A.4**). You can burn the exported QuickTime movie to a CD, email it, or put it on the Web.

- If you'd like to know more about iPhoto, we suggest Adam Engst's *iPhoto 4 for Mac OS X: Visual QuickStart Guide* (Peachpit Press, April 2004).

Figure A.4 Choose File > Export and click the QuickTime tab to show this window. Make sure to check "Add currently selected music to movie" so the song or playlist you selected in the Slideshow window is included in the exported movie.

Still Using iPhoto 2 or iDVD 3?

If you're using iPhoto 2 or iDVD3, there's no option to use a playlist in your slideshow. If you want to string together multiple songs for use in a slideshow, you *can* do it using older iLife tools, though the technique is a bit roundabout. Using iMovie 3, access your iTunes Library and drag songs into the iMovie timeline so they play one after another (see next page). Then, from iMovie's File menu, choose Export, select QuickTime Movie, and then select Expert Settings. Here's the important part, assuming you want to keep things simple: In the Export window, choose Sound to AIFF. The exported file can be added to your iTunes library, where it will then be accessible for use in iPhoto or iDVD.

Another option, equally as roundabout, uses only iTunes: You burn the songs you want to an audio CD, then you reimport the tracks into iTunes, joining them (by choosing Advanced > Join CD Tracks) to create a single new track.

Our opinion? Get iLife '04. It'll save you lots of time.

iTunes in your iLife (Mac Only)

iTunes and iMovie 4

Want to add a little professionalism to your iMovie? Your iTunes tracks can become background music in your iMovie video production. (Of course, this assumes that your movie is for personal use. If you plan to submit it to Sundance, make sure you've secured permissions for any copyrighted music tracks.)

To use iTunes songs in an iMovie project:

1. In iMovie, click the Audio button to expose your entire iTunes Library (**Figure A.5**).

    Just as in iPhoto, you can sort, search and limit what's shown to individual playlists. You can also play songs by clicking the Play button or double-clicking the song.

continues on next page

- Choose a playlist from this pop-up menu.
- Click any column head to sort by that column.
- Song list; double-click to play a song.
- Type a search term here.
- Click to add the selected song at the playhead.
- Click to play the selected song (or the first song in the list if none is selected, or the last song you played). The button becomes highlighted in blue; click it to stop the music from playing.
- Audio button (Shows your iTunes library.)

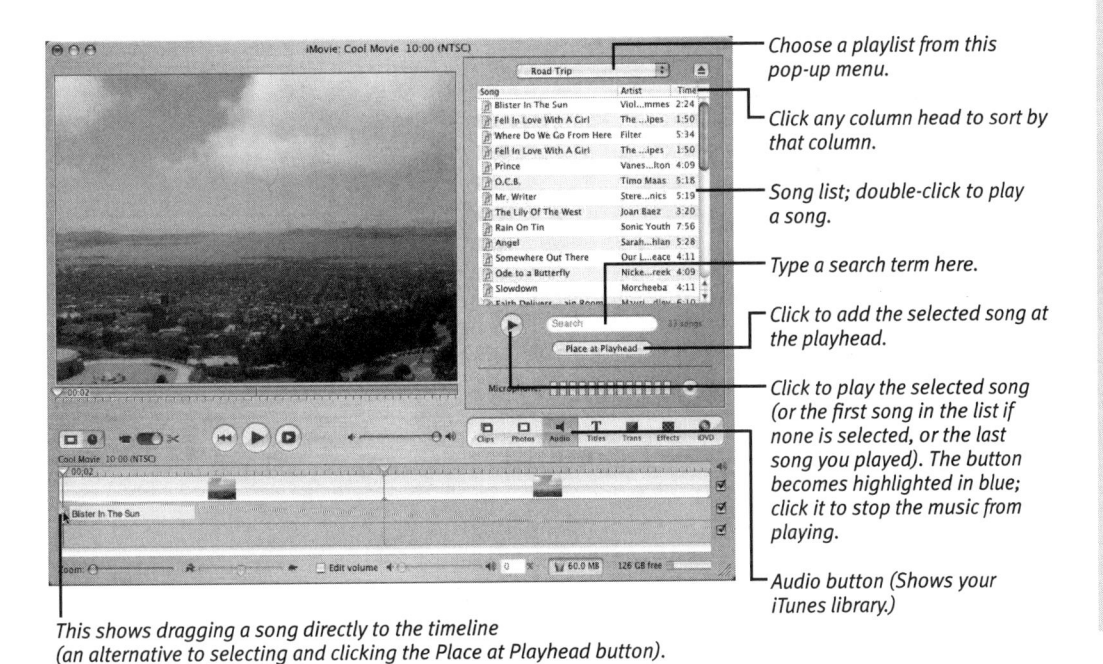

This shows dragging a song directly to the timeline (an alternative to selecting and clicking the Place at Playhead button).

Figure A.5 The iMovie window after you've clicked the Audio button.

209

Appendix A

2. Position the playhead in the timeline where you want the song to begin and do one of the following:
   - Drag a song to the timeline.
   - Select a song and click the Place at Playhead button.

3. Repeat step 2 for additional songs you want to use.

   You can edit the audio you've added in various ways, including fading audio in and out (**Figure A.6**).

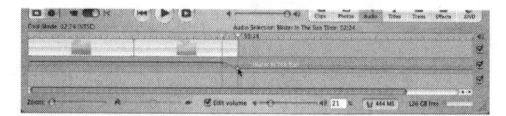

Figure A.6 iMovie provides some sound editing features, like changing the volume of specific segments of the audio.

✔ Tips

- To export your iMovie 4 project to QuickTime, choose File > Share and then click QuickTime at the top of the sheet that appears. The exported movie contains your chosen song mixed in with any other audio (for example, from the video you've included); the final sound track is compressed according to the settings chosen in the pop-up menu (**Figure A.7**).

- Since iMovie compresses audio when it creates a QuickTime movie, you're better off using uncompressed songs from your iTunes Library, if you have any. A Smart Playlist in iTunes in which you specify a condition of "Kind is AIFF" could help you quickly access clips that meet this requirement.

- Check out *iMovie 4 and iDVD 4 for Mac OS X: Visual QuickStart Guide* (April 2004), by Adam Engst.

Figure A.7 The format you choose here determines how the audio is compressed.

210

iTunes in your iLife (Mac Only)

iTunes and iDVD 4

In iDVD, you can add a little polish to your DVD by using iTunes songs either as background music for a menu or as a sound track for a slideshow.

To set an iTunes song or playlist to play when a menu is showing:

1. In iDVD, display the menu for which you'd like background music.

2. Click the Motion button at the bottom of the iDVD window, so that it becomes highlighted green.

3. If the Customize drawer is not open, click the Customize button to open the drawer (**Figure A.8**).

4. Click the Media button at the top of the Customize drawer to show iDVD's Media pane.

5. From the pop-up menu at the top of this window, choose Audio to show your iTunes library.

   The way in which your library is displayed is slightly different than the interface for selecting audio in iPhoto and iMovie: Playlists appear in a field above the song list rather than in a pop-up menu.

6. Make sure the playlist or song you want to use is visible.

   As with iPhoto and iMovie, you can use the Search function, sort by a particular column, and pick a playlist from which you can select an individual song.

7. Drag the playlist or song to the menu area of the main iDVD window, and then release your mouse button when the menu area is selected (that is, has a blue border around it) and a plus sign (+) shows as part of the pointer.

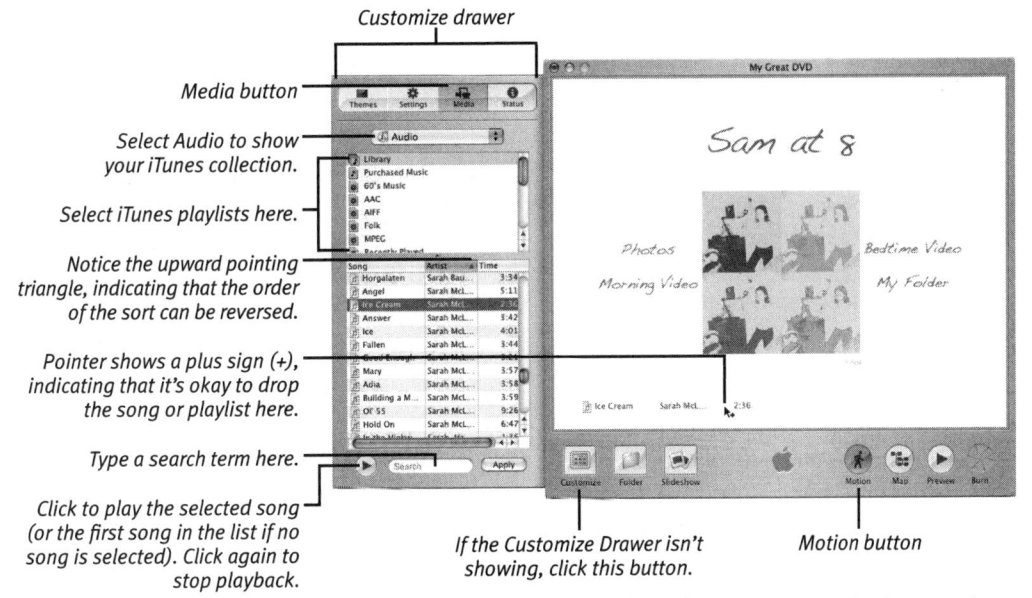

Figure A.8 Drag iTunes songs or playlists from iDVD's Customize drawer to the menu area to set music to play whenever the menu shows.

211

Appendix A

To set an iTunes song or playlist to play during an iDVD slideshow:

1. With the Customize drawer showing your iTunes library (see steps 3, 4, and 5 on the previous page), and the slideshow editor open, drag a song or playlist to the Audio well of iDVD's slideshow editor (**Figure A.9**).

   A document icon appears in the Audio well (**Figure A.10**). The icon matches the icon of the song file as it appears in the Finder; most often this will be an iTunes document icon.

2. In the Slide Duration pop-up menu (**Figure A.11**), specify a length of time for each slide to appear, or select Fit to Audio (which divides the length of your songs by the number of photos in order to determine how long to show each slide).

✔ Tips

- Do you see the bar dividing the playlists from the songs in the Customize drawer (refer to Figure A.9)? Click and drag that bar up, and you'll find that the playlists field disappears; in its place is a pop-up menu from which you can choose a playlist.

- To replace the song or playlist you've dragged to the menu area or to the Audio well in the slideshow editor, just drag a new song to that same location.

- To delete the audio from a slideshow, drag the icon out of the audio well.

- To delete the audio you've assigned to a menu, click the Settings button at the top of the Customize drawer, and drag the icon our of the audio well that's in that pane.

Figure A.9 To use a song for a slideshow, you must first drag it to the Audio well.

Figure A.10 Once you've added a song, a document icon appears in the Audio well.

Figure A.11 Select Fit to Audio if you want the slideshow to be the same length as the song or playlist you have dragged to the Audio well.

iTunes in your iLife (Mac Only)

iTunes and GarageBand

GarageBand, announced in January 2004, is an application that allows you to create music. It's essentially a recording studio in which you can mix prerecorded instrumental loops, your own recorded music, or music you input via MIDI keyboard.

GarageBand's primary interaction with iTunes is different from the other iLife applications in that it contributes *to* your iTunes library rather than borrowing *from* it. (Once a song created in GarageBand is in your iTunes library, it's accessible to the rest of your iLife apps, of course.)

You'll typically want to specify your preferences for how your GarageBand creation appears in iTunes. Then it's a single step to export to iTunes.

To specify song information for iTunes:

1. From the GarageBand application menu, choose Preferences (**Figure A.12**).

2. In the Preferences window, click Export to switch to the Song and Playlist Information pane (**Figure A.13**).

3. Type the name for the playlist in which you want iTunes to place your song, a composer name (probably yours), and an album name.

    The playlist name you provide can be an existing one or a new one that you want iTunes to create specifically to contain your GarageBand songs. The composer name will be used as both composer name and artist name when the song appears in iTunes.

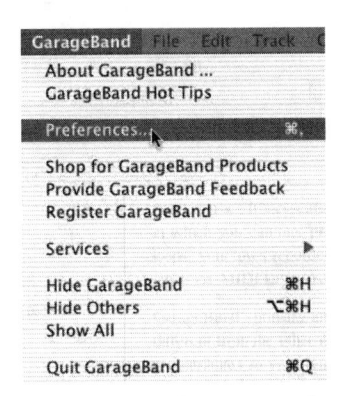

Figure A.12 From the GarageBand menu, choose Preferences.

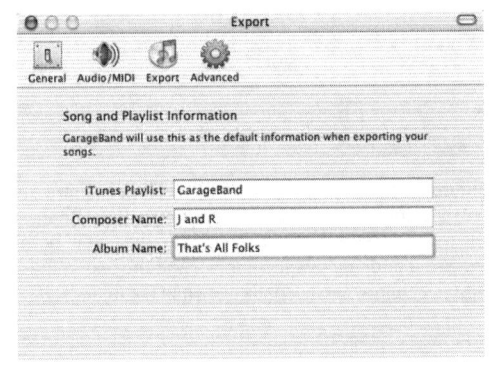

Figure A.13 In the GarageBand Preferences window, click Export to show this pane in which you specify how you want your exported GarageBand creations to appear in iTunes.

213

Appendix A

To export a GarageBand song to iTunes:

◆ From the File menu choose Export to iTunes (**Figure A.14**).

When you next look at your iTunes library, you should find the song in the playlist you specified in the GarageBand Preferences window (refer to Figure A.13); the text in the Composer and Artist columns should match what you entered as composer, and the text in the Album column should match what you entered as album (**Figure A.15**).

✔ Tip

■ You can also drag an MP3, WAV, or AIFF song from your iTunes song list to the GarageBand window; this allows you edit the song with GarageBand or mix it with other audio.

Figure A.14 When you've created a masterpiece (or not), choose File > Export to iTunes.

Figure A.15 The song appears in your iTunes library as you specified in the Preferences window. (Note that the name of the playlist the song is in, the text in both the Artist and Composer columns, and the text in the Album column match what's shown in Figure A.13).

214

AppleScripts for iTunes (Mac Only)

By this point, this book should have made you something of an iTunes power user. If you're a Mac user, you can take it a step further by harnessing the power of AppleScript.

AppleScript is a relatively easy-to-use, English-like scripting language. You can use AppleScript commands to control your computer, accomplishing many of the things you can do with menu commands and buttons, but much faster and more efficiently.

While you can certainly write your own AppleScripts, you don't have to. Others have already done this, and are willing to share these scripts with you at no or low cost. Because the scripts are already written, you don't need to know a thing about the AppleScript language; you simply run the existing scripts.

Why would you want to use AppleScripts in iTunes? Because they reduce the number of steps required to complete a task. For example, one script switches to a new encoder, converts a song for you, and then switches back to your default encoder. Other scripts do things that iTunes doesn't do, such as searching Google for an image for artwork.

In this Appendix, we'll explain how to find and install AppleScripts for iTunes, and then we'll give a few examples.

Finding and Using AppleScripts for iTunes

Anybody can write and distribute AppleScripts, but there's one site that provides the largest and most up-to-date collection of AppleScripts for iTunes: Doug's AppleScripts for iTunes (www.malcolmadams.com/itunes). Doug Adams, the master of the site and an accomplished scripter, has written a good number of these scripts, but many have been contributed by other individuals.

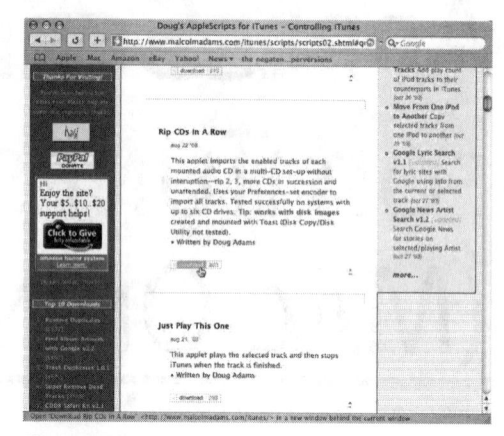

Figure B.1 You can download individual scripts from Doug's AppleScripts for iTunes site, a veritable gold mine of handy scripts for all your iTunes needs.

To download and install scripts from Doug's AppleScripts for iTunes site:

1. If you don't already have a Scripts folder in the iTunes folder of the Library folder of your Home folder (in other words, look in Home/Library/iTunes), create one.

    We'll call this the *iTunes Scripts* folder.

2. Making sure that you're connected to the Internet, navigate your Web browser to www.malcolmadams.com/itunes.

3. Browse or search the Web site to find a script you like, then click the download link to download it (**Figure B.1**).

4. Repeat step 3 for additional scripts you think will be useful.

    The files are downloaded to your hard drive. These are StuffIt *archives*—files compressed with a StuffIt file compression utility—and they should expand automatically after you download them.

5. Locate the downloaded files.

    For each expanded archive, you'll probably find a number of files, one of which is the actual script, and the rest of which are supporting files, such as a read-me file and installation instructions.

AppleScripts for iTunes (Mac Only)

Figure B.2 Once a script is installed in the iTunes Scripts folder, it appears in the Scripts menu in iTunes.

6. Drag the downloaded scripts into the iTunes Scripts folder (see step 1).

   In iTunes, you'll see a Script menu (denoted by a little scroll icon; see **Figure B.2**); when you click it, you'll see the scripts you've installed.

✔ Tip

- If you find other Web sites with scripts you want, you'll download the scripts and put them in your iTunes Scripts folder. The only thing that may differ from your experience of getting scripts from Doug Adams's site is that they may not be compressed with StuffIt; the Web site from which you download should explain what, if anything, you'll need in order to open what you've downloaded.

To run a script:

1. When you download a script, read the accompanying read-me file to find out what it does, and what, if anything, you need to do before running it.

   This typically means selecting a song or playlist in iTunes.

2. Choose the script from the Script menu (refer to Figure B.2).

3. Follow the instructions that appear, enter the requested information, or make requested selections if any.

   The precise actions required vary depending on the script.

✔ Tips

- You can also put scripts in the Library/iTunes/Scripts folder of your computer, if you want them available to all users of the computer.

- If you don't see a newly added script in your Script menu in iTunes, check to make sure you've dragged it to the right folder. If you still don't see the script, try quitting iTunes and reopening the program.

Different Kinds of AppleScripts

In the world of AppleScripts, you'll encounter three kinds of scripts. Some are *applets*, little applications you run by double-clicking them. Others are *droplets*, onto which you drag files. Still others are *Script menu scripts*, which you choose from a menu.

The vast majority of scripts you'll find for iTunes are Scripts menu scripts, and you access them as shown in Figure B.2. A few are applets; while you can double-click these in the Finder to run them, it's usually more convenient to access them from the Scripts menu. There are virtually no droplets in the collections of iTunes AppleScripts that we've found.

217

Appendix B

Some Cool Scripts

Here are summaries of a few of the more than 250 scripts at Doug's AppleScript for iTunes site that we've found particularly useful or just plain fun. Of course, we can't cover them all, there are lots of scripts that we're not mentioning here, for example, that help you manage your library (by locating or getting rid of either duplicate songs or songs for which no file can be found, or by automatically editing song names and artist names). Make sure to check the site yourself!

Find Album Artwork with Google v2.2

This script performs a Google image search using the selected song's album and artist info. With the results shown in your Web browser (**Figure B.3**), you can use any of the techniques described in Chapter 2 to add this artwork to your iTunes songs.

Google Lyric Search v1.1

This script searches Google for the lyrics of the selected song. If it finds the lyrics for the song, you may want to copy some of that text (up to about 256 characters) and paste it into the song's Comments field (**Figure B.4**).

Remove Artwork 2.0

This can be handy if you have a lot of songs with artwork and now find yourself with a limited amount of storage space—perhaps you want to free up more space on your iPod? Use this script to delete artwork from all (or just selected) tracks in the selected playlist. (The artwork can be as much as 100 kilobytes for each song; that adds up when you're talking about thousands of songs!)

Figure B.3 Here, we selected a song in iTunes, then ran the Find Album Artwork With Google script. Who knew one could find so many Carlos Santana images?

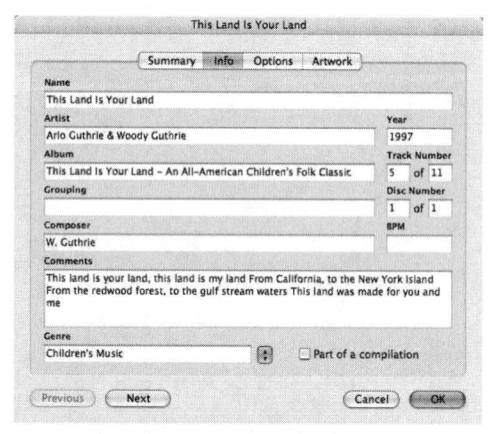

Figure B.4 Add lyrics you find with Google Lyric Search to the song's Comments field.

AppleScripts for iTunes (Mac Only)

Figure B.5 Choose Quick Convert, and pick a converter. This script saves you from the monotony of having to access the Preferences window to choose an encoder every time you want to convert a song to a different audio file format.

Quick Convert

If you find yourself converting a bunch of songs from one audio format to another, and you don't stick to a single encoder, you may be getting frustrated with all the steps involved—having to first open the Preferences window, select the encoder, close it, and then choose the Convert menu—every time you want to pick a new encoder. Instead, use this script to convert all or just the selected tracks of the selected playlist using your choice of available encoders (**Figure B.5**).

iTunes Music Store Player

We think of this as our own 30-second radio station. It plays the previews showing in an iTunes Music Store song list, one after another. The more songs in the list, the longer it will play. For example, in the store you might click Browse, then choose Charts from the Genre list, then Billboard Hot 100 and finally a year (say, 1980). Then, from your Script menu, choose musicStorePlayer\cP; this applet—we don't know why its name doesn't match the name of the download—plays the Music Store's 30-second preview from *each* of the songs in the Billboard list for your selected year. Go ahead and work on something else with those previews playing as background music. If you like something you hear, feel free to switch back to iTunes and make a purchase. If you aren't logged in to the Music Store, it will ask you for a username and password every so often.

SOME COOL SCRIPTS

219

INDEX

A

AAC (Advanced Audio Coding) file format, 28–29
   CD-quality sound, 157
   converting songs to different audio format, 40–41
   media purchased from Music Store, 113
   QuickTime and iTunes, relationship, 9
   transferring media to iPods, 179
accounts (Music Store)
   managing, 121–122
   passwords, 107
   purchase preference settings, 109
   signing in/out, 108
   with/without Apple IDs or AOL screen names, 106–107
Advanced Audio Coding. *See* AAC
Advanced tab, Preferences, 18
   shuffling albums, 65
   streaming buffer sizes, 67
AIFF (Audio Interchange File Format), 28, 30
   CD-quality sound, 157
   converting songs to different audio format, 40–41
   file extensions (.aif, .aiff, .aifc)
      supported for importing into iTunes, 37
      transferring media to iPods, 179
album page (Music Store), 90–91
allowances, (Music Store)
   giving, 119–120
   cancelling, 122
alltheweb Web site, 47
Amazon Web site
   album artwork, 47
   Free Music Download area, 38
annotations, QuickTime movies, 36

AOL screen names (Music Store), 106–107
Apple IDs (Music Store), 106–107
AppleScripts, Doug's AppleScripts for iTunes
   downloading/installing, 218–219
   Find Album Artwork with Google v2.2, 46, 218
   Google Lyric Search v1.1, 218
   Remove Artwork 2.0, 218
archiving songs, 168–169
artist page (Music Store), 92–93
artwork
   adding to songs
      by dragging/dropping, 44–45
      with Information window, 45–47
      sources, 47
   viewing with songs, 62–63
Audible Web site
   Audible Book (.aa) file format
      supported for importing into iTunes, 37
      transferring media to iPods, 179
   downloading books and subscriptions, 43
   inability to burn downloaded files to MP3 CDs, 163
   iTunes Music Store
      compression issues, 103
      volume of available media, 97
   listening to audiobooks on iPods, 187
   media not sharable on iTunes, 195
   using iPod with iTunes, 176
audio CDs
   burning CDs, 156
      preparations, 158–159
      process, 160–161
   importing into libraries
      all songs, 21–23
      creating playlists simultaneously, 132
      individual songs, 24–25
      joining tracks as one song, 25

Index

audio effects adjustments, 78
audio files
    adding links to Internet audio, 42–43
    adding to libraries from computers, 35–36
    downloading
        books and subscriptions, 43
        for fees, 38
        for free, 38–39
    importing, Musicmatch Jukebox files (Windows), 37
    MP3 streams *versus* MP3 files, 42
Audio Interchange File Format. *See* AIFF
audiobooks
    Audible Book (.aa), *versus* iTunes Music Store, 97
    authorizing media for sharing, 200–201
    downloading, 43
    in iTunes Music Store, 101-103
    listening to on iPods, 187
    media not available for sharing on iTunes, 195
    number available, 97
authorized play of purchased music (Music Store), 111
    sharing music, 195, 200–201

B

backup system, library, 170
Billboard Charts feature (Music Store), 97
BMP format, adding as iTunes artwork, 45
books. *See* audiobooks
Breen, Christopher, 173
browsing
    Browser pane, customizing, 68
    library, 50-51
        hiding/showing Browser, 50
    songs in Music Store, 94–95
burning CDs
    audio CDs, 156
        preparations, 158–159
        printing song list, 160
        process, 160–161
    blank disc purchase guidelines, 157
    CD-quality sound, 157
    data CDs or DVDs, 156
        archiving playlist songs, 168–169
        copying files back to iTunes library, 169–170
    disc care guidelines, 172
    gaps between songs, 159
    guidelines, 170–171
    MP3 CDs, 156
        preparations, 162–163
        process, 166–167

    rechecking/converting song format, 164–165
    purchasing burners, 155
    restrictions for purchased music, 161
    supported burners, 154
Burning tab, Preferences, 18
buying media
    Music Store
        with 1-Click, 110–111
        accounts, 106–109
        accounts, managing, 121–122
        allowances, 119–120
        authorized play, 111
        customer service, 115
        file formats of purchased media, 113
        gift certificates, 114–118
        preference settings, 109
        shopping carts, 112–113
    with new Macs, 5
    restrictions for burning CDs, 161
BuyMusic Web site, 38

C

CDDB (Compact Disc Database), importing song data, 23, 124
CDs. *See* audio CDs
Celebrity Playlists feature (Music Store), 97
channel settings, encoders, 33
Cheat Sheet (iTunes) Web site, 83
Check for iTunes Updates, Help menu (Windows), 6
Clean labels (Music Store), 100
Clutter Web site, 46
Compact Disc Database (CDDB), importing data from, 23, 124
consolidating songs on hard drive, 151
Crossfade playback, 25
current song, 58-60
customer service (Music Store), 115

D

data CDs or DVDs, burning, 156
    archiving playlist songs, 168–169
    copying files back to iTunes library, 169–170
deep links, 104
disk images, 11
Doug's AppleScripts for iTunes
    downloading/installing, 218–219
        Find Album Artwork with Google v2.2, 46, 218
        Google Lyric Search v1.1, 218
        Remove Artwork 2.0, 218

Index

dragging/dropping
    artwork to songs, 44–45
    audio files from computer to library, 35

E

Effects tab, Preferences, 18
EMusic Web site, 38
encoding formats
    AAC (Advanced Audio Coding), 28–29
        custom settings, 32–33
    AIFF (Audio Interchange File Format), 28, 30
        custom settings, 32–34
    Audible *versus* Music Store compression, 103
    audiobooks, 101–103
    converting songs to different audio format, 40–41
        Quick Convert, 219
    MP3 (MPEG Layer 3), 28–29
        custom settings, 32–34
    settings
        changing preferences, 31–32
        customizing, 32–34
    WAV, 28, 30
        custom settings, 32–34
Engst, Adam
    iMovie 4 and iDVD 4 for Mac OS X: Visual QuickStart Guide, 210
    iPhoto 4 for Mac OS X: Visual QuickStart Guide, 208
equalizer
    adjusting frequencies, 73
    opening window, 72
    presets
        assigning to streams or songs, 76–77
        choosing, 72
        deleting, 74
        recommended settings, 77
        renaming, 75
        saving adjustments as presets, 74
Essentials feature (iTunes), 97
exclusive items (Music Store), 89
Explicit lyrics (Music Store), 100
exporting song lists, 143

F

fast user switching, 22
Fetch Art Web site, 46
55ware's G-Force, 84
Find Album Artwork with Google AppleScript, 46
firewalls, 203
FlashPix format, adding as iTunes artwork, 45
Fountain Music (Binary Minded Software), 84

frequencies
    adjusting manually, 73
    filter frequency settings, encoders, 34
    saving as presets, 74

G

G-Force (55ware), 84
GarageBand and iTunes, 213–214
Gear Software Web site, 155
General tab, Preferences, 18
genre page (Music Store), 88
    cross-shelved albums, 91
genres of songs, 51
GIF format, adding as iTunes artwork, 45
gift certificates (Music Store)
    email or U.S. Mail, 114–115
    redeeming, 116–117
    redeeming without HTML email, 118
Google
    Applescripts
        Find Album Artwork with Google v2.2, 46, 218
        Google Lyric Search v1.1, 218
    image searches for album artwork, 47

H – I

Heid, Jim, 205
home page (Music Store), 88

ID3 tags, 124
iDVD 4 and iTunes, 211–212
    earlier versions of iDVD, 208
iLife and iTunes, 205
iMovie 4 and iDVD 4 for Mac OS X: Visual QuickStart Guide, 210
iMovie 4 and iTunes, 209–210
importing. *See also* Importing tab, Preferences
    audio CDs
        all songs, 21–23
        checking import status, 23
        individual songs, 24–25
        joining tracks as one song, 25
    data from CDDB (Compact Disc Database), 23
    file formats supported, 37
    songs
        adding to playlists simultaneously, 132
        song lists, 143
    stopping imports in progress, 22
Importing tab, Preferences, 18
    changing preferences, 26–27
    encoding formats, 31
    converting songs to MP3 format, 164

223

Index

InstallShield Wizard (Windows), 9
iPhoto 4 and iTunes, 206–208
   earlier versions of iPhoto, 208
iPhoto 4 for Mac OS X: Visual QuickStart Guide, 208
iPod
   connecting to Windows platform, 175
   copying music from multiple libraries, 184
   ejecting from computers, 178
   file formats transferable to iPod, 179
   iTunes
      disadvantages of using iTunes, 176
      inability to transfer songs from iPod to iTunes, 185
      setting up to use with iTunes, 176–177
      transferring On-The-Go playlists to iTunes, 186–187
      transferring song ratings to iTunes, 189
   iTunes and other portable MP3 players
      transferring songs from Macs, 190
      transferring songs from Windows, 191
   listening to audiobooks, 187
   mini iPod, 173
   playlists
      adding/deleting songs and playlists, 185
      adding songs to On-The-Go playlists, 187
      creating, 186
      transferring On-The-Go playlists to iTunes, 186
      viewing, 184, 186
   rating songs, 189
   updating
      automatic, 181–182
      automatic, disadvantages, 183
      changing preferences, 179–180
      iTunes library changes, 182
      manually, 184–185
   versions
      2.1 with Dock Connector ports, 174
      1.3 with FireWire cables, 174
      Software Updater, 174–175
iTunes
   audio player selection, 15
   customizing, window, 68
   downloading/purchasing with new Macs, 5
   enhancements recommended, 2–3
   and GarageBand, 213–214
   hardware and software requirements, 2
   and iDVD 4, 211–212
   and iLife, 205
   and iMovie 4, 209–210
   installing, 9–11
   interface, 16
   and iPod
      disadvantages of using iTunes, 176
      inability to transfer songs from iPod to iTunes, 185
      setting up to use with iTunes, 176–177
      transferring On-The-Go playlists to iTunes, 186–187
      transferring song ratings to iTunes, 189
      updating iTunes library changes, 180
      updating iTunes library changes after automatic updates, 182
   launching, 12
   other portable MP3 players
      transferring songs from Macs, 190
      transferring songs from Windows, 191
   Preferences window, 17–18
   setting up, 13–14
   toggling between full window and mini player, 69
   versions
      changes, from 3 to 4, 7
      changes, from 4.1 to 4.2, 8
      changes, from 4 to 4.1, 7
      determining, 4–5
      updating, 6
iTunes Cheat Sheet Web site, 83
iTunes Essentials feature, 97
iTunes Link Maker Web site, 105
iTunes Monitor, 198
iTunes Music Store
   accessing from iTunes, 86
   accounts
      managing, 121–122
      passwords, 107
      purchase preference settings, 109
      signing in/out, 108
      with/without Apple IDs or AOL screen names, 106–107
   album page, 90–91
   artist pages, 92–93
   Audible *versus* Music Store compression, 103
   audiobooks, 101–103
      versus Audible Book (.aa) format, 97
      authorizing media for sharing, 200–201
      listening to on iPods, 187
      number available, 97
   basics, 86
   Billboard Charts feature, 97
   Celebrity Playlists feature, 97
   exclusive items, 89
   features, 87
   genre page, 88
      cross-shelved albums, 91

Index

gift certificates
    email or U.S. Mail, 114–115
    redeeming, 116–117
    redeeming without HTML email, 118
home page, 88
iTunes Essentials feature, 97
media not sharable, 195
musicStorePlayercP applet, 219
Muze, biographical information on artists, 92
purchasing media
    with 1-Click, 110–111
    allowances, 119–120
    authorized play, 111
    authorized play, sharing media, 195, 200–202
    customer service, 115
    file formats of purchased media, 113
    preference settings, 109
    shopping carts, 112–113
saving links
    shortcuts or aliases, 104
    URLs, 105
    Web page authoring, 105
songs
    browsing, 94–95
    Explicit or Clean lyrics, 100
    number available, 97
    Parental Advisory Screen, 100
    power searching, 98
    previewing, 99–100
    searching for, 96–97

J–K

JPEG format, adding as iTunes artwork, 45
joining songs, 25

Karaoke (.kar) file format, 37

L

library
    adding to
        audio files from computers, 35–36
        QuickTime movies, 36
    backup system, 170
    browsing, 51
        hiding/showing Browser, 50
    columns
        changing order/size of, 56–57
        hiding/showing, 55
    copying data CD or DVD files back to library, 169–170

importing
    audio CDs, all songs, 21–23
    audio CDs, individual songs, 24–25
    audio CDs, joining tracks as one song, 25
    changing preferences, 26–27
    data from CDDB (Compact Disc Database), 23
    stopping imports in progress, 22
playlists
    accessing for sharing music, 197–198
    adding and importing songs simultaneously, 132
    adding songs, 131
    adding streams, 131
    basics, 129
    copying songs from one playlist to another, 140
    creating, 130
    deleting, 141
    deleting songs, along with playlists, 142
    deleting songs, from library, 138
    deleting songs, from playlists, 137
    importing, 130
    merging, 140
    reordering songs, 139
    Smart Playlists, 133–136
    viewing, 140
renaming, 20
sharing music
    accessing playlists, 197–198
    connecting to, 197
    disconnecting from, 199
    viewing, 196
showing genres, 51
song lists, importing/exporting, 143–145
song searches
    limiting searches, 53
    text strings, 52
viewing list of contents, 20
Link Maker (iTunes) Web site, 105
links (Music Store)
    shortcuts or aliases, 104
    URLs, 105
    Web page authoring, 105
Listen Web site, 38

M

Macintosh
    Apple Web site, CD burners, 155
    AppleScripts
        downloading/installing scripts, 216–217
        examples of cool scripts, 218

Index

Macintosh *(continued)*
  file formats supported for importing
      into iTunes
    Sound Designer II (.sd2), 37
    System 7 sound (.snd), 37
  iTunes
    downloading or purchasing new Macs, 5
    enhancements recommended, 3
    and GarageBand, 213–214
    hardware and software requirements, 2
    and iDVD 4, 211–212
    and iLife, 205
    and iMovie 4, 209–210
    installing, 11
    and iPhoto 4, 206–208
    launching, 12
    Macintosh *versus* Windows, 2
    Preferences window, 17–18
    setting up, 14
  iTunes versions
    determining, 4–5
    updating, 6
    using 2.0.4 with OS 9, 3
  OS X 10.3
    fast user switching, 22
    iTunes disk image, 11
    switching users without logging out, 12
The Macintosh iLife '04, 205
MacPaint format, adding as iTunes artwork, 45
Mark/Space's Missing Sync, 190
Microsoft Update Web site, 3
MIDI (.mid) file format, 37
mini iPod, 173
mini player, 68-69
Missing Sync (Mark/Space), 190
Monitor (iTunes), 198
Moving Picture Experts Group. *See* MPEG
MP3 (MPEG Layer III) file format, 28–29
  burning CDs, 156
    preparations, 162–163
    process, 166–167
    rechecking/converting song format,
      164–165
  converting songs to different audio format,
    40–41
  downloading files for fees or for free, 38–39
  ID3 tags, 124
  MP3 streams *versus* MP3 files, 42
  MP3 Web site, downloading files for fees, 38
  supported for importing into iTunes, 37
  transferring media to iPods, 179
MP3 players, portable, 190-191
MPEG-1 file format, 28
MPEG-2 file format, 28

MPEG-4 (.mp4, .mp4a) file format, 28
  supported for importing into iTunes, 37
MPEG-4 (.mp4b, .mp4p) file format, 28
  media purchased from Music Store, 113
  supported for importing into iTunes, 37
MPEG Layer II (.mp2) file format, 37
MPEG Layer III. *See* MP3
Music folder
  files included in folder, 146
  keeping organized, 13–14
  moving all music files into Music folder, 151
  selecting new Music folder, 150
  structure, 147–149
Music Store (iTunes)
  accessing from iTunes, 86
  accounts
    managing, 121–122
    passwords, 107
    purchase preference settings, 109
    signing in/out, 108
    with/without Apple IDs or AOL screen
      names, 106–107
  album page, 90–91
  artist pages, 92–93
  Audible *versus* Music Store compression, 103
  audiobooks, 101–103
    versus Audible Book (.aa) format, 97
    authorizing media for sharing,
      200–201
    listening to on iPods, 187
    number available, 97
  basics, 86
  Billboard Charts feature, 97
  Celebrity Playlists feature, 97
  exclusive items, 89
  features, 87
  genre page, 88
    cross-shelved albums, 91
  gift certificates
    email or U.S. Mail, 114–115
    redeeming, 116–117
    redeeming without HTML email, 118
  home page, 88
  iTunes Essentials feature, 97
  media not sharable, 195
  musicStorePlayer\cP applet, 219
  Muze, biographical information on artists, 92
  purchasing media
    with 1-Click, 110–111
    allowances, 119–120
    authorized play, 111
    authorized play, sharing media, 195,
      200–202
    customer service, 115

Index

file formats of purchased media, 113
preference settings, 109
shopping carts, 112–113
saving links
   shortcuts or aliases, 104
   URLs, 105
   Web page authoring, 105
songs
   browsing, 94–95
   Explicit or Clean labels, 100
   number available, 97
   Parental Advisory Screen, 100
   power searching, 98
   previewing, 99–100
   searching for, 96–97
Musical Instrument Digital Interface. *See* MIDI
Musicmatch Jukebox files (Windows)
   importing into iTunes, 37
      playlists, 130
   using iPod with iTunes, 176
MusicNow Web site, 38
musicStorePlayercP applet, 219
Muze, biographical information on artists, 92
My Music folder (Windows), 13

N – O

naming/renaming
   equalizer presets, 75
   library, 20
Napster Web site, 38
Nomad Voice File (.nvf) file format, 37

1-Click purchasing (Music Store), 110–111

P

Parental Advisory Screen (Music Store), 100
password for sharing, 195, 197
passwords for accounts (Music Store), 107
Photoshop format, adding as iTunes artwork, 45
PICT format, adding as iTunes artwork, 45
playing media, 58. *See also* sharing music
   controlling volume, 71
   highlighting *versus* speaker icon, 59
   keyboards shortcuts, 60
   making next or previous song current, 60
   moving around in songs, 61
   multiple songs, 64
   obtaining information about current song, 70
   pausing, 59
   preferences, downloads of previews, 100
   skipping songs, 65

Playlist (.pls, .m3u) file format
   MP3 streams *versus* MP3 files, 42
   supported for importing into iTunes, 37
playlists. *See also* songs
   adding streams, 131
   basics, 129
   creating, 130
   deleting, 141
   iPod
      adding/deleting songs and playlists, 185
      adding songs to On-The-Go playlists, 187
      creating, 186
      transferring On-The-Go playlists to iTunes, 186
      viewing, 184, 186
   merging, 140
   Smart Playlists
      creating, 133–134
      creating for audio CDs, 159
      creating for MP3 CDs, 163
      editing, 135–136
      usage ideas, 136
   songs
      adding, 131
      adding and importing simultaneously, 132
      archiving, 168–169
      copying from one playlist to another, 140
      deleting, 137
      deleting along with playlists, 142
      importing, 130
      reordering, 139
   usage ideas, 129
   viewing, 140
PNG format, adding as iTunes artwork, 45
Preferences window
   Advanced tab
      shuffling albums, 65
      streaming buffer sizes, 67
   changing Source and Song text sizes, 69
   Importing tab, 18
      changing preferences, 26–27
      changing preferences, encoding formats, 31
      converting songs to MP3 format, 164
   Macintosh iTunes menu, 17–18
   Sharing tab
      firewalls, 203
      turning sharing on/off, 194–195
   Store tab
      complete downloads of previews before playing, 100
      purchasing media, 109
   Windows Edit menu, 17–18

Index

presets, equalizer
    assigning to streams or songs, 76–77
    choosing, 72
    deleting, 74
    recommended settings, 77
    renaming, 75
    saving adjustments as presets, 74
printing song lists, 160
purchasing media
    Music Store
        1-Click, 110–111
        accounts, 106–109
        accounts, managing, 121–122
        allowances, 119–120
        authorized play, 111
        customer service, 115
        file formats of purchased media, 113
        gift certificates, 114–118
        preference settings, 109
        shopping carts, 112–113
    with new Macs, 5
    restrictions for burning CDs, 161

Q

Quick Convert, 219
QuickTime Image File format, adding as iTunes artwork, 45
QuickTime movies (.mov)
    adding to library, 36
    converting, 41
    relationship with iTunes and ACC encoding, 9
    supported for importing into iTunes, 37
    unavailable for sharing, 195

R

radio streams
    listening to songs, 66
    Smart Playlists, 136
    stopping, 67
    URLs (uniform resource locators), 66
    viewing latest list of categories, 67
rating songs
    iPod, 189
    iTunes
        multiple, 128
        single, 127–128
redeeming gift certificates (Music Store), 116–117
    without HTML email, 118
Remove Artwork 2.0 AppleScript, 218
renaming. *See* naming/renaming
Riehemann, Susanne Z., 83

S

sample rate settings, encoders, 32
sample size settings, encoders, 34
scripts (AppleScripts), Doug's AppleScripts for iTunes
    downloading/installing, 218–219
    Find Album Artwork with Google v2.2, 46, 218
    Google Lyric Search v1.1, 218
    Remove Artwork 2.0, 218
searching
    library, 52–53
    limiting searches, 53
    Music Store, 96–97
        power searching, 98
    text strings, 52
Secrets of the iPod, 173
service packs (Windows), troubleshooting, 3
SGI format, adding as iTunes artwork, 45
sharing music. *See also* playing media
    authorizing computer for sharing purchased music, 200–201
        deauthorizing sharing, 202
    firewalls, 203
    libraries
        accessing playlists, 197–198
        connecting to, 197
        disconnecting from, 199
        viewing, 196
    media not available for sharing, 195
    monitoring users of shared music, 198
    multiple users on one computer, 200
    turning on/off, 194–195
Sharing tab, Preferences, 18
    turning sharing on/off, 194–195
    firewalls, 203
shopping carts (Music Store), 112–113
Shuffle options, 64, 65
slideshows with iPhoto 4 and iTunes, 206–208
Smart Encoding Adjustments, 34
Smart Playlists
    creating, 133–134
        for audio CDs, 159
        for MP3 CDs, 163
    editing, 135–136
    usage ideas, 136
Software Update (Mac), 6
Software Updater (iPod), 175
songs. *See also* playlists
    artwork
        adding by dragging/dropping, 44–45
        adding with Information window, 45–47
        sources, 47
        viewing, 62–63

Index

converting to different audio format, 40–41
deleting, 137-138
equalizer
    assigning presets, 76–77
    opening window, 72
library
    browsing, 51
    browsing, hiding/showing Browser, 50
    columns, changing order/size of, 56–57
    columns, hiding/showing, 55
    searching for songs, limiting searches, 53
    searching for songs, text strings, 52
    showing genres, 51
listening to radio streams, 66–67
Music Store
    browsing, 94–95
    Explicit or Clean lyrics, 100
    number available, 97
    Parental Advisory Screen, 100
    power searching, 98
    previewing, 99–100
    searching for, 96–97
playing
    controlling volume, 71
    highlighting *versus* speaker icon, 59
    making next or previous song current, 60
    moving around in songs, 61
    multiple songs, 64
    obtaining information about current song, 70
    pausing, 59
    playing, 58
    skipping songs, 65
playlists
    adding and importing songs simultaneously, 132
    adding songs, 131
    copying songs from one playlist to another, 140
    deleting songs, 137–138
    deleting songs along with playlists, 142
    importing songs, 130
    reordering songs, 139
    selecting songs, 126
rating
    multiple songs, 128
    single songs, 127–128
song information
    basics, 124
    editing, 125–126
    ID3 tags, 124

song lists
    exporting/importing, 143–145
    printing for burned CDs, 160
start and stop times, 79
visualizer
    controlling visualizations, 82–83
    iTunes Cheat Sheet, 83
    third-party, 84
    using, 80–81
Sony Clié, 190–191
sorting songs, 54
sound. *See* audio
Sound Designer II (.sd2) file format
    supported for importing into iTunes, 37
    transferring media to iPods, 179
    unavailable for sharing, 195
Source pane, customizing, 68
stereo bit rate settings, encoders, 33
stereo modes, encoders, 34
Store tab, Preferences, 18
    complete downloads of previews before playing, 100
    purchasing media, 109
streams
    assigning equalizer presets, 76–77
    Smart Playlists, 136
subscriptions, downloading, 43
System 7 sound (.snd) file format
    supported for importing into iTunes, 37
    unavailable for sharing, 195
System Preferences (Mac), Software Update, 6

T – V

Targa format, adding as iTunes artwork, 45
TIFF format, adding as iTunes artwork, 45

Update Web site (Microsoft), service packs, 3
URLs (uniform resource locators)
    to iTunes Music Store, 105
    radio streams, 66

VBR (variable bit rate encoding), 33–34
VersionTracker Web site, visualizers, 84
visualizer
    controlling visualizations, 82–83
    iTunes Cheat Sheet, 83
    third-party, 84
    using, 80–81
volume, controlling, 71

W – Z

Walmart Web site, 47
Wave (.wav) file format, 28, 30
    CD-quality sound, 157
    converting songs to different audio formats, 40–41
    supported for importing into iTunes, 37
    transferring media to iPods, 179
Windows
    connecting iPod, 175
    Gear Software Web site, CD burners, 155
    iTunes
        downloading, 5
        enhancements recommended, 2–3
        hardware and software requirements, 2
        importing Musicmatch Jukebox files into iTunes, 37, 130
        installing, 9–10
        launching, 12
        Preferences window (Edit menu), 17–18
        setting up, 13
        Windows *versus* Macintosh iTunes, 2
    iTunes versions
        determining, 4–5
        updating, 6
    XP, fast user switching, 22
WMA (Windows Media Audio) file format
    converting to MP3 format, 41
    downloading files for fees, 38

XML files, exporting song lists, 143–145